Anonymous

**Vick's Flower and Vegetable Garden**

Vicks' priced catalogue of seeds, bulbs and plants for 1876

Anonymous

**Vick's Flower and Vegetable Garden**

*Vicks' priced catalogue of seeds, bulbs and plants for 1876*

ISBN/EAN: 9783337377373

Printed in Europe, USA, Canada, Australia, Japan

Cover: Foto ©Lupo / pixelio.de

More available books at **www.hansebooks.com**

# Vick's Flower and Vegetable Garden

THE CULTURE OF FLOWERS is one of the few pleasures that improves alike the mind and the heart, and makes every true lover of these beautiful creations of Infinite Love wiser and purer and nobler. It teaches industry, patience, faith and hope. We plant and sow in hope, and patiently wait with faith in the rainbow promise that harvest shall never fail. It is a pleasure that brings no pain, a sweet without a snare. True, some fail to realize their hopes, but these failures are usually partial, never embarrassing, and are only such as teach us to study more carefully and obey more strictly nature's beautiful laws. Thus we gain, first, wisdom, and then success as the results even of our failures. I have endeavored in a plain and pleasant way to give some suggestions on the philosophy of vegetation that I think will prove valuable, revealing the causes of past failures and insuring future success. Indeed, I have endeavored in the pages of the FLOWER GARDEN to make the subject so plain as to render failure next to impossible, and success almost certain. Experience, however, is the great teacher. The book of nature is open, but its wonderful beauties and mysteries are revealed only to the careful student. Every species of plants have peculiarities which must be studied, and while we can give a few general principles we can furnish nothing that will compensate for the pleasure and profit to be derived from work and study in the garden. Above all things, we caution our readers against over-confidence. There is no one with less confidence in his own skill and knowledge than the experienced gardener. Every season he seeks for new facts; every year adds to his store of knowledge. Do not, for a moment, think that the purchase of a few seeds and the perusal of any work on flower culture will make a florist. The purchase of a drug store and a medical library will not make a physician, nor does the possession of paints and canvas constitute an artist. To become skillful in any art requires both study and practice, and this is especially true where we have to deal with nature's laws. The study of Agriculture and Horticulture has engaged the attention of the wisest from the earliest ages, and yet what wonderful discoveries and improvements have we witnessed in our own day; and we are still learners. Let us all profit by the lessons of the past and become every year better prepared for the duties and responsibilities of life, more fitted to conquer its evils and enjoy its pleasures — learn to plant more carefully and reap a richer harvest of pleasure and profit.

## SUCCESS IN FLOWER CULTURE.

There is great pleasure in success, while failure causes disappointment and pain. It would afford me pleasure to teach every one how to succeed in every case in one short lesson, but success so easily obtained would not be much to boast of, nor minister a great deal to our pride or pleasure. A little difficulty in its attainment sweetens success, and of this sweetness cultivators usually have a full share, for they often have to contend against unfavorable weather, insect enemies, and a host of adverse circumstances. The most skillful sometimes obtain success at considerable cost of labor and patience, while failures are more common than welcome. Many of my readers are of limited experience, some of them just commencing to love and cultivate flowers, and while a few fail, I feel surprised and gratified at the very general success — a little proud, perhaps, at having done something to train up an army of successful florists all over our happy land, the fruits of whose peaceful labor beautify every landscape and perfume every breeze. I have endeavored to make this interesting subject so plain that all may understand the conditions on which success in floriculture may generally be assured.

**Selection of Seeds.**—The selection of seeds is a very important matter, and on the wisdom of the choice success or failure may in a great measure depend. Those who have but little experience should invest money cautiously and in a few of the more hardy and popular kinds, such as Asters, Balsams, Stocks, Petunias, Dianthus, Zinnia, &c., with, perhaps, a few of the more tender and expensive kinds, just for trial. This advice will sound strange to my old friends and customers, but these will please remember that we all knew but little once, and cannot now boast of excess of wisdom, and that one-half my customers are young people, with no experience, yet thirsting for knowledge. I am anxious to encourage this noble army, more than a hundred thousand strong, by a little success rather than to discourage them by a large failure. My desire to spread the love of flowers all over this favored land is far greater than my care to make a few dollars. Half-

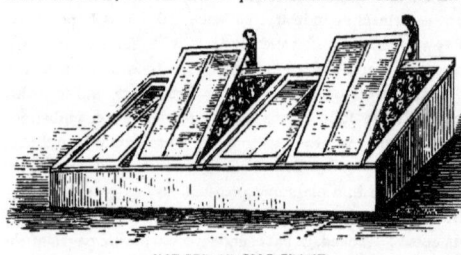

HOT-BED OR COLD-FRAME.

a-dozen flowering plants, well cultivated, will give pleasure, while a hundred neglected, or ill cultivated, will be a source of pain.

Always be careful to get seeds suited to the purposes for which they are designed. If a climber is desired to cover a fence or trellis, the Morning Glory, the climbing Nasturtion, and similar strong growing vines will answer the purpose and give good satisfaction; while some of the more tender climbers will not be likely to come up if planted in such a situation as this, and if they do happen to grow, will not cover the place designed for them, and disappointment will be the result. If the object is a brilliant, showy bed on the lawn, or in the border, the Petunia, Phlox Drummondii, Verbena, &c., will meet your wishes; while a bed of Mignonette, or any of the smaller or less showy flowers, will be entirely out of place. If flowers of taller growth are desired for a showy bed more in the back-ground, the Zinnia, the French Marigold, the Gladioli, &c., are admirably adapted for the purpose, while some very beautiful, low, modest flowers would be worthless. Grave errors are sometimes made, and good flowers condemned merely because they are out of their proper place. For instance, I have known people to sow Calceolaria and Cineraria, and other very delicate seeds, in the open ground and in soils where a Cabbage would hardly condescend to grow, not knowing that they require the most careful treatment in the house, and sometimes tax the skill even of the professional florist. It is possible to destroy the best seeds, and some kinds may be destroyed without much trouble.

**The Soil and its Preparation.**—The best soil for most flowers, and especially for young plants, and for seed-beds, is a rich, mellow loam, containing so much sand that it will not "bake" after hard showers. If we have not such a soil, we must use the best we have, and advantage must be taken of the various plans to ensure the germination of seeds, which we shall describe. It is

also useless to try to grow good flowers on a poor, or a hard, unbroken soil, or in a bed choked with weeds. In either case the plants become dwarfed, arrive at maturity too early, and flower and ripen their seeds before they have attained half their natural size, and about the time a good robust plant would be forming its buds. Such a soil can be much improved by a little sand, or ashes and manure, and by pretty constant working. It must not, however, be handled when too wet. Always drain the flower garden so that no water will be on or near the surface.

**Sowing Seed.** — This is a very important matter, and one in which the young florist is the most likely to fail. Some old and professional florists make sad work here, for knowledge is not only necessary, but care and attention.

BOX HAND-GLASS.     SQUARE HAND-GLASS.

One "*forgot*" may ruin a whole sowing of the choicest seeds. Of course, there are some kinds of seeds that are robust and will grow, no matter how they are treated, just as our weeds grow and thrive under ill treatment; but others require kind and proper treatment, just as almost everything desirable does in the animal as well as in the vegetable kingdom. Many seem to think that seeds will grow anywhere and under any circumstances. They have seen the farmer make a hole and throw in his corn, and in a little while it was up and growing vigorously; they have learned that the seeds of our native trees and weeds grow without planting and care; and from these facts they get the idea that it is of little consequence how or where seeds are sown, so that they are in the ground. But these should consider that the seeds used by the farmer are usually larger and produce stronger and more robust plants than those of the florist, and thus are enabled to bear more hardships and to live under more unfavorable circumstances.

Still, farmers are fast learning that the better they prepare the ground, the more carefully they sow their seed, and the more they study the nature and wants of the plants they cultivate, the better the crops. Another fact should be remembered — that not one seed in a thousand matured by our forest trees and shrubs, produces a living plant. A forest tree will produce seed enough for

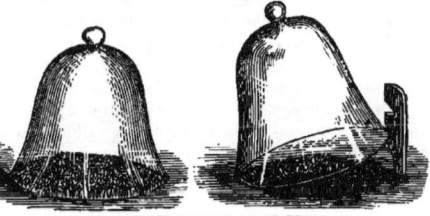

SEEDS PROTECTED BY GLASS BELLS.

an acre of closely set plants, and perhaps not a dozen grow. We cannot afford to purchase costly seeds and lose such a large proportion, which we plant in the same manner. Our weeds are hardy and prolific, very tenacious of life, and are able to propagate themselves under the most unfavorable circumstances; otherwise they would not be generally known as weeds. Most of our troublesome weeds are of foreign origin, the seeds being brought here by accident. The larger part thus introduced have lived for a season and perished unnoticed, while the hardiest became naturalized. If the florist would be satisfied with only the most hardy and prolific flowers, such as would take care of themselves, then he might pursue a careless system of planting and cultivation, and fill his grounds with Dandelions and Poppies; but he craves

PROTECTED BY POTS.

flowers that are not natural to our climate — those that flourish in warmer climes and under more genial skies — their dazzling beauty, their delicious fragrance, must be secured at almost any cost of time and labor. This is well; but having made up our minds to possess the treasures, we must pay the price — we must study their habits and treat them accordingly. None need feel alarmed at these remarks, or think themselves incompetent to the charge of such choice plants without hot-beds, green-houses and professional gardeners. We have known ladies, who, with but little pretensions, equaled the most distinguished florists. There seemed to be magic in their fingers, and everything they touched flourished. It is true that a hot-bed, if properly managed, is of great aid in effecting the germination of seeds, and it is well all should know why this is so.

Causes of Failure.—In the first place, however, we will examine the causes of failure. If seeds are planted *too deep*, they either rot in the damp, cold earth, for the want of warmth necessary to their germination, or, after germination, perish before the tender shoots can reach the sun and air; and thus that which was designed for their nourishment proves their grave.

If the soil is a *stiff clay*, it is often too cold at the time the seeds are planted to effect their germination; for it must be understood that *warmth* and *moisture* are necessary to the germination of seeds. Neither of these will do alone. Seeds may be kept in a warm, dry room, in dry sand or earth, and they will not grow. They may be placed in damp earth, and kept in a low temperature, and they will most likely rot, though some seeds will remain dormant a long time under these circumstances. But place them in moist earth, in a warm room, and they will commence growth at once. Indeed, if seeds become damp in a cold store-room they rot, while if the room is warm they germinate, and thus become ruined, so that seedsmen have to exercise great care in keeping their seeds well aired and dry.

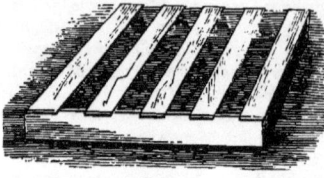

SEEDS PROTECTED BY LATH FRAME.

This accounts for the "sprouting" or "growing" of wheat in the sheaf, when the weather is warm and showery at harvest time, and shows why farmers are so anxious for good harvest weather, so that they may secure their grain perfectly dry. Another difficulty with a heavy soil is that it becomes hard on the surface, and this prevents the young plants from "coming up;" or, if, during showery weather, they happen to get above the surface, they become locked in, and make but little advancement, unless the cultivator is careful to keep the crust well broken; and in doing this the young plants are often destroyed. If *stiff*, the soil where fine seeds are sown should be made mellow, particularly on the surface, by the addition of sand and light mold.

If seeds are sown in *rough, lumpy ground*, a portion will be buried under the clods, and will never grow; and many that start, not finding a fit soil for their tender roots, will perish. A few may escape these difficulties, and flourish.

All of the foregoing cases show good reason for failure, but there is one cause which is not so apparent. The soil, we will suppose, is well prepared, fine as it can be made, and of that loamy or sandy character best fitted for small seeds. We will suppose, too, that the seeds were sown on the surface, with a little earth sifted over them, and that this was not done until the season was so far advanced as to furnish the warmth necessary to secure vegetation. Under these very favorable circumstances many seeds will grow; and if the weather is both warm and showery, very few will fail. But if, as is very common at the season of the year when we sow our seeds, we have a succession of cold rain storms, many of the more tender kinds will perish. A night's frost will ruin many more. If, however, the weather should prove warm and without showers, the surface will become very dry, and the seeds, having so slight a covering, will be dried up and perish as soon as they germinate, and before the roots attain sufficient size and strength to go down in search of moisture. Of course, the finer and more delicate seeds, and those natural to a more favorable climate, suffer more than those that are more robust.

SEEDS GROWING IN POTS.

Hot-Beds and Cold-Frames.—It is to overcome these evils that hot-beds are useful. By being protected at the sides and ends with boards, and covered with glass, they confine the moisture which arises from the earth, and thus the atmosphere is kept humid and the surface moist, and the plants are not subjected to changes of temperature, as a uniform state can be maintained no matter what the weather may be. The bottom heat of the hot-bed warms the soil, and enables the grower to put in his seed early, and obtain plants of good size before the soil outside is warm enough to receive the seed. Care, however, is required to prevent scorching the young plants. In bright days, the heat is intense inside the frame, and unless air is freely given, or some course taken to obstruct the rays of the sun, most likely a great portion of the plants will be ruined. Some time since, I was called to examine a hot-bed, as the seeds planted did not grow, when I found they had been all burned up, except a few along the edges that were shaded

by the sides and ends of the frame. When the sun gets pretty warm, give the glass a thin coat of whitewash. This gives a little shade, and, with some air during the middle of bright days, will make all safe. The *hot-bed* is made by forming a pile of horse manure with the straw used for bedding, or leaves, some three feet in height. Shake all together, so that straw and manure will be equally mixed. It may be sunk in the ground a foot or eighteen inches, or made on the surface. On this place about five inches of good mellow soil. Then set the frame and keep it closed until fermentation takes place and the soil is quite warm. It is better to wait a day or two after this, and then sow the seeds. The principal advantages of a hot-bed can be secured by what is called a *cold-frame*. This is simply a hot-bed frame, with sash, as shown in the engraving, placed upon a bed of fine, mellow earth, in some sheltered place in the garden. By the exclusion of air and the admission of sun, the earth becomes warm, and the moisture is confined, as in the hot-bed. After the frame is secured in its place, a couple of inches of fine earth should be placed inside, and the frame closed up for a day or two before the seeds are planted. As the cold-frame depends upon the sun for its warmth, it must not be started as soon as the hot-bed, and in this latitude the latter part of April is soon enough. Plants will then be large enough for transplanting to the open ground as soon as danger from frost is over, and, as a general thing, they will be hardier and better able to endure the shock of transplanting than if grown in a hot-bed. A frame of this kind any one can manage. Watering occasionally will be necessary; and air must be given on bright, warm days. Shade also is necessary. These frames, when so small as to be conveniently moved by the hand, are called *hand-glasses*. A simple frame or box, with a couple of lights of glass on the top, will answer a very good purpose, though when small it would be better to have the front of glass. A very good hand-glass is made of a square frame, with a light of glass at each side and on the top. These contrivances, though so simple as to be made by any one handy with tools, are exceedingly useful, as they prevent the drying of the surface of the ground, and afford the plants shelter from sudden changes of the temperature, cold storms and frosty nights. The engravings show several forms of which they may be made. Seeds may be sown in the house in pots, &c., but the greatest difficulty is that in pots the soil dries very rapidly, and young plants are apt to suffer. A very good plan is to cover the pots with glass, as we have shown in the engraving, removing it occasionally for air, &c. Where very fine seeds are sown in pots, the watering, unless carefully done, generally results in great injury. A wet paper placed over the top of the pot will afford moisture enough for the germination of fine seeds. If pots are used it is well to sink them to the rim in a box of moss, or something of the kind, that will hold moisture, and prevent the drying of the earth in the pots. A shallow box may be used to advantage, sowing the seed carefully in narrow drills.

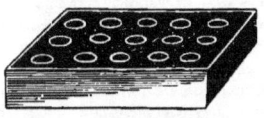

POTS OF SEED SUNK IN MOSS.

When these conveniences are not to be had, make a bed of light, mellow soil, in a sheltered situation in the garden; and as soon as the weather becomes settled, and the ground warm, sow the seeds, covering them with a little fine earth, and if very small sift it upon them. Some one has given as a rule that seeds should be covered twice the depth of their own diameter; that is, that a seed one-sixteenth of an inch through should be covered one-eighth of an inch. Perhaps that is as near correct as any general rule can be. If the weather should prove dry after sowing, it would be well to cover the beds of very small seeds with damp moss, or what is better, with evergreen boughs or boards, or something that will afford partial protection from the sun and wind. A very good plan is to nail lath to a frame, as shown in the engraving, leaving the open spaces about as wide as the lath. Seeds do not require light for their germination, and will grow quite as well in the dark as the light until they are above ground. Bell-glasses are convenient both for in-doors or garden use, only care must be given to afford plenty of air, especially on bright days, and shading may be necessary. An inverted flower pot answers almost as good a purpose, but when the young plants are up they will need light, which can be afforded for a few days, and until the plants are large, by elevating the pot, as shown in the engraving. Light and air should be furnished as soon as the plants are above ground, or they will become weak and pale. Of course, it is designed that

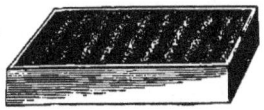

SEEDS IN A BOX.

5

plants from the *hot-bed*, *cold-frame* and *seed-bed* shall be transplanted to the border or beds where they are to flower, and these helps are intended mainly for *Tender* and *Half-Hardy Annuals*, described in an article on the Classification of Flowers, on another page. The *Hardy Annuals* may be sown where they are to flower, though, with the exception of a few varieties difficult to transplant, it is best to sow all in a seed-bed.

All seeds of hardy and half-hardy Annuals, and Perennials, and, in fact, nearly all flower seeds, can be sown in the South in the autumn. The plants are thus enabled to make vigorous growth in the early spring, and become well matured before the heat of summer. The Perennials should be sown so early as to make a fair growth before winter sets in. Then they will flower the next summer. The Hardy Annuals generally do best sown rather late, so that the seed will remain in the ground and be ready to start at the first approach of spring.

**Transplanting.** — Sowing seeds and transplanting, in fact, all the operations of the garden, should be done with neatness; no crooked, irregular rows are admissable in the flower garden. The engraving shows how easily lines are marked in a bed with a rod or ruler. After plants in the seed-beds have obtained their second leaves and made an inch or two of growth, they should be removed to the garden beds or border. This should be done on a dull, showery day, if possible, if not, the plants may require shading after removal until they become established. In transplanting in dry weather, always give the plants as they stand in the seed-bed a good soaking with water, and also the soil to which they are to be removed, an hour or so before removal. In removing, disturb the roots as little as possible. If the plants are not too thick, there is no need of injuring the roots; and in sowing, it is well to have this in view, and sow evenly and thinly. As soon as the young plants come up, if too thick, a portion should be removed. A few plants, with long tap-roots, will not bear removal well. The Larkspurs are difficult; and these and the Poppies, and plants with like roots, should be sown where they are to flower.

MARKING FOR PLANTING.

Still, there are few plants but can be removed when young, with proper care. Sweet Peas, Candytuft, and a few flowers of similar character, that do best if sown early as the ground can be got ready, should always be sown where they are to flower.

**Disappointed Cultivators.** — Many years of experience and careful estimates have convinced me that while nearly all of my customers succeed in growing excellent flowers from the seeds they receive, and are not only satisfied, but enthusiastic over the result, some two or three per cent. totally fail, or fail to such an extent as to feel quite dissatisfied with the expenditure and labor of the season. To this small number I cannot give much space, but will make a few remarks that may be profitable and prevent disappointment in the future.

Some are disappointed because flowers do not prove what they expected. It should be remembered that I do not agree that flowers shall meet the expectations of any person. The first thing is to ascertain what it is right to expect. Not the notion of any person, but the description I have given must be the standard. The descriptions and drawings are not exaggerated, yet they represent plants and flowers that have been well grown; neglected, half-starved plants will present a very different appearance.

Full length Portrait of some unhappy woman's husband. The man who thinks it nonsense for wife and girls to make flower beds.

Any specimen of the animal as well as the vegetable kingdom will become dwarfed and deformed, and lose every trace of beauty by ill-treatment and neglect. Then the descriptions in the GUIDE must be understood. If I call some little delicate flower, like a Lobelia, a fine variety, you have a right to expect it to be a fine Lobelia; but have no right to expect it to be as large, fine and showy as an Aster, a Ten-Weeks Stock, or a Zinnia, or any

other of our large, brilliant flowers. It is fine in its place, but not fine for a display in the garden. A pen-knife is good for the purpose for which it was designed, but it is not exactly fitted for wood-chopping. I advertise *double* Zinnias, *double* Stocks, &c.; but you have no right to complain and think you are cheated if one-fourth should come single, but should pull up the single ones as fast as they show their character, and enjoy the good instead of mourning over the bad. Many varieties of double flowers do not give seed, so we have to obtain double seed by fertilizing the single flowers with the pollen of the double, and by other slow and difficult processes known to the experienced seed-grower. These operations are usually only partially successful, and, as a necessary consequence, some of the seed will give single flowers; and yet intelligent men, and correspondents of the press, and officers of Agricultural societies, and others who ought to know better, often scold, and write complainingly because seed purchased as double produced single flowers.

Portrait of the fortunate woman's husband, who makes wife and children happy and home pleasant.

Again, I advertise separate colors of Phlox Drummondii, Dianthus, Asters, &c. Occasionally, with some of these, you will find a little mixture of color. This, with some things, can not be avoided, even with the greatest care. There always has been, and always will be, a little uncertainty in growing flowers from seed. They are prone to mix and "sport." If it were not for this disposition, we could never obtain new varieties. When plants or trees are grown from cuttings, or are produced by budding or grafting, all mixture is the result of carelessness, accident or fraud. This is not the case with plants produced from seed. While many varieties come almost or quite true from seed, with good care, others are far less reliable in this respect. All I can promise is that I have done all that human care and skill can do to produce distinct colors, and when there is very much uncertainty in regard to color I advertise them only as "mixed colors." For this reason I advertise only "mixed colors" of many varieties.

Occasionally we hear complaint that seeds do not grow — perhaps one or two varieties failed out of a hundred, and the cultivator is like the shepherd in the Scriptures, who left the ninety-nine in the wilderness and went in search of the lost one. This was well for the shepherd and the sheep, but is not a good plan for florists and flower seeds. If you have ten or twenty varieties, and all grow nicely but one or two, just enjoy the success, instead of making yourself miserable over failures. The best and most skillful gardeners will fail occasionally, and neither the seed nor the gardener be very much to blame. Every professional gardener knows this. There is a wonder — a mystery — in vegetable as well as in animal life. Our friends fail, droop and die — our little ones pass away just as they are taking deep root in our hearts. We feel the deathly pangs, but cannot save. But the variety that failed was the one of all you most desired. Of course, what we cannot have we always want the most. The fish that escapes from the hook is always the largest.

The woman whose flower seeds never come up unless they are scratched up.

The woman whose flower seeds all come up.

But, if you fail to any great extent, make up your mind there is trouble somewhere — some mismanagement — and resolve to find it out, if possible. Don't jump at the conclusion that the seed was bad, because it is not true, and thousands will praise the seed you condemn as bad. By concluding that you are all right and the seed all

wrong, you will not only lose the seed, but the benefit of experience. It will not help the matter to say that seeds of your own growing came up in the same beds, unless you had just the same varieties. As a general rule, the finer the varieties of flowers the less vitality in the seeds. One may grow almost anywhere and anyhow, the other require the most favorable circumstances for its germination. This is particularly the case with most double flowers, even of the same species or variety. A single Aster will give more seed than a hundred of double, and the seed will be larger, and produce earlier, stronger plants, and will grow under unfavorable circumstances, where the seed from the double flower would decay. Hence, if there happens to be three seeds from a single plant in a package, if all should grow, these three plants would produce flowers before any others, and those not acquainted with the facts would say at once, "all my Asters are going to be single." If through a bad season or soil all the Aster seed from the double flowers had died, and only the more robust from the single flower lived, of course, the complaint is, "I had only three plants from a package of seeds, and that was plenty, for they were very poor flowers." A beautiful flower is often obtained at the sacrifice of the vigor, and not unfrequently the constitution, of the plant. After laboring long and anxiously to secure some desired improvement, it is not uncommon, just as success seemed about to crown our labors, to find all our hopes blasted on account of some defect in the plant — a grand flower secured and a healthful plant ruined.

## THE LAWN AND GARDEN.

Man may be refined and happy without a garden; he may even have a home, I suppose, without a tree, or shrub, or flower; yet, when the Creator wished to prepare a proper home for man, pure in all his tastes and made in His own likeness, He planted a garden and placed this noblest specimen of creative power in it to dress and keep it. A few suggestions on the Improving of Grounds and the Adornment of Rural Homes may be useful, and prevent a great many expensive and troublesome mistakes.

In the first place, the space in front of the house, and generally the sides exposed to view from the street, should be in grass. No arrangement of beds, or borders of box, or anything else, will look so neat and tasteful as a well kept piece of lawn. It can also be kept in better order at less cost than in any other way. Mixed beds of flowers or shrubbery in the most conspicuous part of the garden is always unsatisfactory. Get a good plat of grass, and dry, neat walks, and all other things will soon follow with but little trouble.

The very first thing needed in improving ground is to secure good drainage. Have good drains made to carry off all waste water from the house and surplus water from the soil. These can be made of stone, laid in any way that will leave an open and secure space for the water to pass through, though where drain tile can be obtained they are as good as anything and usually cheaper. The drains should be from two to three feet deep. Cut a trench as wide as is needed for convenient working, and as deep as you have determined is necessary, and lay the stone or tile at the bottom, being careful that the work is well done, for this is the foundation of all improvement, and the correction of any failure is made only with a good deal of trouble and expense. This secures a dry soil at all seasons of the year, and a healthy growth of plants or trees.

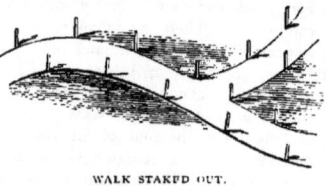

WALK STAKED OUT.

The next thing is to prepare the soil and make the walks. Make no more roads than are absolutely necessary, as many walks divide the lawn and greatly disfigure it. Of course, there must be a bold walk to the front door, and one passing from this to the rear of the house, and in general no more will be necessary. These must be made in the most convenient places — in those one would naturally take in going from one place to another.

If the ground to be improved is only a small lot, it can be done best by the spade, and it is not well to endeavor to do it with the plow. In that case, mark out the walks first. Do this by setting up little sticks on the line you design for the road, as shown in the engraving, changing them until you get just the curve that seems graceful and pleasant to the eye. Put a row of

sticks on each side of the road, measuring carefully so as to get the width uniform. Another plan for securing the desired curve to walks is the use of a stout line. The idea is shown in the engraving. Next, remove the earth from the walk to about the depth of eighteen inches, using it to fill up any low places. The walks, of course, have somewhat the appearance of ditches. The operator is now prepared to pulverize the soil with the spade. Have it done thoroughly,

LOCATING WALK WITH LINE.

sending the spade well down, and completely inverting the soil, but leaving about six inches on each side of the walk undisturbed for the present, so as not to break the line of the road. All stones found in digging should be thrown into the roads, and often sufficient will be found to fill within six or eight inches of the surface; if not, enough can be procured usually without much difficulty. The stone cutter's yards and the stone piles in the roads and fields generally furnish abundant material. When the walks are filled with this rough material to within six inches of the surface of the soil, the ground being raked off nice and smooth, dig the six inches left undug on the edges of the walks, being careful to keep the edges true and as originally staked out, and then set a turf about six inches wide for a border to the walk, as shown in the engraving, keeping the turf as low as the level of the adjoining soil, or a little lower, and to do this, remove three or four inches of the soil where the turf is to set, according to its thickness.

A good deal of this rough work can be done in the autumn, so as to leave only the finishing up in the spring; but if commenced in the spring, it should be hurried up so as to get the grass sown as early as possible, for grass seed will not start well unless it has the benefit of spring showers. Lawn Grass sown about the first of September, so as to have the benefit of autumn rains, will usually make a fine growth before frost, and be in excellent condition in the early spring, almost appearing like an old lawn by July. All being done as previously advised, sow the grass seed on the well prepared surface, raking it in, and if pretty dry, it is well to roll the soil after sowing. Sow Blue Grass, or a preparation of the most desirable grasses for lawns, sold as Lawn Grass, at the rate of *four bushels to the acre.*

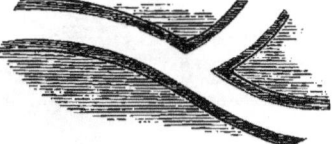

WALKS WITH TURF EDGING.

In our Lawn Grass we always put a little Sweet Vernal Grass, on account of its delightful fragrance. If you use Blue Grass, get a little Vernal and use with it, a pound or two to the acre. Most persons also like a pound of White Clover to the acre. If the grass is sown early in the spring and the weather is at all favorable, by the first of July the lawn will look pretty green, and from the middle to the last of July will need cutting, and after that must be cut as often as the little Lawn Mower can get a bite. These Lawn Mowers are a real blessing, for not one in ten thousand can cut a lawn properly with a scythe, and therefore our lawns, before the introduction of these Mowers, always looked wretched.

It will be strange if a great army of weeds do not appear with the grass, but do not take it for granted that these weeds came from the grass seed sown, because if you had not sown any grass the weeds would have been just as abundant. The farmer who finds the weeds among his corn and potatoes never imagines that he planted them with the seed. As soon as the grass and weeds get high enough to be cut with a scythe or Lawn Mower, cut close and evenly, and repeat this as often as possible. The weeds will soon disappear. A few perennial weeds, like Docks, Thistles and Dandelions may be removed by cutting the roots as far down as possible with some narrow, sharp implement. Two or three such cuttings will destroy them.

After sowing the grass, finish the walks by covering the rough stones with five or six inches of gravel, as clean as can be procured. It is best to leave the finishing of the walks until the last,

SECTION OF WALK.

because, even after sowing the grass seed, at raking it in, a quantity of stones will be gathered, and

9

you will need a place to put them and the walk will need the stones. A section of the road when done will appear as shown in the engraving, and will be always dry and free from weeds and grass. If the earth should wash from the lawn and cause weeds to start, sow salt along the edges and you will see no weeds for a season.

In very small places it would, perhaps, be as cheap to sod the whole, instead of sowing grass seed. Where this is desirable, good turf can be procured from the roadside or pasture, and it should be well and neatly laid. In large places the plow can be used instead of the spade, and with great economy of labor. In that case the whole lot should be well plowed and dragged before the walks are staked out. After this, stake the walks and remove the earth the necessary depth, using it to level off the low places. There will always be a good deal of work for the spade and rake, even when the plow and drag have been used.

Two great errors are usually made, both by gardeners and amateurs; one destroying the lawn by cutting it up with unnecessary walks and flower beds, the other producing the same result by almost literally covering it with trees and shrubbery. Grass cannot grow well among the roots and under the shadow of trees and shrubs, and no lawn can look well cut up in sections by numerous roads. Most of the little lawns we see in this country are almost entirely destroyed by one or both of these causes. The main part of the lawn should be left unbroken by any tree or shrub, as a general rule, and if any tree is admitted it should be only an occasional fine specimen, like a Purple Beech, or Magnolia, or cut-leaved Birch. The shrubbery should be in clumps or groups, in proper places, and so thick as to cover all the ground. The soil under them should be kept cultivated and clean like a flower bed. A tree or two in certain appropriate places for shade, is, of course, desirable; but plant for the future, not for the present, and always have in view the size and form and habits of the trees when full grown, and not their present small size, and, perhaps, delicate form. Every curve should be a sensible one; that is, have a reason for its course, either real or apparent; therefore arrange your planting so as to make an apparent necessity for every turn. The idea is shown in the little sketch accompanying, where the walk curves to accommodate the trees.

The great difficulty with American gardens is that they are too large, and not sufficiently cared for. If we gave the same amount of labor on a quarter of an acre that we now expend on an acre, the result would be much more satisfactory. No one should have more ground in garden than he can keep in the very highest state of cultivation. It is this kind of excellence that affords pleasure, while failure or partial success is a source of pain. It is not only a fault to cultivate too much ground, but even too many flowers. Some seem anxious to obtain and grow everything. This is not best, especially where there is not a good deal of time and money to be devoted to the work. A choice selection is best, and I like every cultivator of flowers to have a pet or hobby. Take, for instance, the Pansy, and make it a pet. Obtain the choicest seed, and give the plants the best of care, and you will see to what wonderful perfection it can be grown. In a few years you will tire, perhaps, of this. Then adopt the Balsam, or Stock, or Aster. Always have something choice—something grown better than any one else is growing it—something you have reason to be proud of. It will astonish you to see how flowers thrive under such petting, and what a wonderful exhibition they make of their gratitude.

PLANTING FOR CURVED WALKS.

Some persons may think from what we have said in favor of grass in front of the house in preference to beds of flowers, that we are no friend to these beautiful treasures—these delightful children of the field and garden, who speak to us in every fragrant breath and lovely tint and graceful form, of Him who spake from naught this matchless beauty. Far from this. A home without the children of the field, and flowers of the family, we might, perhaps, enjoy, but we have never had to endure the trial. I only wish them to be treated in a proper manner. In the center of the lawn, especially if opposite a window, it is well to make a round or oval bed, and on the borders or near the edges of the lawn, beds of various graceful forms. A few plans for these we give.

These beds should be filled with flowers that will keep in bloom during the whole season, and it is best generally to have but one kind in a bed. Phlox Drummondii, Verbena, Portulaca, and the scarlet Geraniums, are well adapted for this purpose, and occasionally it is well to

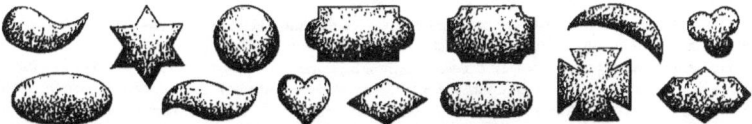

introduce the ribbon style. The plan is to set plants of the same height and color in a row, several rows forming the bed, and giving it the appearance of the stripes in ribbons, as shown in the engravings below. To make a bed of the kind select flowers of similar height and habit. Of course, if one row loses its flowers the effect is spoiled. If a circular bed is made, the rows toward the center may be taller than the outside rows. A very cheap and pretty ribbon bed can be made by using the different colors of the same flower, like Phlox Drummondii, and for a beginner we know of no flower as good. These beds, it must be remembered, are for the adornment of the grounds, and they furnish no flowers for the house—no presents for friends, no bouquet for the dining room, or for schools or churches, or the sick room. These we must have. So, just back of the lawn, make generous beds of flowers that you can cut freely—Asters, Balsams, Zinnias, Stocks, Mignonette, Sweet Peas, &c. In these beds you can also grow the Everlasting Flowers for winter use. It is best to make such beds oblong, about four or five feet in width, so that one can reach half way across, with alleys or paths between.

RIBBON BED.

RIBBON BED.

A few well filled vases are a fine and appropriate decoration of any grounds if kept in good condition with healthy plants. The evaporation from baskets and vases is very great, much more than is generally supposed, as every side is exposed to air, sun, &c., and they must receive a copious supply of water every evening to keep the plants in a healthy condition.

Another very pretty ornament for the garden is the Rockery, made of rough stones, tastefully laid up, with earth sufficient for the growth of plants suitable for this work. Low growing plants with succulent and ornamental foliage are appropriate to the rockery — Portulaca is admirable. I would like my readers who have had no experience in this kind of garden ornamentation to try a specimen in some retired quarter of the garden, so that if it proves a failure no harm will be done. We give an illustration of a bed of this kind.

ROCK-BED.

## CLASSIFICATION OF FLOWERS.

THE flowers of our gardens, besides those produced by shrubs, trees, etc., are HERBACEOUS PERENNIALS, BIENNIALS, ANNUALS and BULBOUS.

HERBACEOUS PERENNIALS are plants which die down to the ground every autumn, but the roots continue to live, and new branches and flower stems are thrown up for many years. Some continue indefinitely, but others die after three or four years, like the Sweet William; but if the roots are divided every year, they will continue to live and increase. These are called *Imperfect Perennials.*

BIENNIALS are those that flower the second season after the seed is sown, and then die, unless particular care is taken to preserve them, by dividing the roots, or retarding the flowering at the usual time by removing the buds. Some of these classes flower the first season under favorable circumstances, as when the seed is sown early.

ANNUALS flower the first season, perfect their seeds, and then die. Some varieties that are grown as Annuals in a Northern climate, are either Perennials or Biennials in their Southern home, where there are no severe frosts. Annuals flower in a few weeks or months after being planted, and can be depended upon for a brilliant show. Annuals are classed as *hardy*, *half-hardy* and *tender*. Hardy Annuals are those that, like the Larkspur, Candytuft, etc., may be sown in the autumn or very early in the spring, in the open ground. The *half-hardy* varieties will not endure frost, and should not be sown in the open ground until danger from frost is over. The Balsam and the Marigolds belong to this class. The *tender* Annuals generally require starting in a green-house or hot-bed to bring them to perfection, and should not be set in the open ground until the weather is quite warm. The Cypress Vine and the Sensitive Plant belong to this class; but, fortunately, very few of our fine Annuals. Some of them do tolerably well if sown in the open ground the latter part of May, but very great success is not to be expected in this way. It must be admitted, however, that these distinctions are not well defined, and it is difficult to say where some kinds belong. In a climate sufficiently South, of course, those kinds we describe as tender are perfectly hardy.

BULBS are divided into *Hardy*, *Holland* and *Tender*. The *Hardy* includes all that will bear a Northern winter. *Holland*, those exclusively grown in Holland, like Hyacinths, Crocuses, Tulips, &c. *Tender*, those, like the Gladioli and Tuberose, that will not bear freezing, and therefore must be planted in the spring.

---

We make a rather different division in this work, and one which, we think, will be found quite convenient.

1st. ALL KINDS that PRODUCE FLOWERS the same SEASON the SEED IS SOWN, are arranged in one Department, under the heading of ANNUALS. This Department includes the following subdivisions: *Climbers, Everlastings and Ornamental Grasses*.

2d. Under the name of PERENNIALS, all plants produced from seed that bloom the second season after planting.

3d. GREENHOUSE, describing the leading plants grown from seeds adapted to Greenhouse culture.

4th. BULBS AND PLANTS. This Department has two divisions: *Tender Bulbs and Tubers*, embracing all those tender bulbs, like the Dahlia, Gladiolus, Tuberose, &c., that will not bear frost, and consequently must be planted only in the spring in a Northern climate. *Hardy Plants and Bulbs*, embracing all the Lilies, Pæonies, and other things that will endure our winters, and consequently can be planted either in the fall or spring.

5th. HOLLAND BULBS. This Department embraces Hyacinths, Tulips, and all other Bulbs known as Holland Bulbs, and these must be planted in the autumn.

THE first and most important section of our FLOWER GARDEN is composed mainly of ANNUALS, that is, those plants that live but one season. The seeds are sown in the spring, the plants arrive at maturity in the early summer, bud, blossom, ripen their seeds, and die in the autumn, having performed their entire mission. This class of plants, from their nature, are valuable treasures to both the amateur and professional gardener. There is no forgotten spot in the garden, none which early flowering bulbs or other spring flowers have left unoccupied that need remain bare during the summer; no bed but can be made brilliant with these favorites, for there is no situation or soil in which some of the varieties will not flourish. Some members delight in shade, others in sunshine; some are pleased with a cool clay bed, while others are never so comfortable as in a sandy soil and burning sun. The seed, too, is so cheap as to be within the reach of all, while a good collection of bedding plants would not come within the resources of many, and yet very few beds filled with expensive bedding plants look as well as a good bed of our best Annuals, like Phlox, Petunia or Portulaca, and for a vase or basket many of our Annuals are unsurpassed. Though we risk our reputation for good taste, perhaps, in making this statement, yet we have seen nothing better, and few things that we shall remember longer or more pleasantly than a vase filled almost entirely with the striped Petunia, and showing all day and every day hundreds of flowers. To the Annuals, also, we are indebted mainly for our brightest and best flowers in the late summer and autumn months. Without the Phlox and Petunia and Portulaca and Aster and Stock, our autumn gardens would be poor indeed, and how we would miss the sweet fragrance of the Alyssum, Mignonette and Sweet Pea if any ill-luck should deprive us of these sweet favorites. Many of our beautiful climbers, such as the Convolvulus and Cobœa scandens, and nearly all our Everlastings and Ornamental Grasses are included in this section.

This Department, however, embraces some Perennials, but only those that flower the first season, though they do not die at its close, like the Annuals. Among these are the Pansy, Dianthus, Antirrhinum, &c., that live for several years under favorable circumstances. In our country, however, most of these are usually short-lived, and are really only to be considered as hardy Annuals. Under the influence of spring showers and summer suns they mature rapidly, and flower so freely that by autumn the plants are so exhausted they cannot endure the rigor of our winters, and in the spring are usually worthless, if not entirely lifeless. By removing a portion of the flowers in the summer, and encouraging a vigorous growth, this class of plants will remain in perfection at least two years. If seed is sown late in the spring, or even in summer, young plants will give but few, if any, flowers the first season, and the second summer will be in perfection. Many of the flowers that we treat as Annuals, sowing fresh seeds and growing new plants every year, because the plants are destroyed by frost in the autumn, are really Biennials or Perennials in their Southern home.

### ABRONIA, Nat. Ord. *Nyctaginaceæ*.

BRONIAS are trailing plants, with prostrate branches, several feet in length, and bearing clusters of sweet-scented flowers; somewhat resembling the Verbena, both in flower and habit of plant, though more robust. The Abronias are natives of California, and in their natural home make a beautiful flowery carpet. The yellow variety, *arenaria*, delights in the most barren sand hills, and on the borders of the Pacific Ocean, within a few feet of high water, with no other sign of vegetation around, we have seen the clean white sand hills made gay by this pretty plant, which is known on the coast of California as the Sand-plant. *Umbellata* is a delicate pink with a good deal of fragrance.

The seed does not always germinate freely, and the plants in some sections do not seem to grow with their native vigor. Start the seed under glass, first removing the husky covering. The Abronias, when they succeed, are deservedly admired, and therefore have some warm friends.

### ADONIS, Nat. Ord. *Ranunculaceæ*.

The Adonis, a native of Europe, is of the easiest culture. The finely cut foliage is rather pretty. The flowers, by no means abundant, are of an intensely deep blood red color, and cup shaped. The legend is that this flower sprang from the blood of Adonis, when he was wounded by the boar. It will grow well in the shade or under trees, and this we consider its principal recommendation. A clump under a tree or in a shady corner of the garden, or under a hedge, or near a rustic summer house, is desirable, but we would not recommend it for small gardens or limited collections. It is an every day plant and will fill a modest place very satisfactorily; but if we attempt to make much of it, or put it on exhibition it will disappoint and mortify us. Flowers, like people, have places where they do themselves and their friends credit, while in other situations there is general disappointment and mortification. Seeds may be sown in the garden, and plants should be about a foot apart.

### AGERATUM, Nat. Ord. *Compositæ*.

A Mexican flower, of a brush-like appearance, not showy in the garden, but prized by florists, because it bears a great many flowers, and keeps in bloom a long time, and is, therefore, desirable for bouquet making. In fact, there are very few flowers that will work up to better advantage, and give a more chaste appearance to a small bouquet than the white or delicately tinted blue Ageratum, and as it will grow well in the house, is always a favorite with both amateurs and florists. Its name has reference to the long continued flowering of the plant, and also of the fact that the flowers will remain fresh for a long time after being gathered, and a very liberal translation would be *ever-young*. It is well to start the seeds under glass, and then transplant to the

flowering fled. Take up the smallest plants in October, and pot them for winter use. If no glass is to be had, select a mellow soil and a sheltered spot for the seed bed, and cover the seeds but slightly. Set plants six or eight inches apart to form a bed in the garden. A few seeds sown the latter part of August, if the soil is kept moist and shaded, will make young plants fit for potting for winter flowers.

## AGROSTEMMA, (Viscaria,) Nat. Ord. *Caryophyllaceæ.*

The annual Agrostemmas, or, more correctly, *Viscarias*, are very pretty, free blooming and hardy annuals, making desirable beds and useful for cutting. The flowers are something like a single Pink, and are borne on long, slender stems. The plants are of a rather straggling habit, and produce abundance of flowers with but very little foliage, so that a single plant, or a few plants set widely apart, do not present a very pretty appearance; but when planted thickly in a bed, form a mass of color quite satisfactory, resembling a good bed of the bright colored Phlox Drummondii. This flower was introduced into England from Sicily more than a hundred years since, and is still quite popular and common in English gardens, and is considered effective in producing a mass of bright color. We have had very good results in sowing this seed in the bed where it was intended to bloom, thinning out the plants but very little, if any. We have been much pleased with it as a plant for edgings for beds of Gladiolus or other tall plants. Grows about twelve inches in height, and should be set about six inches apart.

## ALONSOA, Nat. Ord. *Scrophulariaceæ.*

The Alonsoas are natives of Chili and Peru, and when first introduced into Europe were treated as green-house plants, but of late years have been generally cultivated as tender or half-hardy annuals. Young plants removed to the house or green-house in the autumn will continue to flower during the winter. The flowers are small, but of remarkably brilliant colors, in which respect they are excelled by very few of our richly colored flowers. We have succeeded best by sowing seed under glass and transplanting, in this latitude about the first of June, and as the plant is inclined to be hard-wooded, any young plants taken up and potted will assume a shrub-like form and continue to grow and flower for a long time. This flower has been cultivated for about fifty years, and the improvement since its introduction has not been marked.

## ALYSSUM, Nat. Ord. *Cruciferæ.*

The Sweet Alyssum is one of those modest plants that everybody likes and every one must have. Its pretty little white flowers are so purely white, and so useful in making up all kinds of small bouquets, and its fragrance, while sufficiently pronounced, so very delicate, reminding one of the peculiar aroma of the hay-field, that no florist feels satisfied unless he has a little bed of Alyssum that he can resort to at all times when delicate flowers are needed. The Alyssum grows freely from seed, either under glass or in the open ground, though it does not germinate freely in the open ground in dry, hot weather. For a low, white edging or border, the Alyssum is excellent, as its habit is good, and height only about six inches. The little black flea that destroys Cabbage and Turnip in the seed-leaf is exceedingly fond of Alyssum, and will destroy whole beds. Dusting with fine ashes is of advantage, and if a little fine snuff is mixed with the ashes the effect is better. The Alyssum was first found wild on the shores of the Mediterranean, and is now found growing on the rocky cliffs of some parts of the English coast, but is supposed to have become naturalized; that is, the seeds were accidentally carried from gardens to the fields and woods by birds or some other means.

## AMARANTHUS, Nat. Ord. *Amarantaceæ*.

The Amaranthus embraces a large class of plants, and some of them so diversified in character that, to the casual observer, they hardly seem to belong to the same family. They are mainly, however, valuable for their ornamental foliage, the leaves of most varieties being highly colored, while in some the form as well as color is desirable. The present popularity of ornamental leaved plants for bedding out renders this class more than usually interesting The great difference of habit makes it necessary to give engravings of the varieties, showing the more marked distinctions. The drooping flower shows *A. caudatus*, sometimes called Love Lies Bleeding, a rather coarse plant, yet graceful and excellent for autumn decoration, with racemes of flowers sometimes two to three feet in length. Another variety, Prince's Feather, has flowers nearly similar, but arranged in erect spikes. The smallest engraving represents *bicolor*, *tricolor* and several other sorts of about the same habit, though differing in color. The large engraving gives a very good representation of *salicifolius*, or the Fountain Plant, a free growing plant that sometimes reaches a height of five feet or more, and is a very pretty object in a suitable position. The Amaranthus are half-hardy plants, and use-

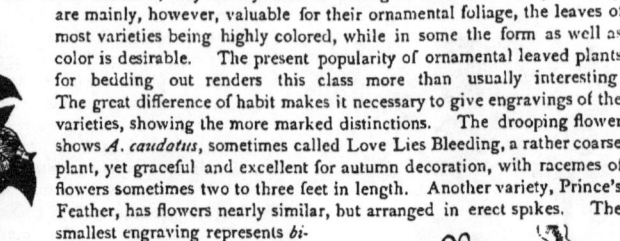

ful in many situations, as the back-ground of a flower bed, a bed on the lawn, or as an ornamental hedge. In a rich soil, where plants make a vigorous growth, the varieties with bright colors sometimes become dull. It is unfortunate that we cannot always rely on the color, no matter how fine the plants from which the seeds are derived, but success is most assured in a warm, dry season, and in a light or rather poor soil. The Amaranthus is a native of the East Indies, but has been in cultivation in Europe since the days of Queen ELIZABETH, and in America since its first settlement. The name is a favorite with poets, and means never-withering. The leaves of the species of Amaranthus are wholesome food, and many varieties are eaten in their native countries, like Spinach.

## ANAGALLIS, Nat. Ord. *Primulaceæ*.

The genus Anagallis is remarkable for the beauty of its flowers, for even our wild scarlet Pimpernel, or Poor Man's Weather Glass, is one of the prettiest of our small wild flowers. The improved garden varieties are very desirable for small beds, edgings, baskets, &c. The plants usually do not exceed six inches in height, and when set in a bed thickly, cover the ground with a constant profusion of rich flowers. The Anagallis has representatives among the wild flowers of a large portion of the world, from some of which importations have been made to America and Europe, and the hybrids obtained by our florists exhibit great improvement. Sow under glass, if possible, and set the plants not more than six inches apart. The Anagallis is one of those honest, every-day flowers that, while it will not astonish any one, cannot fail to meet the anticipations of every lover of flowers.

### ANTIRRHINUM, (Snapdragon,) Nat. Ord. *Scrophulariaceæ.*

The Antirrhinum, perhaps better known by its old and popular name, Snapdragon, is one of the very best of our Perennials, and one that always gives a good account of itself the first season, blooming abundantly all the first summer, even until after frost. Sometimes the plants suffer in winter, especially when permitted to exhaust themselves by excessive flowering, but they generally flower well the second season, and sometimes the third. When it is desired to keep the plants for flowering the second or third season, never allow seed to form; and if one half the plant is cut down to near the surface of the ground about the middle of summer, new vigorous shoots will be produced for the next season's flowering. They exhibit a fine variety of colors and are exceedingly brilliant. Sow either in the frame or garden, early in spring. Easily transplanted. Set six to nine inches apart. The Antirrhinum is easy to grow and sure to please, and we ask those who do not cultivate this flower to give it a trial.

### ARGEMONE, Nat. Ord. *Papaveraceæ.*

The Argemones are free blooming hardy annuals, with large flowers, resembling a single Poppy, while the leaves are armed with slender prickles, and very much resemble Thistle leaves, hence the Argemone is known almost every where as the Prickly Poppy. Natives of Mexico and Peru, and some of the species were introduced into Europe more than two hundred years since.

The plants grow two feet in height and make a very good low screen or hedge, for which purpose set the plants about ten inches apart in the rows. The foliage is not only large and very pretty in form, but of a pleasant light green color, and it can be easily imagined that with its large, Poppy-like flowers a hedge of Argemone must be an interesting object. Very few summer hedges will look better. The engraving shows the flower less than one-half the natural size.

### ASPERULA, Nat. Ord. *Rubiaceæ.*

Asperula azurea setosa is a profuse blooming hardy little annual from the Caucasian Mountains, and only introduced to cultivation a few years since. It is of dwarf habit, growing less than a foot in height, and bearing many clusters of small, light blue or lavender, sweet-scented flowers. This is one of the class of pretty, neat little flowers which some persons admire on account of their delicate beauty, and which many condemn as weedy and worthless, because they make no show in the garden. For making up in small bouquets the Asperula is all that can be desired.

The engraving shows the habit of the plant as well as the size of the flower, and from this a pretty good idea may be obtained of the use to which it is adapted. We design to be quite particular on this point, because many of our choicest little gems are evil spoken of, just because their friends do not give them a proper introduction.

## ASTER, Nat. Ord. *Compositæ*.

The Aster was popular when we had our little garden nearly half a century ago. We used to call it then CHINA ASTER, but those children who wished to be very nice would say *Reine Marguerite*, and would often get laughed at for preferring so hard a name, just because it was French. The Aster was sent to France from China by a Missionary, and the English name means *China Star*, while the French is *Queen Daisy*. Is was then a single, showy flower, bearing not much more resemblance to the Aster of to-day than the Mayweed does to the Dahlia. However, we thought it very pretty, and it afforded us a great deal of pleasure. We never see a poor single flower come up among the good ones, and we occasionally find such, but we are reminded of early days and childish friendships. We thought an engraving showing the character of the Aster as it was when imported might be interesting to our readers, and therefore give a small sketch. The Aster now is a general favorite, and its popularity is on the increase. For an Autumn show of flowers, we were about to say, we have not its equal, but we are reminded that when we get enthusiastic over any of our special favorites, we are ready to say the same thing about a good many. Perhaps we can safely say that for an autumn display it has no successful rival among the Annuals. Give the Aster a deep, rich soil, and mulching with coarse manure is very beneficial, and if extra fine flowers are needed for exhibition or any other purpose, a little liquid manure occasionally will give the most gratifying results. Plants may be grown in the hot-bed, cold-frame, or a seed-bed in the garden, but to obtain good flowers the Aster plant must be strong and "stocky." A plant that is what gardeners call "drawn" will never produce very fine flowers. A "drawn" plant is one that, by being crowded in the seed-bed, or some other cause, has become tall, slender and weak. The Aster transplants easily. Twelve inches apart is the proper distance for making a showy bed of the large varieties; the dwarf kinds may be set six inches or less. It is not best to have Asters flower too early in the season, and there need be no haste in starting seed in the spring, for the Aster, like the Dahlia, is essentially a Fall flower, and the flowers are always the largest and most perfect and enduring in the showery weather and cool, dewy nights of Autumn. The tall varieties with large flowers need a little support, or during storms of wind and rain they are often blown down and their beauty destroyed when in full blossom. Set a stake in the ground near the main stem, so that its top is only about two-thirds the height of the plant. Then fasten the main branches to this stake, not in the way too common, which is merely to pass a string around the whole plant, stake and all, thus injuring both foliage and flowers. The proper way is to attach several strings to the stake, so that they will not slip down, then pass each one around two or so of the main branches in a kind of loop or sling, so that the plant will retain its natural position, and may be swayed by the wind without receiving the least injury. We have endeavored to show how this is done in the accompanying engraving. Asters are so very dissimilar in habit,

ranging from the little dwarf, scarcely six inches in height, to the stately plant of more than three feet, and bearing flowers almost as large as a Pæony, that a few words seem necessary to prevent persons purchasing what they do not desire. The smallest of the family is the little *Dwarf Bouquet*, represented in the engraving, fig. 9, which presents a bouquet of flowers about five or six inches in height, with scarcely a leaf. These are excellent for borders around beds. The *Dwarf Pyramidal Bouquets*, represented by engraving, fig. 10, make plants from ten to twelve inches in height. Next in height is the *New Schiller*, about fifteen inches, which we represent on this page. It will be seen to be of very peculiar habit, the leaves being almost entirely at the base of the plant, and drooping. Another class, like the *Imbrique Pompon* and *Chrysanthemum-flowered*, grow from eighteen inches to two feet in height, while the tallest class, represented by the *New Rose*, *Perfection*, and others, range from two to three feet.

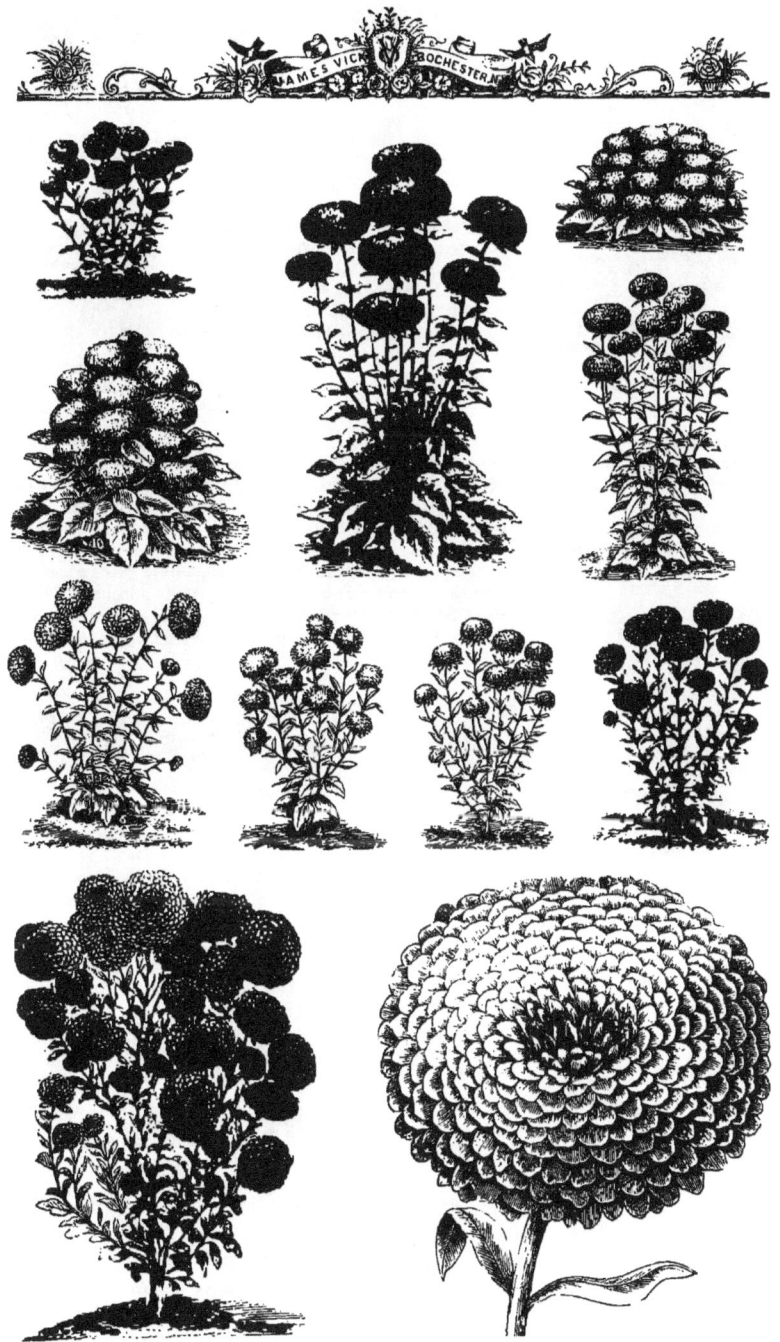

## BALSAM, (Impatiens,) Nat. Ord. *Balsaminaceæ*.

ALSAMINA, like the Aster, is one of the most beautiful and popular of our Annuals. Like that flower, too, it is an old favorite, and so much improved during the last quarter of a century, that it scarcely bears a resemblance to the old flower. We give an engraving of the *Balsam*, which many of our readers will recognize as the *Lady's Slipper* of other days; and though they formerly thought it handsome, and have a right to think so now, now, if they wish, yet it

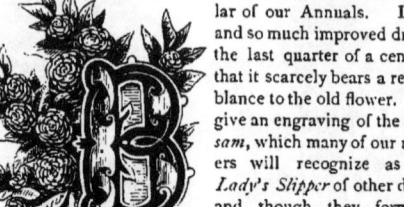

must be acknowledged there is a great improvement in this flower, and that the poor, single blossom so prized because associated with years and thoughts and friends of the past, is far inferior to the double, rose-like flower of to-day. Our climate is wonderfully adapted to the growth of the Balsam, and with a good, rich soil, and decent care, plants and flowers of the greatest excellence are produced. In some parts of Europe the Balsam requires a great deal of nursing to secure good plants, almost hot-house treatment. No flower pays better for a little extra care, in the way of enriching the soil, a little guano water and the like. We have grown side branches of Balsam two inches in diameter at the base, two feet in length, and perfect wreaths of flowers. Sow in a frame or in a sheltered bed in the garden in the spring, as soon as the weather is rather warm. Transplant when the second leaves have made a little growth. Set the plants ten or twelve inches apart, and when the side branches appear, pinch off all but three or four, and pinch out the center shoot.

Those left will then grow strong, and the flowers will not be concealed by the foliage, as is the case when the plant is left unpruned. A very good way is to keep all the side shoots pinched off, leaving only the leading one. This will grow two or three feet in height, and be a perfect wreath of flowers. Treated in this way, they will bear close planting. Some people, however, prefer the Balsam unpruned, and we advise to try several plans. It is quite interesting to watch the results of such treatment. The engravings show the effects of pruning. Fig. I, Dwarf Balsam of natural growth; fig. 5, same pruned to five branches; fig. 2, common Balsam of natural growth; fig. 3, plant pruned to one branch; fig. 4, pruned to three branches; fig. 6, flower of natural size. The Extra Dwarf Balsams grow only about six inches in height, while the tall varieties often reach nearly three feet in a rich soil. With the choicest seed the Balsam occasionally insists on giving only semi-double flowers, and no one can tell why. Many think that old seed produces flowers more double than new.

OLD BALSAM.

BALSAM IMPROVED.

## BARTONIA, Nat. Ord. *Loasaceæ*.

Bartonia aurea is a very showy, half-hardy annual. It is a native of California, and was found there nearly forty years ago by the unfortunate DOUGLAS, who discovered so many ornamental annuals in California and South America, which he introduced to European florists, and who finally sacrificed his life to his botanical zeal by falling into a pit placed to entrap wild cattle, on the Sandwich Islands, while on a botanical excursion. The leaves are somewhat thistle-like in appearance, gray and downy. The flowers are double the size shown in the engraving, of a very bright, metallic yellow, and exceedingly brilliant in the sunshine. It likes considerable moisture, and in a drouth the young plants sometimes suffer. We saw it flowering beautifully, in June, on the mountain sides in the neighborhood of the Yosemite Valley, but not in large quantities. As it does not bear transplanting very well, we sow seed in the garden early, and in that way get good plants and flowers.

## BRACHYCOME, Nat. Ord. *Compositæ*.

The Brachycome iberidifolia is a daisy-like flower, found on the banks of the Swan River, in Australia, and sometimes called Swan River Daisy. It is an elegant little plant, growing only about eight inches in height, of a branching, compact habit, with deeply cut foliage and abundance of flowers, of the size and appearance of which our engraving will give a good idea, and bearing more resemblance to the Cineraria, perhaps, than any other flower. Colors blue and white, with a dark eye. For a bed or mass, set the plants six or eight inches apart. Neither this simple description nor the engraving will give the reader a sufficiently favorable idea of the pretty, daisy-like flowers, and the compact, rounded form of this beautiful plant, which is deserving of far more attention than it has ever received.

## BROWALLIA, Nat. Ord. *Scrophulariaceæ*.

The Browallias are excellent, free flowering, half-hardy annuals, mostly from South America. The flowers are beautiful and delicate, the engraving showing the natural size. Seeds grow quite freely and the plant gives abundance of bloom. Plants about eighteen inches in height, and should be set a foot apart. This, though not a showy, is a very interesting class of flowers; in fact, they belong, like the Clarkia, the Nemophila, and Whitlavia, to a modest, and therefore unappreciated, family, which we like much better than we usually say, because they are not showy enough to please everybody, and we do not like to be the cause of disappointment, even to unreasonable people. For several years past, however, the taste for the culture of the more delicate flowers has been rapidly improving, and instead of being scolded for over-praising some little favorite, it will be recollected, many readers have complained because we said so little when so much could be spoken with truth. With this progress we are well pleased.

### CACALIA, Nat. Ord. *Compositæ*.

ACALIAS are pretty half-hardy annuals, with small, tassel-like flowers, and from the form of the flower, often called Flora's Paint Brush. The flowers are borne in clusters on slender stalks, about a foot or so in length. The appearance of the Cacalia in the bed is quite satisfactory, and for cutting these little flowers are always in request. There are two varieties, scarlet and orange. Sow seed under glass, and set the plants in the flowering bed about six inches apart. This little flower is a native of the East Indies. The principal merit of the flower is that it continues in bloom from early summer until late autumn, throwing up its tall branching and tasseled flower stems, and furnishing flowers for cutting every day for several months.

### CALANDRINIA, Nat. Ord. *Portulacaceæ*.

A very pretty genus of plants, with somewhat succulent stems and fleshy leaves, as might be expected, being of the Purslane family. The plants are more or less prostrate, some varieties as much so as the Portulaca. The best of the species are natives of South America. They endure heat and drouth like the Portulaca, and are peculiarily well adapted for rock work, mounds, &c. Flowers large, abundant and continuous through the summer. The engraving shows the flower about one-third the natural size of most of the varieties. It is best to treat the Calandrinia as a half-hardy annual, and sow under glass, but very good success may be had by sowing in the open ground, especially in a light, sandy soil.

### CALENDULA, (Marigold,) Nat. Ord. *Compositæ*.

The Calendula is the old and well known Marigold family which every one knows, but may not recognize by this name. The name was given because some of the species were supposed to be in flower every month of the Calendar. The *C. officinalis* is the old Pot Marigold, which, according to the old belief, possessed wonderful medical virtues, and as a pot herb had great merit, and which now some Englishmen think gives a delicious flavor to a leg of mutton. The English name is a corruption of Mary's gold, on account of the value of this plant as a pot herb to English cottagers' wives. The single varieties are not much cultivated, but the double are still popular.

### CALLIOPSIS, Nat. Ord. *Compositæ*.

The genus Calliopsis embraces a very useful and brilliant class of hardy annuals. The plants are tall, usually two or three feet in height, and though of slender habit are of vigorous growth. The flowers embrace every shade of yellow, orange and rich, reddish brown, verging to red or crimson. Some varieties are finely marked. The flowers on slender foot stalks, and very abundant, so that when sown in groups, which is the best method, the effect of the waving flowers is very fine. Our engraving shows one of the varieties with a beautiful eye, and the real English of the Greek word Calliopsis is "*Beautiful Eye.*" Seed may be sown in the open ground or under glass.

### CALLIRHOE, Nat. Ord. *Malvaceæ*.

A species of Mallow-like plants, natives of America, with large, purplish flowers, about twice the size of the engraving, and showing a white center, which gives the flower a very beautiful appearance. They are five-petaled, and about two inches across. The filaments of the stamens are united in a columnar tube, which bears a tuft of many stamens at the end. Height of plant about two feet, though there is a dwarf variety, growing only about one-half this height. Seeds under favorable circumstances will grow freely in the open ground. Thin out the plants so that they will be about a foot apart. The Callirhoe commences to flower when only about six inches high, and gives abundance of its pretty flowers through the summer until frost.

### CAMPANULA, Nat. Ord. *Campanulaceæ*.

The Campanulas are a large genus, embracing a great many beautiful and popular Perennials, like the Campanula Medium, or Canterbury Bell, which we shall describe in the department devoted to flowers that bloom the second season. In the *Campanulaceæ* there are supposed to be over two hundred species, and natives of the colder portions of America, Asia and Europe, and scarcely any found in warm countries. The famed Blue Bells of Scotland, (the Hare-bell of America,) is the best known species. There are quite a  number of annuals of great value for forming masses, as they are neat in habit, hardy, and free bloomers. Seed may be sown in the open ground or under glass. In the flowering bed plants should be five or six inches apart, so as to form a mass and entirely cover the soil. The flowers of the annual varieties are small compared with the perennials, and the prevailing colors white, blue and rose. They are simple, neat little flowers, not very desirable as single plants, but quite effective in masses.

### CANNA, Nat. Ord. *Marantaceæ*.

The Cannas are stately plants, with broad green, highly ornamental leaves, giving to our Northern gardens a tropical appearance, exceedingly pleasant. Although the Canna looks well when grown singly, yet we must look for the most desirable effects when grown in clumps or groups, or when to the Canna is devoted a whole bed on some portion of the lawn. There are several varieties, the leaves of some being entirely green, while in others the leaf-stem, midrib and veins are red. Some kinds also grow three or four feet in height, while others are of a somewhat dwarfish habit, being only about two feet. The Canna is also very useful, when grown in pots, for indoor decorations, such as halls, porches, etc. The Canna makes good large plants from seed the first season after planting only under favorable circumstances, so that those who depend upon seeds for their show of plants for the summer, should encourage growth in every possible way, therefore, soak the seeds in hot water for several hours before planting. In a cold climate, seed must be sown under glass, and indeed it is well to grow the plants in pots, so as to get them of good size before the weather is warm enough to turn them into the garden, for unless the plants are strong when set out they will not produce much effect the first year. Many of my customers on the rich soils of the Southwest succeed admirably with the Cannas, not only making a fine show the first summer, but plants of enormous size. In ordinary places, where there is no convenience for hot-bed, potting, &c., it is well to purchase roots, which can be obtained of good size in the spring. In the autumn take up the roots and keep them in the cellar in sand, to be planted again the following spring. The flowers are pretty but not showy.

## CANDYTUFT, (Iberis,) Nat. Ord. *Cruciferæ*.

The Candytuft is an old, popular, hardy annual that every one at all conversant with flowers is acquainted with. It is the same flower now that it was two hundred years ago, the improvement in its character being very slight.  Although the Candytuft grows so freely that it is not considered necessary to give it any particular care, yet it appreciates a little extra culture, as those who take a plant or two for extra good treatment will be fully aware after the trial. A little manure water occasionally, with a thorough softening of the soil around the the plant, and a thinning out of the too numerous clusters of buds, will produce heads of flowers three inches across. The Candytufts are a treasure in the hands of the florist for bouquet making, especially the white varieties, because the flowers are so small and the white so pure, and because by sowing a little patch occasionally flowers can be had at any time, winter or summer. Several times, crimson, carmine and other bright colored Candytufts have been announced among the Novelties, but until this summer we never found any better than the old purple, or much different. We now have a good bright rose, which is a most valuable acquisition. Seed should be sown where the plants are to bloom, either in the fall or as early in the spring as possible. The general form of the Crimson, Purple, Lilac etc., is shown in the engraving; also the Rocket, which bears its flowers in spikes.

## CASSIA, Nat. Ord. *Leguminosæ*.

Cassia chamæcrista is a very good annual indeed, with pretty, light green foliage, like the Sensitive Plant, and plenty of bright, golden yellow flowers 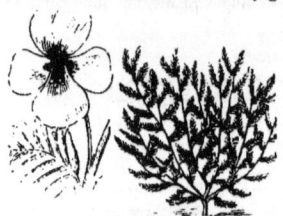 It is of dwarf, compact habit, about eighteen inches in height, has the appearance of a little hard-wooded shrub, and makes a very pretty border. It is a native of the West and Southwest, and entirely worthy of culture. Persons who see this flower first in its wild state are so delighted with it, and so anxious to have others share their pleasure, that samples of both flowers and seeds are sent us by the hundred. We judge from the demand made upon us for seeds by European seedsmen and florists, that this native American is attracting considerable attention. Sow under glass or open; set plants a foot apart.

## CATCHFLY, (Silene,) Nat. Ord. *Caryophyllaceæ*.

There are a great many Silenes with small flowers and not very great beauty. The prettiest of all is *S. Armeria*, and generally known as Lobel's Catchfly, named after LOBEL a distinguished old botanist of Flanders. Nearly all the species of this genus have a viscid moisture on their stalks, in which it is said flies are sometimes entrapped, therefore the Catchfly part of the name. The Silene Armeria is a free flowering hardy annual, growing over a foot in height, with small flowers, red, white or rose.  Set plants six inches apart so as to form a clump.

## CELOSIA, Nat. Ord. *Amarantaceæ*.

The Celosias are interesting and singular annuals, and when well grown, from seed of good quality, never fail to please the grower and attract the attention of his friends. In Europe they are grown in pots for floral exhibitions and also for table decorations, but in most parts of America they grow so freely in the open ground that this treatment is not necessary to form most superb plants, though for exhibition purposes extra good plants in pots would be very convenient and useful. There are two desirable forms of the Celosia, the Cockscomb and the Feathery, the former being the most curious and far the most popular. When true, the latter forms a feathery head that is very pretty, but it is not always reliable, and we have discarded all but one or two varieties of this form that usually come good and true. Of the old-fashioned Cockscomb, represented by the small engraving in the center, seed can now be obtained of excellent quality, that with good culture, in a rich soil, will give heads from six inches to a foot across, and some who read this article will, no doubt, be ready to say they have grown them nearly twice this size, for in the rich soils of the West, and with comparatively good culture, they make combs of wonderful size. Four years ago we obtained a new Cockscomb from Japan, which we named the *Vick's Japan Cockscomb*, and which far excels every other variety in the brilliance of its color and the beauty of its comb. We kept it on our own grounds on trial for two years, and was so charmed with its great beauty as well as its distinctness of character that in 1873 we offered the seed for sale. It not only sustains its original character, but seems to like the Amercan climate and soil. Last summer it was more brilliant than ever before. The usual form of the plant is shown in the first engraving at the left, while the cut on the right exhibits the usual form of the combs, with a bright scarlet edging ruffled like the most delicate lace. In many specimens the comb is so nicely cut as to resemble the finest coral both in form and color, and this appearance we have endeavored to show in the lower engraving at the right. Some of the side branches also assume this square instead of the comb form. Occasionally a plant has the form of the lower engraving at the left, being a mass of combs with scarcely a leaf. The branches from the roots to the smallest leaf-veins are scarlet or crimson. It flowers earlier than the old varieties and keeps in bloom until frost. The seed germinates readily in the hot-bed, and will bear plenty of bottom heat, but needs abundance of air. The form of the feathered Celosia is shown by a drawing of a branch, found at the right of the central engraving. A spike of Celosia spicata rosea may also be seen at the left. These spikes are pinkish, three or four inches long, and nearly an inch in diameter, and may be cut and dried like an Everlasting, retaining both form and color nearly as well as the Helichrysums. This flower is known in some locations as the Lady's Finger.

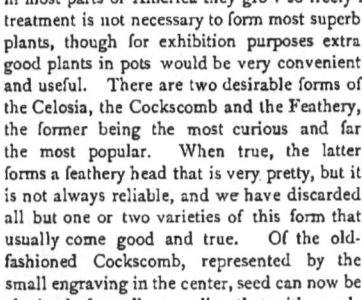

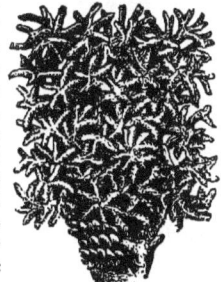

### CENTAUREA, Nat. Ord. *Compositæ*.

The Centaureas are a very large family, and some of the members bring no very great credit to the household, many English farmers think when they see the Blue Bottles among the Wheat, and the Knapweed in the pastures. It is, of course, a little flattering to our national pride to be able to say that the handsomest and best of the tribe are Americans. Some English Botanists, we know, think that one bad fellow emigrated from America, naturalized, and took up his abode in England, but we have never acknowledged the truth of this charge, and do not design to do so without better proof. The Centaureas are perfectly hardy, and some of the best varieties are really fine. *C. Americana*, is sometimes called Basket Flower, because the calyx has the appearance of a basket filled and overflowing with the hair-like petals. We have endeavored to show the appearance of this flower in the engraving.

### CENTRANTHUS, Nat. Ord. *Valerianaceæ*.

There are several varieties of perennial Centranthus, differing not very materially from the Valerians, that is, for the purposes of the florist. *C. macrosiphon* is a very pretty annual species, for which we are indebted to Spain. It has a light green, hollow, almost transparent stem, delicate branches, with light, glaucous leaves. The flowers are small and borne in clusters, as shown in the engraving, and for a pretty bed or mass of delicate flowers, or for a little reserve for cutting, we may search a long time before we find anything to surpass the little Centranthus. The word *macrosiphon* means long-tubed, and as will be seen by the engraving, these flowers have long, slender tubes. We have had no difficulty in getting a good growth from the seed, either in the open ground or under glass.

### CHAMÆPEUCE, Nat. Ord. *Compositæ*.

The Chamæpeuce is a very singular and rather elegant Thistle-like plant, with the prettiest variegated leaves and the sharpest spines imaginable. It is perennial, living several years, but not blooming until the second year, though this is of very little consequence, as the beauty is in the foliage and not the flowers. It is perfectly hardy in this section, the self-sown seed having produced plants on our grounds for several years. It is much used in some parts of the world for decorative purposes, a good plant in a pot, looking quite as well as a young Century Plant or any thing of this character.

### CLEOME, Nat. Ord. *Capparidaceæ*.

The Cleomes are very good half-hardy annuals, obtained, we believe, first from South America, and now pretty generally cultivated. At first it was thought to be a green-house annual, but latterly has been classed with the half-hardy annuals in England, and in America it does exceedingly well, flourishing in our hottest, driest seasons. The Cleomes have very singular flowers, as will be seen by the engraving, the stamens looking like spider's legs. The Cleome is a plant well worthy of culture. Growth about eighteen inches, and plants should be set about a foot apart. Start the seed under glass, or in a warm sandy soil.

### CLARKIA, Nat. Ord. *Onagraceæ*.

When once in the County of Essex, in England, wandering about in search of flowers and their intelligent cultivators, we neared an old-fashioned village, called St. Osyth, and in its neighborhood we saw immense fields ablaze with bright colors, acres each of pink, red, white, purple, lilac, and which a closer view proved to be masses of Clarkia, being grown for the seed. Wherever a mass of bright colors is desired, the Clarkia is the most effective annual in the hands of the English florist. It suffers with us in hot dry weather. Seed sown in autumn will give good early spring flowers.

### COLLINSIA, Nat. Ord. *Scrophulariaceæ*.

The Collinsia is a very pretty, free blooming, hardy annual, that we always liked, but never so well as since we saw it growing wild in California, and which we mistook when at a distance for some new species of Lupin. The marbled, or many-colored, flowers are in whorls of five or six blossoms, and three or more of these whorls on each flower stem. The upper lip of the flower is white or pale lilac, and the lower one dark purple. About eighteen inches in height. We have had very good success with fall planted seeds in a dry soil, but would hardly like to advise this plan generally.

### CONVOLVULUS, Nat. Ord. *Convolvulaceæ*.

Every one knows the Convolvulus major, the old and loved Morning Glory, which will be found described among the Climbing Plants, but all are not conversant with the Dwarf Convolvulus, *C. minor*. It is a dwarfish plant, of a trailing habit, each plant covering a circle perhaps two feet in diameter, or more. The flowers are about two-thirds the size of those of the Morning Glory, and a bed of the Dwarf Convolvulus forms beautiful mass; and were it not that the flowers are closed during the latter part of the day, the same as Convolvulus major, few plants would give more satisfaction. The engraving shows the flower one-half natural size.

### CREPIS, Nat. Ord. *Compositæ*.

The Crepis are pretty plants that almost every one would like in a large collection, but which we would not recommend to those who cultivate but few flowers, except once for trial or acquaintance. There is great pleasure in forming a personal acquaintance with strange flowers by culture, just as much as in traveling among new scenes in strange lands; at least, so we think. There are several varieties of the Crepis, yellow, purple, pink and white, all hardy annuals, about one foot in height, and bearing delicate, pretty flowers. The engraving shows the full size of the flower. Plants should be about eight or ten inches apart. Seed will germinate if sown in the open ground, but we generally put a pinch or two in the hot-bed.

### DATURA, Nat. Ord. *Solanaceæ*.

ATURA is a large, strong-growing plant, with trumpet-shaped flowers, the best varieties bearing blooms six inches in length, mostly white, and sometimes tinted with a delicate blue. No one ever flowered a good Datura for the first time who was not a good deal more than pleased, and no one ever had a blooming plant in his garden that did not receive a large share of the attention and admiration of visitors. This is due very largely to its great size and purity of color. There are several double varieties, in fact, the Datura seems to double in almost every style, but we prefer the single kind. The roots of one variety, *Wrightii*, will usually endure the winter and flower for several seasons, but any of the roots can be preserved in a cellar, like Dahlia roots. Plants two feet in height; set plants two feet apart.

### DELPHINIUM, Nat. Ord. *Ranunculaceæ*.

The Delphiniums are beautiful, free blooming, popular plants, and generally known as *Larkspurs* on account of the peculiar formation of the flower, which has a fancied resemblance to the spur of that favorite European song-bird, the Lark. There are several very desirable Perennials, which will be found described in the proper department, and also quite a number of annuals, all hardy and good. The Larkspurs prefer a cool soil and season, plenty of moisture, and a little shade will do no injury. Sow the seeds in the autumn, or very early in the spring, so as to have the benefit of cool, early, showery weather. Among the annuals, the Rocket varieties are perhaps the favorites. They send up a tall spike, as shown in the engraving, which gives the name, and a bed of these varieties is truly gorgeous. The appearance of a good double flower is shown in the small engraving. There are several varieties that make rather large, branching plants, and as these have abundance of flowers on strong stems, are especially desirable for cutting. A somewhat new variety, called *Candelabrum*, is shown in the engraving. The branching varieties grow about two feet in height, and should be planted about eighteen inches apart. The Rockets should be set in rows five or six inches apart. Sow the seed where the plants are to bloom. Larkspurs continue in flower only a short time.

### DIDISCUS, Nat. Ord. *Apiaceæ*.

The Didiscus cœruleus is a truly handsome Australian plant, about two feet in height, with numerous umbels of sky blue flowers. The appearance of both plant and flower we have endeavored to show in the engraving. While, like others we have before described, we do not think this flower will ever become generally cultivated, yet it is too pretty to be omitted from our list. If seeds are sown and plants well forwarded in the hot-bed, bloom may expected about the first of July; but if in the open ground, not until the latter part of the month. It is better, if possible, to sow under glass.

## DIANTHUS, Nat. Ord. *Caryophyllaceæ.*

A splendid genus of the most beautiful perennials grown. The *Sweet William*, (*Dianthus barbatus,*) the Carnation and Picotee, (*D. caryophyllus,*) and the Garden Pink, (*D. hortensis,*) belong to this genus; but, as they do not flower until the second season, will be described in the proper place. The species known as *D. Chinensis*, embracing the old Chinese Pink, very much improved of late years, and the new and superb varieties from Japan, known as *D. Heddewigii* and *laciniatus*, are among the most brilliant and useful of our garden flowers. The last two run into many varieties, the result of hybridization, with flowers of monstrous size and varied and rich in coloring. Plants of the tall growing sorts are from twelve to fifteen inches in height, while the dwarf kinds make handsome low, compact bushes, excellent for the garden and unsurpassed for pots. Seed may be sown in the spring, under glass or in a seed-bed. Easily transplanted. Set the plants from six to twelve inches apart, according to varieties—the dwarf sorts only about six inches. The Dianthus flowers freely during the whole summer. If the flowering is checked by pruning, so as to keep the plants vigorous, they will usually survive the winter well, and make most beautiful plants the second season, even much

better than the first. If allowed to flower too freely, they are sometimes so weakened as to be unable to bear the winter without suffering great injury, if they escape destruction. Seed sown late in the spring will produce strong young plants for the second season's flowering. The Dwarf sorts especially, and, in fact, all kinds, make very good house plants, if not kept too warm. In this family there has been very great improvement in the past few years, so that now flowers grown from seeds of the common China Pink are far superior to anything known among the China or Japan Pinks ten years ago. The engraving shows a flower of a good double Pink, of natural size. The single varieties are so brilliant in color that they are prized by some persons even more than the double sorts, and for beautiful markings and rich coloring few flowers equal the single Japan and China Pinks.

## DOUBLE DAISY, (Bellis,) Nat. Ord. *Compositæ.*

Every one knows and loves the Daisy. It has been the favorite flower of the poets from CHAUCER down. Even the Daisy of the field is beautiful and poetical. The cultivated double kinds are so good, and their merits so well known, that they need neither description nor praise at our hands. Unfortunately our climate is too dry for the perfection of the Daisy, and it is only in early spring or in favored locations, or where water is freely used, that we can see the Daisy in its prime. Plenty of water and shade, however, will do the work. Plants of good sorts can usually be procured, but seed sown either in the hot-bed or open ground

will produce plants that will give a few late flowers the first season. A portion coming from seed will always be single, and these can be removed. The plants should be about six inches apart when set, so that when in perfection they will about cover the ground. For a single line or border, the Daisy is unsurpassed. Plants do not always bear a Northern winter without injury, and sometimes suffer in dry seasons. A cold-frame in winter, and a cool North border in summer, will insure success.

### ERYSIMUM, Nat. Ord. *Crucifera*.

RYSIMUMS are very good and perfectly hardy annuals, of the Mustard family. They form fair looking plants about eighteen inches in height, with clusters of yellow or orange, fragrant flowers, and plant and blossom resemble the single Wallflower, though both flowers and clusters are smaller. Late in the season the Erysimum is very desirable for cutting, and although not a flower that we would select as one of the best six, yet it is one we would not like to dispense with and also one that improves with acquaintance. Some time when you need flowers for loose bouquets or decorations, try the Erysimum.

### ESCHSCHOLTZIA, (California Poppy,) Nat. Ord. *Papaveracea*.

The Eschscholtzias are the most showy of our yellow-flowered annuals. This we well knew, but the exceeding brilliance of these flowers when grown in masses we did not realize until we saw thousands of acres in their native home, California, shining like seas of molten gold. The plant is of low growth, the tallest varieties being less than a foot in height, while the dwarf kinds are not more than six inches. The leaves are finely cut, and glaucous green in color. There are now several distinct varieties, white, yellow, orange, &c., but the old yellow, known as the California Poppy, is quite equal to the best. Seed may be sown in the garden where plants are to flower.

### EUPHORBIA, Nat. Ord. *Euphorbiaceæ*.

The Euphorbia marginata is a pretty annual, making a plant nearly two feet in height and having the appearance of a shrub or miniature tree. The largest of the leaves are nearly two inches in length, growing smaller as they near the tops of the branches. The leaves are very pretty light green, surrounded by a margin of clear, snowy white, on the large leaves merely a line, becoming wider as the leaves get smaller, until the smallest are nearly or quite pure white, as are also the flower bracts. It grows abundantly west of the Mississippi, and is called Snow on the Mountains, and we thought this a very appropriate name, as we noticed it growing upon the plains, within sight of the snow-fringed mountains. For a bed of ornamental-leaved plants few things we are acquainted with will give more satisfaction.

### EUTOCA, Nat. Ord. *Hydrophyllaceæ*.

The Eutocas are another pretty class of California annuals, all having blue flowers, though of different shades. They are coarse growing plants, but the flowers of the dark colored sorts are intensely blue. They do best in a warm sandy soil, at least give more flowers in proportion to their foliage than if in a rich strong soil. The Eutocas are very desirable for cutting, because a flowering branch when placed in water will keep in bloom for many days. It seems almost strange that we are indebted to California for so many of our nice annuals. The lover of flowers, and particularly if acquainted with annuals, in traveling in California finds it hard to persuade himself that he is not in a cultivated garden, and often we found ourselves unconsciously looking for the house, the host, and the gardener.

### FENZLIA, Nat. Ord. *Polemoniaceæ.*

FENZLIA DIANTHIFLORA is a very neat little plant, bearing a perfect mass of small flowers. In fact both plant and flower are miniature in size. The flowers are rosy tinted, with a yellow throat, surrounded by dark colored spots. This little plant is a native of California, and we think must grow up among the mountains or in the shady canyons, for it seems to require both shade and moisture, and suffers materially in the garden in a hot, dry season. It is very desirable for pots or baskets, or for window or conservatory decoration, forming a globular mass of flowers, four inches in diameter, and constantly in flower, when the plant is healthy and strong.

### GAILLARDIA, Nat. Ord. *Compositæ.*

GAILLARDIA is a really good bedding annual, the plants being strong, constant bloomers through the whole summer, and each plant covering a good deal of ground. The plants are somewhat coarse, and the flowers by no means delicate, yet a good bed of Gaillardia will bring no discredit upon the taste of the cultivator. The Gaillardias are natives of Texas and other Southern States, and are known by the common name of Blanket Flower in some sections of the South, under which name we have received many specimens of seed and flowers.  Half-hardy annuals; bear transplanting well, and should be set from twelve to eighteen inches apart.

### GILIA, Nat. Ord. *Polemoniaceæ.*

Gilias are free-flowering, hardy annuals, growing from six to ten inches in height, with clusters of small, delicate, yet bright, lively flowers, that make very pretty little masses or clumps, but do not look well in very large beds or masses. The Gilias, like so many of our fine annuals, are natives of California, and were discovered and introduced into Europe about forty years since. Plants of most of the varieties flower very early, often in the seed bed, and almost as soon as out of the seed-leaf. The flowers are small, borne in panicles, and desirable for cutting. Quite hardy,   and seed may be sown in the open ground, but if transplanted should be removed when small.

### HELIANTHUS, (Sunflower,) Nat. Ord. *Compositæ.*

HELIANTHUS is the well known old fashioned Sunflower; coarse, tall plants, from four to eight feet in height, with bright yellow flowers. The best double varieties produce a very good effect among shrubbery, and when used as screens, etc. The Sunflower is a native of Peru, and in old times was regarded with some reverence as a flower sacred to the sun, and was worn by the virgins of the sun at the great festivals of the Incas. It is no doubt the flower alluded to by Ovid, when he represented Clytia as pining to death for love of Apollo and being changed by the pitying god into a flower which turned to the sun. The Sunflower is hardy and annually reproduces itself from self-sown seed. Many are now turning their attention to the growth of the Sun-flower for the production of oil, and as food for poultry, and Prof. MAURY published a series of articles endeavoring to prove that for the destruction of malaria in swampy districts it was invaluable, we have no doubt equaling the *Eucalyptus.*

## HUNNEMANNIA, Nat. Ord. *Papaveraceæ.*

Hunnemannia fumariæfolia is a beautiful herbaceous perennial, from Mexico, but one, we regret, not hardy in Northern latitudes. Fortunately, however, the plant makes a rapid growth,

arrives at maturity and flowers the first season. We, at the North, therefore, can treat the Hunnemannia as an annual, and by sowing the seed every spring enjoy its beauty as well as those who are blessed with a more favorable climate. The plant makes a growth of about two feet; the flowers are bright yellow and tulip-formed. We are always pleased with this flower, and can, therefore, recommend its culture.

## KAULFUSSIA, Nat. Ord. *Compositæ.*

AULFUSSIAS are pretty, little, free flowering, hardy annuals, having the appearance of single Asters, but the ray florets curl back in a very curious way, after the flower has been expanded a short time. The plants make a low growth, only being about six inches in height, and would be excellent for bedding, only that they make their growth early in the season, and bloom and ripen their seed long before we are prepared to dispense with any bedding plant that has been enlisted in the work of ornamenting our lawns or gardens. There are many,

however, who, despite this fault, are very much attached to the pretty little Kaulfussia. The colors of all the varieties are good, and of some very intense.

## LEPTOSIPHON, Nat. Ord. *Polemoniaceæ.*

EPTOSIPHONS are low, pretty, hardy, California annuals, growing less than six inches in height, and bearing clusters of delicate little flowers. Like many other California annuals, they do not seem to bear our hot dry summers very well, but do not suffer by either wet or cold. They are so perfectly hardy that we have always succeeded by sowing seed late in the autumn or at the earliest

possible moment in the spring, as we have advised for Clarkia. This course produces early spring flowers in abundance. A border on the north side of a fence or building suits them exactly.

## LINUM, (Flax,) Nat. Ord. *Linaceæ.*

Linum grandiflorum rubrum is a very fine half-hardy annual, with beautiful, bright crimson flowers that continue all through the summer. The habit of the plant is neat and slender, like all the Flax family, and it grows to eighteen inches or more in height. When planted a foot apart, this Flax makes a very good bed. We have endeavored to show, in the engraving, the habit of the plant, and also the appearance of the flower, which is of a brilliant scarlet color, and about the size shown in the engraving. Seeds germinate best in the hot-bed, but will do pretty well if sown in the garden in a light soil. Perennial varieties will be found described in the proper department.

## LOBELIA, Nat. Ord. *Lobeliaceæ.*

Lobelias are a class of plants of great beauty and remarkably useful to the gardener, being adapted to a great variety of ornamental purposes. Some of the Lobelias are strong, hardy perennials, like our Cardinal Flower. The annual varieties are mostly of a trailing habit, bearing immense numbers of small flowers, and are particularly adapted to baskets, vases, etc., where drooping plants look so graceful; they are also freely used as edgings for beds of ornamental-leaved and other bedding plants. A few varieties form compact, almost globular, little plants, and one of these we have shown in the engraving. This style is superb for edgings of beds, pots, and like purposes, which the habit will suggest to the thoughtful florist.

## LUPINUS, (Lupine,) Nat. Ord. *Leguminosæ.*

The Lupins are a well-known genus of very conspicuous plants, and there are very few people that are not acquainted with some of the varieties. We have cultivated the Lupin for a couple of scores of years, have seen it in the best gardens of Europe, and yet we never realized its wealth of beauty until we met it in its California home. Here we saw the little, dwarf Lupin, scarcely six inches in height with its pretty, miniature flowers, and the mammoth plant full six feet, with flowering stems stretching themselves out like giant arms. Here we saw the white, the yellow, the blue, the variegated,—Lupins of every hue. We returned with greater love than ever for this old-fashioned flower. All the Lupins are hardy, and seed can be sown in the open ground. The Lupin has a tap root and does not transplant well.

## LYCHNIS, Nat. Ord. *Caryophyllaceæ.*

The Lychnis family are mostly perennials, but flower the first season under good treatment, and endure the winter unusually well. Some, like *L. Chalcedonica*, are old friends, but of late years florists have greatly improved this flower, and the better varieties now give flowers as large as Japan Pinks, and of a great variety of colors, such as rose, red, and white. To obtain good flowers the first summer, seeds should be started under glass and transplanted as early as the weather will permit. The taller varieties are excellent for planting among shrubbery. A piece of shrubbery looks quite sombre a great part of the season, and the sooner we learn to light up our shrubberies with tall, bright flowers, the better. The engraving on the right shows one of the improved, large varieties, *Haageana;* at the left, *Chalcedonica*, both less than half natural size.

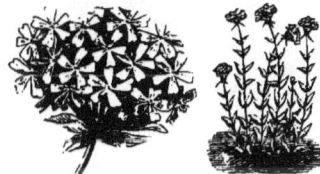
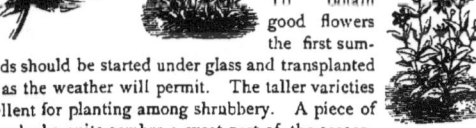

## MALOPE, Nat. Ord. *Malvaceæ.*

ALOPE differs from the Mallow, botanically, principally in the shape of the capsules, and their arrangement, but to the florist the principal difference is in the superior size and beauty of the Malope flower. The only varieties we would recommend for culture are M. grandiflora, a bright purplish flower, more than three inches across and M. grandiflora alba, pure white, and about two inches. The Malope is a strong growing plant, three feet in height. Seed may be sown under glass, and then plants will bloom very early; or in the open ground, with a later, but quite as strong a growth.

## MARIGOLD, (Tagetes,) Nat. Ord. *Compositæ.*

Marigold, or Tagetes, as the French and African Marigolds are called, are so well known that no general description will be necessary, as they have been cultivated for more than two hundred

years. The French Marigold, no doubt, came from Peru, or some part of South America, while the name of the African indicates its true origin. Both are tall, coarse plants, the African being the more robust, often reaching more than two feet in height. The flowers large, some being four inches across, double, in color yellow, orange, and brown. There are several dwarf varieties, growing only from six inches to a foot in height. A comparatively new variety, *signata pumila*, makes a beautiful plant, almost a perfect ball, a foot or more in diameter, and covered with hundreds of single yellow flowers, as shown in the engraving. The leaves are finely cut, almost fern-like, and the plant continues to increase in beauty until frost.

## MARTYNIA, Nat. Ord. *Pedaliaceæ.*

The Martynias are coarse, robust, hardy annuals, of a spreading habit, requiring at least three feet of space to perfect their growth. They are natives of Louisiana, Texas, Mexico, and farther South. The engraving gives a front view of the flower, which is tubular, and about an inch in length. The colors are yellow, white and purple, and one variety, *formosa*, is sweetly fragrant. The seed-pods are very curiously formed, as will be seen by the little engraving, and they grow six inches or more in length; the variety called *proboscidea* having the largest

pods, and these, when about two-thirds grown and quite tender, are much prized for pickles.

## MEDICAGO, Nat. Ord. *Leguminosæ.*

There are several varieties of Medicago more or less cultivated for their curious seed-pods. These we have never thought worthy of description in the GUIDE, as the flowers are by no means beautiful; yet there is considerable demand for the seed-pods by those who use them for the manufacture of rustic picture frames, and other rustic work. We, therefore, give engravings of two of the best, one called Snail, and the other, Bee-hive, or Hedge-hog; of the appropriateness of these names we leave our readers to judge.

## MESEMBRYANTHEMUM, Nat. Ord. *Ficoideæ.*

The Mesembryanthemums are pretty, half hardy annuals, with delicate, succulent, almost transparent leaves and branches. The two most popular varieties in America are those commonly known as Ice-plant and Dew-plant. Both are excellent for baskets, vases, pots, etc., the Ice-plant having thick, fleshy leaves and stems, covered with little shining globules, which it will take some investigation to convince the spectator are not "truly ice." The flowers are small, white, and unimportant. The Dew-plant has a smooth, light green, pretty, dewy-looking leaf, a graceful slender, habit, and a very pretty pink flower. Both are drooping plants, and therefore, with their pretty foliage, peculiarly adapted to basket and vase work. The increased attention given to these graceful decorations has made the Mesembryanthemums and other plants adapted to this work very popular. The culture of plants with pretty ornamental foliage that can be grown from the seed early in the spring so as to produce a good effect during the season, should be encouraged, as it places very large resources in the hands of the gardener at a mere trifling cost.

## MIGNONETTE, (Reseda,) Nat. Ord. *Resedaceæ.*

We need not describe the Sweet Mignonette, that every one knows and everybody loves, and yet very few cultivate, compared with the many who might thus show their love for this sweet little flower. In Europe, especially in England and Germany, we noticed Mignonette growing in every possible place and in every imaginable receptacle. For the wealthy, beautiful and costly Mignonette pots and boxes are provided, that will elegantly adorn the window sill, or nicely fill and beautify any niche or bracket. Those not blessed with so much of earthly good use ordinary flower pots, while the children press into the service broken teapots and old crockery of every conceivable pattern. Seeds of Mignonette can be sown at any season, so that by having pots prepared at different times a succession of flowers can be secured, and Mignonette adorn the button hole and perfume the house at all times.

The florists of Europe have introduced several new varieties of Mignonette among their novelties, claiming for them much superiority over our old and well loved Sweet Mignonette; but these claims, we have always found, on trial, to have but little foundation in truth. The *New White*, with a larger flower and more robust growth, and a little whiter in color, is the only new kind of merit.

## MIRABILIS, Nat. Ord. *Nyctaginaceæ.*

Mirabilis Jalapa is the well known Marvel of Peru, a native, we believe, of South America, and also of the West Indies, and first found in Peru, soon after the discovery of the country, when everything from that strange land was considered marvelous. It was at one time supposed that the root of this plant furnished the Jalap of commerce, hence the name, but this was found to be untrue. It is also known as the Four-o'clock, because its flowers expand about that time in the evening and fade the next morning. By the French it is called Belle of the Night. It is really a good plant, about two feet in height, well branched, with bright foliage, fragrant flowers, desirable colors, and fine markings. Plants should be about two feet apart. It makes a nice summer hedge if set in a row about a foot apart. Seed should be planted in the open ground, where the plants are desired. The Mirabilis is generally treated as a half-hardy annual.

The roots, however, may be taken up in the autumn and preserved like Dahlias, during the winter; but as plants are obtained so readily from seed, and flower so soon, this course is seldom practiced. The flower shown in the engraving is about two-thirds the natural size.

## MIMULUS, Nat. Ord. *Scrophulariaceæ*.

The Mimuli, sometimes called Monkey Flowers, are beautiful, tender looking plants. The branches are almost transparent and quite succulent, and are easily broken by the wind. For baskets under the shelter of verandahs, vases, and for culture in the house, not many plants will give more satisfaction. M. cardinalis does very well in the garden. Flowers of the Mimulus are very brilliant.

## MYOSOTIS, Nat. Ord. *Boraginaceæ*.

Perennial plants, that flower the first season if sown early, bearing small white and blue flowers. Delight in a rather moist situation. Fine for moist rock-work. All the blue varieties are commonly called Forget-me-not. M. palustris is the old and popular Forget-me-not. 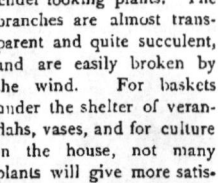 The branches cut and placed in water will continue to bloom a long time, almost as well as if on the plant, and will often make roots, and considerable growth. Seed may be sown in the hot-bed and transplanted as early as possible, or may be sown in the open ground in the spring, so as to get a good growth before the hot, dry weather of summer.

## NEMOPHILA, Nat. Ord. *Hydrophyllaceæ*.

NEMOPHILAS are pretty, delicate, hardy annuals, throwing up their slender flower stems a few inches. The leaves are very pretty in form, and of a delicate, lively green, and, if the plants are grown in masses, have a mossy appearance. The flowers are mainly blue and white, and of the forms shown in the engravings. They are native Americans, and yet flourish much better in the moist climate of Britain than here. Nemophilas were first found fifty years since, in shady, moist places on the banks of the Missouri River. This fact shows why they will not better endure our hot, dry summers. No annual is grown with greater success in England than the Nemophila, and we hardly think as extensively. On the high land in Calaveras County, California, and in the neighborhood of the big trees, we saw acres of Nemophilas, beautifying the waste land, and finer than we ever saw them in the gardens of Europe or America.  They do best if sown in a frame and transplanted early, as the hot sun injures the flowers; but do finely all summer, if planted in a rather cool, shady place. Set about six inches apart. A few plants set early among spring-flowering bulbs, such as Tulips, etc., flower splendidly, and a few seeds scattered over the beds of bulbs will render a very good account of themselves in the early spring.

## NIEREMBERGIA, Nat. Ord. *Solanaceæ.*

The Nierembergias are very pretty plants with delicate, whitish flowers, tinted with lilac, and with a deep purplish lilac blotch in the center. The plant is slender and delicate, bearing abundance of flowers the whole summer. The Nierembergias are tender perennials, and are therefore suitable for house culture, or they may be treated as tender annuals, and will flower early in the season, if transferred from the frame or the green-house to the garden, when there is no danger of frost. They are natives of South America, and are worthy of more general culture. For baskets, vases, etc., we cannot recommend the Nierembergia too highly. The engraving shows the flower of natural size, and is a fair representation of its form, but the engraving representing the appearance of the plant does not give so good an idea of its character.

## NIGELLA, Nat. Ord. *Ranunculaceæ.*

The Nigellas are curious, hardy annuals, with finely cut leaves, and very curious, showy flowers, which, from their singular construction, have acquired many odd names, as Love-in-a-Mist, Devil-in-a-Bush, etc. Seeds grow very readily, and may be sown in the open ground early in the spring, and in most sections in the autumn. They are natives of Asia Minor, Egypt, and other Eastern countries, and the seeds, being aromatic, are extensively used both by oriental cooks and physicians. Indeed, they are supposed by Egyptian ladies to improve the complexion; but as their ideas of a good complexion may not agree with Western notions, perhaps it would not be well to try the experiment. Both seeds and leaves, we believe, are used in India to prevent the ravages of moth and other insects among clothing.

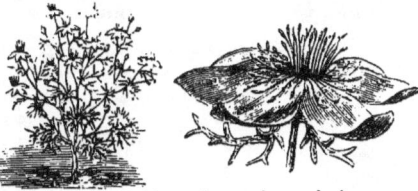

## NOLANA, Nat. Ord. *Nolanaceæ.*

Nolanas are trailing, hardy annuals, the plant fleshy and succulent, and with flowers very much resembling Convolvulus minor, but with more substance. The Nolana prefers a light soil, and it is seldom too hot or dry to suit its wants. The Nolana is a native of Peru and Chili. Seed may be sown in the border where the flowers are desired, or in a seed-bed in the garden, to be transplanted as needed. Excellent for rock-work, baskets, etc. The Nolana delights in the same treatment, soil, &c., as the Portulaca, and may be used with the best effect in situations where our old Portulaca would be desirable. This class of plants, the natives of Southern climes, that delight in heat and drouth, are our choicest treasures in midsummer, when the thermometer is above ninety much of the day, without a drop of rain for weeks.

## ŒNOTHERA, (Evening Primrose,) Nat. Ord. *Onagraceæ*.

ENOTHERAS are a very fine genus of showy plants, opening their flowers suddenly in the latter part of the day, and making a most brilliant exhibition during the evening and early in the morning. Some of the large varieties will attract as much attention as anything that can be grown. They certainly look like things of life, as they open with a nervous motion that cannot only be seen but heard. The low, white variety, *acaulis alba*, is a marvel of beauty, producing flowers four inches across, pure white, and one or more flowers appearing each successive evening. Most other varieties are primrose yellow.

## OBELISCARIA, Nat. Ord. *Compositæ*.

The Obeliscarias are coarse plants with showy flowers. The best, *O. pulcherrima*, exhibits a strange commingling of red, brown and yellow. The engraving gives a very good idea of the form of this flower, with its curious, acorn-like center, and drooping petals, or rather, the ray-flowers. These ray-flowers are of a rich, velvety crimson, edged with yellow. The central cone, or disk, is brown until the ray-flowers expand, and they are bright yellow. The flowers are borne on pretty long stems, and plants are about eighteen inches in height. The Obeliscaria we cannot call beautiful, but it is interesting.

## OXYURA, Nat. Ord. *Compositæ*.

Oxyura chrysanthemoides is a very pretty, free-flowering, little hardy annual, one of the very many pretty things for which we are indebted to California. The plant is neat in habit, branching, about eighteen inches in height; the flower is daisy-like, size and form being very well represented in the engraving. The color is of the most delicate lemon yellow, with a clear, white edging. The effect of these two colors is very pretty. The only possible objection to this plant is the fact that it does not continue in flower all the summer, like the Phlox, Petunia, etc.

 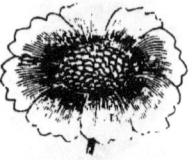

## PALAFOXIA, Nat. Ord. *Compositæ*.

ALAFOXIA HOOKERIANA is a fine, new annual. There are several species, but the best is the one we describe, which is of a dwarf, branching habit. The flowers are rosy crimson, with a dark center, and continue in flower well through the summer. We have uniformly sown the seed of this flower under glass, judging from its appearance and place of nativity, Texas and Mexico, that this would be the best treatment, but some of our correspondents have succeeded by sowing in the open ground. Set the plants about ten inches apart.

## PANSY, (Viola tricolor,) Nat. Ord. *Violaceæ*.

The Pansy is the little Heartsease of Europe, become somewhat naturalized in America, and wonderfully improved by cultivation. It was about sixty years ago that this flower first attracted the special notice of florists, their attention being called to it by the great success of a lady amateur. We give an engraving of the Hearts-ease as it is found wild. The French call it *Pensee*, and this is, no doubt, the origin of the common name, Pansy. The Pansy is now a popular flower with both florists and amateurs, giving abundance of bloom until after severe frosts, enduring our hard winters with safety, and greeting us in the earliest spring with a profusion of bright blossoms. It will flower better in the middle of the summer, if planted where it is somewhat shaded from the hot sun, and especially if furnished with a good supply of water, but in almost any situation will give fine flowers in the spring and autumn. If plants come into bloom in the heat of summer, the flowers will be small at first; but as the weather becomes cooler, they will increase in size and beauty. Often plants that produce flowers two and a half inches in diameter during the cool, showery weather of spring, will give only the smallest possible specimens during the dry weather of summer. To have good flowers, the plant must be vigorous, and make a rapid growth. No flower is more easily ruined by ill treatment or adverse circumstances. Seed may be sown in the hot-bed or open ground. If young plants are grown in the autumn, and kept in a frame during the winter, with a little covering in the severest weather, they will be ready to set out very early in the spring, and give flowers until hot weather. If seed is sown in the spring, get it in as early as possible, so as to have plants ready to flower during the spring rains. Seed sown in a cool place in June or July, and well watered until up, will make plants for autumn flowering. The Pansies make a beautiful bed, and are interesting as individual flowers. No flower is so companionable and life-like. It requires no very great stretch of the imagination to cause one to believe that they see and move, and acknowledge our admiration in a very pretty, knowing way.

## PERILLA, Nat. Ord. *Labiatæ*.

The Perilla Nankinensis is one of the best of the ornamental-leaved annuals. It has a broad, serrated leaf, of a purplish mulberry color, and makes a well formed plant, as represented in the engraving, and eighteen inches or more in height. It is very desirable for the center of a bed of ornamental-leaved plants, and we can recommend it also for a low screen or hedge, and such hedges will be found exceedingly useful in many situations. The Perilla is one of the plants that is good for some special work, indeed, almost invaluable, but in an ordinary collection of flower seeds would not be desirable. We are induced to mention this fact here, because, last season, a gentleman wrote us that we had better leave this plant out of our collection, as it was no better than a weed—and, perhaps, he was right, for a weed is any plant out of place. An Aster among a bed of Petunias would be a weed.

### PETUNIA, Nat. Ord. *Solanaceæ*.

Just fifty years ago, the White Petunia was found by a botanical explorer in South America, at the mouth of the Rio de la Plata. For seven years the florists of Europe were delighted with this poor, white flower, when a Purple Petunia was discovered in Brazil. Since that time, 1830, the improvement of this flower has been constant. About fifteen years since the floral world were surprised by the announcement of a *double* white Petunia. It was only semi-double, but now we have them well doubled, of all colors, and as large as any one can wish. Seed sown in the spring will produce flowering plants in June that will continue to bloom abundantly until frost, and may be sown in a cold-frame or hot-bed, or in the open ground. Set the plants about eighteen inches apart. They come pretty true from seed, though not reliable in this respect, being inclined to sport. The Petunia as at present cultivated embraces three distinct classes. The grandiflora varieties make quite a strong, succulent growth, and the stems and leaves are sticky to the touch. These bear a few very large, magnificent flowers, often from three to four inches across. They bear but few seeds and these are obtained at great expense of labor. In the open ground they give no

seed, so plants for seed must be grown in pots on stages, sheltered from rain and dews, and fertilization is accomplished by hand, the pollen being distributed with the aid of a camel-hair brush. Of course, seed obtained in this way is always expensive, but the wonderful size and the richness of the coloring well repays the cost. In this class we have a Fringed Petunia, new and unique. The Double Petunia gives no seed, and those that will produce double flowers are obtained by fertilizing single flowers with the pollen of the double, in the manner previously described. The third class is the small flowered varieties. The plants are of a slender, wiry growth, but cover a good deal of ground. They bear an immense number of flowers, from early summer until frost, and seed freely in the open ground. A well filled circular bed, six feet in diameter, will display continually, without a day's intermission, thousands of flowers. We know of no annual, and but few flowers of any kind, that will make a more brilliant bed. Our engravings show one of the small-flowered varieties of natural size, and a double flower much reduced.

### PHACELIA, Nat. Ord. *Hydrophyllaceæ*.

The Phacelias are hardy annuals, very much resembling the Eutocas, and, we believe, all natives of America. Most of the varieties are blue, though there are some white. This flower does not really possess much merit, though pretty fair as a border plant, and good for bouquet making. We only recommend two varieties. P. tanacetifolia alba, presenting a very remarkable appearance from the strings of whitish flowers that appear to have just unrolled, the long, black hairs with which it is covered, and the singular stamens, which project far beyond the corolla of the flowers. P. congesta is somewhat less robust, not so hairy, and flowers light blue.

## PHLOX DRUMMONDII, Nat. Ord. *Polemoniaceæ.*

No annual excels the Phlox for a brilliant and constant display. Indeed, if confined to one plant for the decoration of the lawn or border, the *Phlox Drummondii* would be my choice over any annual or perennial with which I am acquainted. It seems to have every desirable quality for this purpose. The colors range from the purest white to the deepest crimson, including purple, and yellow, and striped, the clear eye of the Phlox being peculiarly marked. Seed may be sown in the open ground in May, or in a cold-frame or hot-bed earlier in the season; and in either case, from June, during the whole summer and autumn, they make a most brilliant bed of showy yet delicate flowers.

A good bed of Phlox is a sight that dazzles the eye with its brilliancy. The Phlox, in a good, rich soil, will grow more than eighteen inches in height, but as there is not sufficient strength in the main stem, it will not stand entirely erect. A foot apart is about near enough to set the plants, unless the soil is very poor. If too thick, they suffer from mildew. The Phlox makes a very good border or low summer hedge. The finest effect, however, is produced by planting each color in a separate bed or in ribbon fashion, its constant bloom making it very desirable for these purposes. Indeed, we know of no annual or perennial that will give a more brilliant and constant mass of color. The Phlox is a native of America. It was first discovered in Texas, in 1835, by DRUMMOND, a collector sent out by the Glasgow Botanical Society. It was the last new plant he sent home, as he soon after died in Cuba. The buds, just before opening, look like a flame, and hence the name, Phlox, or Flame. I grow from five to ten acres of Phlox every year, devoting much time and means to its improvement, and have no hesitation in saying my strain of Phlox Drummondii is the best the world produces. Indeed, I have already introduced several new varieties, showing much improvement either in form or coloring, and have several more on trial, among them one with a pretty fringed edge; another, very large, of unusual substance, and perfect, rounded form; and if I should, in a year or two, introduce a good, double, annual Phlox, I would be more pleased than surprised. There is no difficulty in starting new and improved varieties. The difficulty is in getting their character so well established that the seed will be reliable, that is pretty sure to produce a good portion of flowers like the one from which the seed was saved.

## POPPY, (Papaver,) Nat. Ord. *Papaveraceæ.*

The Poppies are not only well known to every cultivator of flowers, but to almost every one, and yet few know a real good Poppy. There are some very fine perennials, which we shall mention when describing plants that do not flower the first season from the seed. The good annual varieties are numerous, ranging in size from the little Ranunculus-flowered, an inch in diameter, to the Pæony-flowered, four or five inches across. They also present an almost endless variety of colors and markings. The true Opium Poppy, the variety used for growing Opium, is a large, white, single flower. The Poppy has a strong tap-root, and is, therefore, difficult to transplant, and it is better to sow the seed early in the spring where the plants are to flower. The Poppies are all perfectly hardy.

## PORTULACA, Nat. Ord. *Portulacaceæ*.

The Portulaca is a popular, hardy, creeping annual, each strong plant covering a space about a foot in diameter, with salver-shaped flowers, of every color imaginable, except blue, and striped, and these colors of the most intense brightness. The Portulaca delights in a warm sun and a sandy soil, and the drouth is never too long nor the heat too intense for this beautiful little salamander. When everything else is perishing for lack of moisture, the Portulaca will give its largest flowers and brightest colors. We well recollect when the Portulaca gave us but very few colors, and a double flower would have been a wonder. Now we have all the colors that heart can desire, and flowers as double as roses and almost as large. The Portulaca does not like a clay soil nor black muck. It makes a brilliant bed on the lawn, but as the plants are low it is best to raise the bed in the center. Sow the seed in the open ground early, or under glass. The plants can be transplanted even in full flower, and in making a ribbon bed with Portulaca, we always wait until the first flower opens, so as to be entirely sure of the colors. Only one possible objection can be made to the Portulaca, and that is that its flowers are fully open only in sunshine; like the sun-dial, it counts only the bright hours. The perfectly double Portulaca forms no seed, so that seed must be saved from semi-double flowers; and from fifty to seventy-five per cent. of plants from this seed will give double flowers.

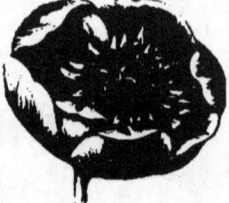

## RICINUS, (Castor Oil Bean,) Nat. Ord. *Euphorbiaceæ*.

RICINUS. Plants with very ornamental foliage and showy fruit, of stately growth and quite a tropical appearance. With other ornamental-leaved plants, they make a most attractive bed on the lawn, and are also desirable when grown as single specimens. Plant the seed in the open ground, in a dry situation, and as early as safe in the spring. The same soil and treatment that will give good early corn is just suitable for the Ricinus. In the latter part of the summer the splendid spikes, composed of the seed-vessels, will be quite gorgeous. Some of the varieties have spikes of a beautiful metallic green, others of a fine, almost transparent pink and scarlet, which seem to illuminate the grounds. There is no ornamental-leaved plant for outdoor decoration for ordinary use equal to the Ricinus. For a clump or bed, the Ricinus should be planted about three feet apart. For a screen, and nothing is better fitted for such a purpose, about two feet apart. Plants range from five to ten feet in height, except a dwarf variety, which seldom exceeds three feet.

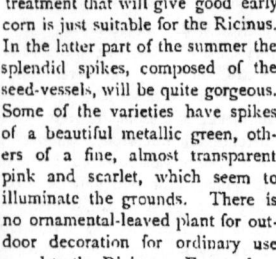

## SALPIGLOSSIS, Nat. Ord. *Scrophulariaceæ*.

ALPIGLOSSIS is a very good half-hardy annual, with flowers of peculiar richness, and very delicately and beautifully pencilled. Indeed, the delicate, yet almost gorgeous markings, are a matter of surprise to many who grow this flower for the first time, and do not expect so much in so small, and apparently simple, a flower. The ordinary height is about two feet, but there is a dwarf kind that grows only about one foot in height. When the plants are set pretty closely together, say about eight or ten inches, they make a very fine bed.
Seeds may be sown under glass, but they will do well in the open ground, especially if the soil is light, and always do best in a sandy soil. The flower shown is about one-half natural size.

## SALVIA, Nat. Ord. *Labiatæ*.

Very ornamental plants for beds or borders, growing freely in any light, rich soil; from eighteen inches to two feet in height. Their beautiful spikes of gay flowers are produced in the greatest profusion. Must be treated as tender annuals, and plants should get a good start in the hot-bed, and not be planted out before the weather is warm. Very little success must be expected from sowing seed in the open ground, unless in a very favorable climate. They make fine fall and winter ornaments for the house or conservatory, and grow from two to three feet in height. The variety known as S. splendens is the beautiful autumn flower known as Scarlet Sage. Plants that are in a thrifty condition can be taken up in the autumn, before frost, and potted, and they will bloom well into the winter.

## SANVITALIA, Nat. Ord. *Compositæ*.

Sanvitalia procumbens flore-pleno is a pretty, low, or creeping, plant, especially suited for baskets, and bearing a great many double, daisy-like flowers, of a bright yellow color. It was introduced some six years since, and we felt very much disappointed with it, because more than half the flowers were only semi-double, and with a very poor black center, but for a year or two there has been considerable improvement. Seeds germinate quite freely. We sow generally under glass. A good plant will cover a space more than two feet in diameter, and will flower from July, if sown pretty early, until killed by frost.

The foliage is clean, abundant, of a fresh, lively green, and the habit of the plant good in all respects, making it a desirable drooping plant, one that will give general satisfaction.

## SAPONARIA, Nat. Ord. *Caryophyllaceæ*.

The Saponarias are little, low, delicate plants, growing a mass of little leaves and miniature flowers, the latter just about the size shown in the engraving. For a small pot, or edging, there are few little things prettier, for they entirely cover the ground with their bright little leaves and star-like flowers. There are two varieties desirable, a deep pink and a white. Setting alternate plants of white and pink produces a very nice effect in a border. We once saw a very pretty, small, circular bed filled with Saponaria, a row of each color; but it is only suited for small beds, alone; as a border or edging for beds filled with stronger plants, it is very desirable.

### SCABIOSA, (Mourning Bride,) Nat. Ord. *Dipsaceæ*.

The Scabiosa, called all-the-world-over, Mourning Bride and Mournful Widow, has been so long a popular garden flower that nobody knows where it was discovered or when first cultivated. We don't know that we can call it a very beautiful flower, and yet it is an old friend, and we like it, and it gives a great variety of colors, from white almost to black, and it grows freely and healthily, and we always grow it, and always intend to; and it cuts beautifully for large bouquets, and is an excellent flower every way. The tallest varieties grow eighteen inches in height, the flowers being supported on long, wiry stems. The dwarf sorts are about a foot in height. Seed may be grown in the garden or under glass. Plants, if thrifty in the autumn, not weakened by over-flowering, often flower the second season. A variety, S. stellata, bears curious seed-pods, shown in the engraving at the right, and these dried, work up well with Everlastings. Indeed, they look much like dried flowers, besides being very singular. There is also a double variety, so called, the plant being dwarf in habit, and the flower smaller and more compact than the old sorts. It is a neat variety and better for bouquets than the old kinds. There is a little perfume to these flowers, and they are known by the name of Sweet Scabious.

### SCHIZANTHUS, Nat. Ord. *Scrophulariaceæ*.

An interesting and beautiful class of plants that may be treated as half-hardy annuals, but that are not often seen in our gardens, and are really better adapted for house culture. They are not exactly of a climbing habit, and yet are so slender that they need support, and when this is provided will grow from two to three feet in height, and bear hundreds of pretty two-colored flowers, looking like little butterflies. Winds, rain and the hot sun often injure plants in the garden. The seed should be sown under glass, if possible. A really beautiful flower for the house. The name signifies cut flower, and it is really interesting and good.

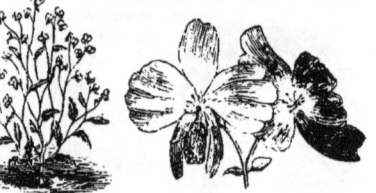

### SENSITIVE PLANT, (Mimosa,) Nat. Ord. *Leguminosæ*.

The Mimosa pudica, called Sensitive Plant from the singularly sensitive nature of the leaves, is really a pretty plant, but its chief merit is in the amusement it provides the children, and in fact, everybody. No one seems to get tired of observing the habits of this plant. When a leaf is touched it immediately begins slowly to close, and if touched near the base of the leaf-stalk, not only will the leaflets close up but the leaf-stalk droop as if broken. Start the seed under glass, and do not transplant to the open ground until the weather is warm. A plant or two reserved for the house will afford a good deal of pleasure during the winter. A very good way is to start a young plant in a pot in the spring at transplanting time, and sink the pot in the earth to the rim. Before the nights get cool in the autumn, remove the pot to the house, first re-potting into a larger pot, if necessary.

## SPRAGUEA, Nat. Ord. *Amarantaceæ*.

The Spraguea umbellata is a really pretty plant, and as curious as it is beautiful. The leaves are rounded, somewhat succulent, and arranged in a crown-like cluster, as shown in the engraving. The flowers form dense umbels, on leafless flower stems, six inches or more in length. The blossoms are pink, and though not an everlasting flower, with a very little drying will equal the best for winter use. The Spraguea is a native of California, but we saw it there only in one place, within reach of the spray of the Nevada Falls, and there it grew most luxuriously, and when we informed the ladies that these flowers were   everlastings and would keep for years, every one appropriated a good bunch as a memento of the Yosemite and Nevada Falls. Sow the seed under glass or in a sheltered bed in the garden.

## STOCK, TEN-WEEKS, (Mathiola annua,) Nat. Ord. *Cruciferæ*.

The Ten-Weeks or Annual Stock presents nearly or quite all the requisites of a perfect flowering plant—good habit, fine foliage, beautiful flowers of almost every delicate and desirable tint,

delightful fragrance, early flowering, and abundance of blossoms. Although not a constant bloomer like Phlox, Petunia, etc., the flowers endure for a long time, and the side shoots give a succession of flowers under favorable circumstances for months. Indeed, the growth and flowering seems almost perpetual, where the plant can obtain a needed supply of moisture. Cool, dewy nights and moist days are the delight of the stock. The best seeds of this flower are grown by German florists, in pots, on stages, in open houses, the object being to protect the plants from rains and dews, and severe winds. The double flowers give no seeds, but by crowding several plants into small pots, thus starving them, and by other operations known to skillful flower seed growers, seeds are produced that will grow plants with double flowers. Three-fourths of the plants raised from the best seeds will usually produce double blossoms. Seeds may be sown in the open ground, or in the hot-bed or cold-frame; but if transplanted, let this be done when the plants are quite small, just out of the seed-leaf. They should be removed from the seed-bed before they become "drawn," or slender, or the flowers will be poor. Make the soil deep and rich. Set the plants about twelve inches apart. If the plants that are not too far advanced are taken up carefully in the autumn, and potted, they will flower elegantly in the house in the winter. It is a good plan to sow a few late in the season for this purpose. After growing in the house they can be put out in the ground, and will generally flower well the second season.

## TROPÆOLUM, Nat. Ord. *Tropæolaceæ*.

ROPÆOLUM. A very splendid class of half-hardy annuals, generally known as the Nasturtium. Flowers of all the different shades of yellow, orange and red. This flower has of late been much improved, the blossoms being larger and more brilliant than the old-fashioned sorts. The varieties of *T. majus* and *T. Lobbianum* (*hybridum*,) will be found described among the Climbers; but when allowed to run on the ground, and pegged down, they make a brilliant bed. *T. minus* and its varieties are dwarf, round-headed plants, about a foot high, and in Europe are very popular, and make very fine beds. Indeed, on the Dwarf Tropæolums, among the annuals, the gardeners of England almost entirely depend for a mass of brilliant colors, while the Clarkia furnishes masses of the more delicate shades.

## VERBENA, Nat. Ord. *Verbenaceæ*.

ERBENA. Every one knows the Verbena, and almost every one has bought the little, sickly plants, in small pots, with one little tuft of flowers, but every one does not know that good, healthy plants can be produced from seed as readily as almost any tender annual, plants that will perfectly cover a space three feet in diameter, flower well in July, and continue strong and healthy until destroyed by frost. Another strange fact not generally known, is that nearly all Verbenas raised from seed are fragrant, the light colored varieties particularly so. Sow the seeds under glass early in the spring, and transplant after three or four inches of growth. There is a variety, a native of the Rocky Mountains, with pink flowers, so hardy that it will generally endure our winters and flower the second season.

## VINCA, Nat. Ord. *Apocynaceæ*.

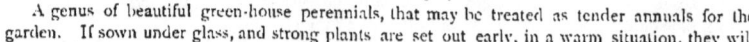

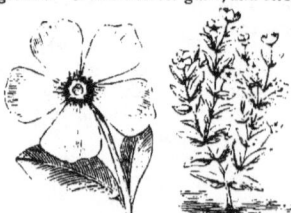

A genus of beautiful green-house perennials, that may be treated as tender annuals for the garden. If sown under glass, and strong plants are set out early, in a warm situation, they will flower beautifully in the summer and autumn, and may be potted for the house before frost. Not suitable for out-door sowing, in northern latitudes. In the Southern States the Vinca does admirably, growing almost like a weed. There are several varieties, rose-colored, white, and white with red eye. The engraving shows the flower about one-half the natural size. The leaf is a beautiful dark green, thick, smooth and shining, somewhat like the Laurel or Camellia. A well grown plant will be about eighteen inches in height. We write this in the garden, with a bed of Vincas before us, and it is difficult to moderate our praise.

## WHITLAVIA, Nat. Ord. *Hydrophyllaceæ*.

HITLAVIA. The Whitlavia is a pretty little California annual, with delicate foliage and drooping clusters of beautiful bells, of the size of the engraving, blue and white. The plants are perfectly hardy, proof against cold and wet, but suffer often in dry, hot weather, like Nemophila and many other California annuals. For a shady spot there are very few little flowers that will give more real pleasure. The flowering branches, if cut while the lower buds are about opening, will continue fresh in water for several days, every bud opening, and are elegant for a small, slender vase.

## ZINNIA, NEW DOUBLE-FLOWERED, Nat. Ord. *Compositæ*.

INNIAS must be familiar to all our aged readers, for as far back as we can recollect, the old single variety was grown under the name of Youth and Old Age in almost every garden. The Double Zinnia we may call a new flower, for it has been introduced but a few years, and has found itself so well adapted to our climate that the double Zinnias in America seem a different and better flower than the Zinnias we see growing in Europe. The plant usually grows two feet in height, at least seventy-five per cent. give flowers almost as beautiful and quite as double as the Dahlia. A plant that commences flowering in June will grow larger and handsomer, and the flowers better every day until destroyed by frost. Tie a string around the stem of a flower, or mark one in any other way, and that flower will be found perfect in six weeks from the time it was marked. Having taken particular pains in improving the Zinnia, I think my strain is excellent; indeed, my Zinnias have been pronounced by florists from England, France and Germany the best in the world. Seed will do well sown under glass, but must not have much heat, and plenty of air. Seed will, however, grow well in a bed in the garden, and transplant as safely as a Cabbage plant, and this should be done as early as possible, and when the plants are small; cold, rough weather will do them good. The plants begin to blossom when quite young, and the first flower is not usually good. Set them about eighteen inches apart. — The largest flowers are sometimes nearly six inches across. The Zinnias are coarse plants, and we do not suppose every one will be pleased with them, but we must remember that there are always places in the garden where large, and even coarse, plants look well, and those that are more delicate are useless.

THE CLIMBERS furnish us with nature's drapery, and nothing produced by art can equal their elegant grace. As the Lilies surpass in beauty all that wealth or power can procure, or man produce, so these tender Climbers surpass all the productions of the decorator's skill. They are entirely under the control of the skillful gardener and tasteful amateur, and under their guiding hands make the unsightly building or stump bloom with beauty. The strong growing varieties can be made, in a short time, to cover fences, arbors and buildings, and give both grace and shade. Those of more delicate growth are invaluable for pots, baskets, and other decorative purposes.

The Climbing Plants are nearly all well adapted for culture in vases, and are particularly well fitted for baskets and the decoration of balconies, &c. No hanging basket can look well unless furnished with graceful trailing plants, which not only have great beauty in themselves, but throw a mantle of beauty, if not of charity, over everything unsightly about the basket or its filling. Several Climbers will be found among the Perennials, but, of course, all the varieties described in this Department flower the first season. Some of our annual Climbers are natives of tropical countries, and while they do well in the garden, with a little care, are really better for house culture and for baskets, verandahs, etc.

### CALAMPELIS, Nat. Ord. *Bignoniaceæ.*

Calampelis scabra, or perhaps more properly Eccremocarpus scaber is a very excellent climber, with neat foliage, and bright orange flowers borne in racemes, and blooms profusely the latter part of the season. The seeds are made to vegetate with some difficulty, and should be grown in a hot-bed or green-house. Good, strong plants should be grown before setting them in the garden, and it is not best to trust the plants in the open ground in a climate like most of the Middle and Northern States until the first of June. The Calampelis, however, is well suited to house culture, where it will always give good satisfaction and prove valuable; but being a native of Chili, will not endure the changes and harshness of a Northern climate, even in the summer, except under favorable circumstances. As, however, it is not common,  and very pretty, the Calampelis well pays for a little extra care on the part of the tasteful florist.

### CARDIOSPERMUM, Nat. Ord. *Sapindaceæ.*

Cardiospermum Halicacabum is a curious, half-hardy annual, from India, we believe, though some of the species are found in almost all tropical countries. It is called Ballooon Vine, and Love in a Puff, on account of the inflated seed-capsule seen in the engraving. In some countries the leaves are cooked and eaten, and in others the plant is supposed to contain very great medicinal properties. With us it is only valuable as a good summer climber, and really more curious than beautiful. Sow seed under glass, and if planted in the garden, find it a sheltered situation. Like many southern climbers, it needs favoring in the garden, but gives a good account of itself in the house.

### COBŒA, Nat. Ord. *Polemoniaceæ*.

The Cobea scandens is one of the most beautiful of our climbing annuals, on account of its large size, rapid growth, fine foliage, and large, bell-shaped flowers, about an inch and a half across and two inches in length. When strong plants are

set out early in the spring, and in a good soil, they often grow twenty or thirty feet in length, branching freely, and covering a large surface. Plants commence to flower when quite young and continue in bloom until removed or killed by frost. In the autumn, plants can be taken up with care, potted, and removed to the house where they will flourish and flower during the winter. The flowers are at first green, but gradually change to a deep, violet blue. The seed requires some care in starting, and much success is not to be anticipated in sowing the seed in the garden. Put the seeds in moist earth, edge down, and do not water until the young plants appear above the surface, unless the pots are in a warm place and the earth becomes exceedingly dry. Cobœas set in a row, two feet apart, supported by brush six feet high, make an elegant screen.

### CONVOLVULUS, Nat. Ord. *Convolvulaceæ*.

Convolvulus major, the old Morning Glory, is the best known and most popular, and all things considered, we are almost prepared to say the best annual climber we possess. The seeds germinate so readily that they can be grown in the garden in any corner where the plants are needed, and almost at any time. The flowers we need tell no one are beautiful, and of a great variety of colors. Their growth is so rapid that they cover an arbor or trellis in a very short time, though it is important that support should be supplied as soon as the young plants show a disposition to run, for if this is neglected too long they willl not readily attach themselves. The only fault that can be urged against the Convolvulus is the fact that its flowers are open only in the early part of the day, the brightest about sunrise, but a sight of a good "patch" of these flowers in the "dewy morn" is a feast for a whole day, and quite enough to tempt any lover of the beautiful to rise early to see and enjoy their glory. Indeed, we have known several fits of early rising induced by the beauty of the Morning Glory, and yet, we are glad to say, without serious results.

### DOLICHOS, Nat. Ord. *Leguminosæ*.

Very beautiful climbing plants, resembling the running bean, but the flowers are more beautiful, as the common name (Hyacinth Bean) indicates. The seed-pods are as pretty as the flowers,

being, in the purple-flowered variety, a beautiful purple, shining as though freshly varnished. The large varieties grow from six to twenty feet in height, but the growth upward may be checked by pinching off the tops. Plant the seeds in the garden where the plants are desired, selecting as warm and dry a spot as possible. Give just the treatment required for our more tender running beans, like the Lima. Most of the varieties are eaten in some parts of Europe. A dwarf white variety grows only about four or five feet in height. The Dolichos is not only the prettiest of our bean-like climbers, but is one of the ornamental species that not only flourishes in the hot weather of summer, but rejoices in heat, drouth and a warm, sandy soil. This makes it particularly valuable to Americans, as our flowering beans usually suffer in a dry time.

### GOURDS AND CUCUMBERS, (ORNAMENTAL,) Nat. Ord. *Cucurbitaceæ*.

The Gourds are a coarse class of plants, liked principally on account of their curiously formed and often strangely colored fruits. The foliage, however, is abundant, the leaves generally large, and useful for covering old trees, fences, arbors, etc. The culture is the same as required for squashes, melons, etc. Some people are curious in collecting and growing all the odd formed and colored Gourds they can procure, and in Europe we saw some very large and varied collections. This, however, is a "hobby"

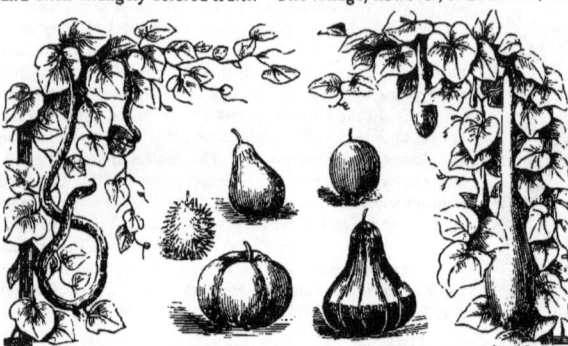

we do not much admire, for we can get more real beauty with far less trouble. However, we garden for pleasure, and if it is obtained in this way, we certainly shall not complain.

### IPOMŒA, Nat. Ord. *Convolvulaceæ*.

Under the name of Convolvulus we have described the Morning Glory, which is by some called Ipomœa purpurea; but the Ipomœas proper are a genus of very beautiful Convolvulaceæ, widely distributed over all warm climates, and a few extending into North America. Some of the varieties of Ipomœa are exceedingly large and fine, excelling even the best Convolvulus. Others, like the Cypress Vine, which we show in the engraving, have small flowers, of the brightest colors, and the most delicate foliage imaginable. The Ipomœa is generally more delicate than the Convolvulus, and should be classed among the tender annuals, and therefore will succeed best if started in the hot-bed, and afterwards planted in a sheltered and warm situation. The Ipomœas are all desirable for pots, baskets, etc., for the house. For hanging baskets and green-house decoration, the Ipomœas hold a prominent place, and will well repay for any extra care they may require.

### LOASA, Nat. Ord. *Loasaceæ*.

The Loasa is a good climber, with curious, handsome flowers, which it bears in great abundance. The flowers are of the size shown in the engraving, bright in color, being yellow and red. The branches are covered with stinging hairs that give pain when touched, so that a good deal of care must be exercised when handling the plants. The Loasa is a native of Chili and Peru, and though seldom seen in American gardens, is quite commonly found in some sections of Europe. A plant or two will give a good deal of pleasure for a season or so, until one becomes familiar with it, and we have known several important lessons taught by the Loasa, to thoughtless people who are so apt to handle and pick flowers in other people's gardens; a very thoughtless practice.

## MAURANDYA, Nat. Ord. *Scrophulariaceæ*.

The Maurandya is a graceful, rather delicate climber from Mexico, bearing flowers very much resembling the Antirrhinum, the principal difference being in the mouth. The Maurandya  is almost too delicate for out-door culture in the Northern and Middle States, but does remarkably well for baskets, vases, etc., in sheltered positions. Plants should be grown in the hot-bed or green-house, and if designed for the garden, should not be put out until the weather is quite warm; late in the spring or early summer. Few climbers do better for greenhouse culture. Growth of plant, five or six feet, and the foliage abundant, a very desirable trait in a climbing plant, as half the beauty, at least, of a climbing plant is its foliage. The flowers of the Maurandya, however, are of good size and form and color, being about the size and appearance of Digitalis or Antirrhinum, and the colors different shades of blue, white and mauve, and the whole plant pleasant to look upon.

## PEAS, FLOWERING, (Lathyrus,) Nat. Ord. *Leguminosæ*.

The Flowering Peas are among the most useful and beautiful of all our hardy annuals. Nothing can be better for large bouquets, as the flowers are lively and delicate, varying in color from white to the darkest purple imaginable, and including the most lively pinks; and as fragrant as Mignonette. For a hedge or screen, or little groups supported by common brush, the Sweet Pea is not excelled. If the soil is rich they will grow five feet in height, and continue to flower all the summer unless the season is too hot and dry. The Pea luxuriates in a cool, moist soil, and in a damp season. Cut the flowers freely and do not allow seeds to form except on a few plants which are designed for seed-bearing. Sow the seed four inches deep, and as early in the spring as possible. Don't wait for fair weather. Hoe the earth towards the plants a little, as for common garden peas, but do not form a ridge, and furnish support early. Use plenty of seed, so that they will not be further than an inch apart. The engraving shows flowers of about the natural size. I am anxious to encourage the culture of this sweet flower. There  are several varieties called winged, on account of a wing-like attachment to the seed-pod. They are not really climbers, but creepers; the flowers are small, and they are hardly worth cultivating.

## THUNBERGIA, Nat. Ord. *Acanthaceæ*.

The Thunbergias are good annual climbers for the garden, but very much better for the house and conservatory, where they grow well and flower beautifully. They need support, like  all the climbers, but we have seen them do well when allowed to run over the ground, making a very pretty bed. For baskets and similar purposes, the Thunbergia should be more generally used, as it is far superior to a score of weedy plants that seem, strangely, to have been adopted for this work. The Thunbergia starts rather slowly at first, but when it begins to run makes a rapid growth. The engraving shows the flowers of natural size, but they form usually more in clusters. The seed requires conservatory or hot-bed treatment, but plants are grown easily from cuttings. The flowers are white, buff, or orange, generally with a dark eye.

## TROPÆOLUM, Nat. Ord. *Tropæolaceæ*.

Tropæolum majus is a fine climber, growing ten or twelve feet in height, comprising several varieties, differing in the color of both flower and foliage. In some the leaves are a bright, lively green, in others very dark. The flowers are of all shades of yellow, scarlet, striped and spotted. The engraving of trellis shows the habit of the plant. Seed may be planted in the open ground, or under glass. T. Lobbianum is very desirable for the greenhouse, and will answer well for a summer climber when started in the house. T. peregrinum, of which we also give an engraving, is the popular Canary Flower. The Tropæolums grow freely from cuttings, and are admirable for the house in the winter. For large baskets and vases, especially for hanging baskets, they are exceedingly desirable, drooping over the sides to the ground, making a charming and graceful display of foliage. When the branches have become as long as desired, they should be pinched off. Some gardeners think Tropæolums are of so rampant a growth that when planted in baskets they rob more delicate plants of their share of nourishment, but we have never found this a serious objection, especially where water was given pretty freely; and a basket exposed to the air on every side, without plenty of water, is only a snare and a delusion. If any trouble of this kind is noticed, pinch the shoots back freely, and this will check the growth of roots. It is a good thing to have a few vigorous plants, those whose growth need checking instead of encouraging, as an abundance of foliage is thus secured beyond a contingency. We give an engraving of the Tropæolum flower of full natural size, and can recommend the family as worthy a place in any garden, and an honorable position among the choicest of our annual Climbers.

# EVERLASTINGS

The Everlasting, or Eternal Flowers, as they are sometimes called, have of late attracted a good deal of attention in all parts of the world, and are becoming generally cultivated. The plants do not appear very important when the garden is gay with scores of Flora's choicest gems, and are, therefore, often considered hardly worth saving, and the flowers remain ungathered. In the winter, however, when it is desirable to decorate church or school room or home, the Everlastings are a treasure. These flowers lessen the regret we all feel when the season of blossoms is over, because they enable us to transfer a little of summer beauty to the parlor. They retain both form and color for years, and make excellent bouquets, wreaths, and every other desirable winter ornament. The flowers should generally be picked as soon as they expand, or a little before, and hung up in small bunches, and so that the stems will dry straight. If the bunches are too large they will mildew. The *Gomphrenas* must not be gathered until fully developed. Those who are familiar with the usual style of winter decoration, and realize how gloomy a room is made by the heavy, dark wreaths of cedars and hemlocks, unrelieved by a flower or berry, or any bright color, will thank us for urging them to save every flower that will keep its color during the winter. Make all wreaths light and airy, and enliven them with bright flowers.

### ACROCLINIUM, Nat. Ord. *Compositæ*.

The Acroclinium is one of the most beautiful of the everlasting family. It is of strong growth, about eighteen inches in height, and bears a great number of pink and white daisy-like flowers, with a yellow centre. They should be gathered the first day they open, or even before fully open, and dried. If allowed to remain too long on the plant, the center becomes black in drying, but if gathered young they retain their natural color. The engraving shows the size of the plant, and the appearance of the flower when fully expanded.

There are two varieties, a bright pink and a clear white, and both indispensable.

### AMMOBIUM, Nat. Ord. *Compositæ*.

Ammobium is a small but very pretty little flower, pure white, and therefore very useful in making up. The plant, which grows about eighteen inches, is stiff and angular in appearance. This is one of the hardiest of the everlastings. Some florists use this flower very liberally, even in the summer, in the making of small bouquets. Like the Acroclinium and very many of our everlastings, it is a native of Australia.

The bud, as shown in the engraving, is very pretty.

### GOMPHRENA, Nat. Ord. *Amarantaceæ*.

A well known Everlasting, sometimes called English Clover. Flowers should not be picked until well matured and of full size, near the end of summer. The seed of the Gomphrena does not germinate very well in the open ground, and it is therefore best to sow it in a hot-bed if possible. Set the plants about a foot apart. About eighteen inches in height. Fine for the garden as well as for drying. Makes a good summer hedge. If the cottony coating which surrounds it is removed, the seed will be more certain to grow, as in wet weather it may cause rot.

### HELICHRYSUM, Nat. Ord. *Compositæ*.

An exceedingly handsome class, mostly large and showy plants, of great value for winter bouquets and other floral ornaments. The flowers are large and full, and of a good variety of colors. Plants generally about two feet in height. Cut just before the flowers fully expand. Even the buds are handsome and make up beautifully. Always save a few buds to use with the flowers. Plant about a foot apart. Seeds germinate readily, even in the open ground. The colors are, white, yellow, and red of very many brownish shades. It is the largest and boldest and one of the best of the Everlastings.

### HELIPTERUM, Nat. Ord. *Compositæ*.

Helipterum Sanfordii is one of the prettiest little everlasting flowers that grows, as all will believe after a look at the engraving, and when we inform them that it is a truthful representation of a cluster of these flowers, of the natural size, and that they are a deep, rich, golden, shining yellow. The plant, which is about a foot in height, and branching, bears very many of these clusters. They should be taken when the buds are about opening, tied in bunches and hung up in a shady place, and the flowers will open in the drying process, and will retain their brightness and color for very many years. The Helipterum is found wild in Australia, and we believe, in sections of Africa.

### RHODANTHE, Nat. Ord. *Compositæ*.

The Rhodanthe is one of the prettiest and most delicate of the Everlastings. It has been in cultivation for many years, and we have seen it in Europe in the conservatories, where it was once much prized as a pot plant, and a good specimen, bearing a hundred of its pretty flowers is really a beautiful object. The Rhodanthe is a native of Northern Australia. Some care is necessary in starting the seeds, but after good plants are grown we never fail to obtain flowers in abundance. The flowers should be gathered before they fully expand, as if allowed to grow too long, they open too much and lose their beautiful bell form.

**WAITZIA**, Nat. Ord. *Compositæ*.

The Waitzias are an interesting class of annuals, bearing their dry or everlasting flowers in clusters. The flowers are very good, though showing too much of the centre, which becomes discolored unless picked early. With this precaution, however, they make a desirable addition to our stock of Everlastings. All the varieties have yellow flowers. The seeds are very fine and should be sown under glass, or much success is not to be anticipated. Sometimes when we give such instructions, some people are just contrary enough to try to show us we are mistaken, and that they can succeed in growing plants in the open air, and generally succeed because they are determined to do so; zeal and determination are the elements of success, and the open ground often furnishes the warmth and moisture necessary to germinate the most delicate seeds.

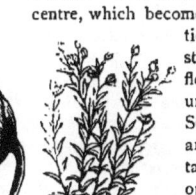

**XERANTHEMUM**, Nat. Ord. *Compositæ*.

Xeranthemums are free-blooming annuals of a very neat, compact habit, and growing less than a foot in height. The leaves are silvery and flowers abundant on strong stems, and are purple, blue and white. There are both double and single varieties, specimens of both of which are seen in the engravings. Seeds germinate freely; plants transplant well when small, and should be set about ten inches apart.

**GYPSOPHILA**, Nat. Ord. *Caryophyllaceæ*.

The Gypsophilas, though not Everlastings, are among the most valuable flowers we have for bouquet making, either green or dried. Every one knows that florists add much to the beauty of bouquets by a delicate net-work of fine flowers, which appear like an airy veil, toning down the bright colors. For this purpose the Gypsophila is used, and we commend it to our readers as one of the most desirable plants known for ornamental purposes. It dries admirably, and is a treasure in winter. It flowers the first season, but will continue to bloom several years.

**STATICE**, Nat. Ord. *Plumbaginaceæ*.

The Statice is an extensive series of herbaceous plants, bearing their small flowers in panicles. They are not Everlastings, but, like the Gypsophilas, are of very great value for drying, as they retain their color when dried, and work up with the true Everlastings in bouquets and floral ornaments to very great advantage. They are also equally useful in summer for bouquets of fresh flowers. There are several annuals, almost as many perennials, yellow, pink, rose and blue. We give an engraving of one of the best varieties, S. latifolia. For others, see seed list.

 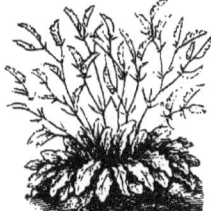

## ORNAMENTAL GRASSES.

AGROSTIS NEBULOSA.

THOSE who grow Everlastings for winter decoration will need a few of the Grasses to work up with them. If the grasses would retain their color, as do the flowers, it would be a great blessing, but they lose, even when dried with care in the shade, most of their green color. In Europe, the Grasses are grown extensively and dyed of various colors, and in this condition we import them, and many varieties are really elegant, especially the *Stipa pennata*. Even without this coloring they will be found very useful. Some persons are quite ingenious in dyeing the Grasses, and make them look very pretty with a little coloring matter. We know that this coloring of flowers and grasses is not exactly in good taste, as a rule, but we are almost ready to say, anything to enliven winter, and these Grasses do look pretty when worked up judiciously — not lavishly — with winter wreaths. Cut about the time of flowering, tie up in little bunches and dry in the shade. Those that flower the second year, like the *Stipa* and *Bromus*, must be marked in some way or they will be destroyed for weeds, as they look so much like common grass. We have lost a good many crops for the want of this caution. They are perfectly hardy, and will endure the winter just as well as any of our wild grasses. The *Agrostis nebulosa* is a very fine grass, indeed, so very fine and small that we can hardly represent it in an engraving. *Briza maxima* is the well known shaking grass, really one of the most valuable of our grasses. There are several varieties of Briza, all but maxima quite small. *Erianthus Ravennæ* is a perennial grass, perfectly hardy, and the best large grass we know of for a northern climate — much better than Pampas Grass, which it resembles. The flower stems are ten feet in height. *Stipa pennata* is the beautiful Feather Grass, really the most graceful and beautiful of all the small grasses. We show it as growing, just as the plant begins to flower, and also a bunch of the perfected grass, as often used for winter ornament. We have named only a few of the best varieties, but a full list of all desirable kinds will be found in our regular seed list of varieties. Many will be surprised that we have not in this page spoken of the beautiful Pampas Grass, which perhaps has no rival where the winters are not very severe, but in the Northern and Middle States it suffers sorely in the winters. Almost every one, also, has some favorite variety, and almost any of the grasses, if gathered at the proper time and well cured, are useful and handsome in the winter. Cut the grasses before the flowers open, tie up in little bunches, and hang them in the shade. When sufficiently dry, pack them away out of the dust. Somewhat of a variety is secured by cutting grass at different stages of growth.

BRIZA MAXIMA.

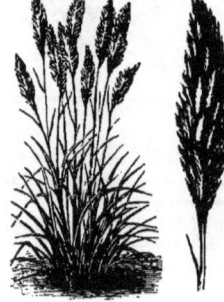

ERIANTHUS RAVENNÆ.

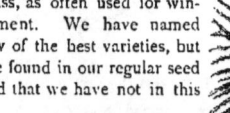

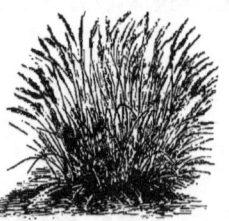

STIPA PENNAT..

# PERENNIALS

IN this section will be found those Biennials and Perennials that do not flower until the second season. The first summer the plants merely grow and gather a store of strength for next summer's flowering, and a stock of material for the next season's flowers. The seed may be sown in early spring with the Annuals, or later in the summer; but if sown late, give the seed-bed a cool, damp place, or keep the ground shaded and quite moist by artificial shading and watering, until the plants appear, or very likely the seeds will not germinate. This class of flowers do not usually keep in bloom a long time, and therefore are not suited for the lawn, where a continuous show of flowers or pretty foliage is absolutely necessary. To many, however, the border of Perennials is the most interesting part of the flower garden. Every day almost it exhibits something new — some flower in bloom that we did not expect to see, or whose development we had been anxiously watching and awaiting. A pleasure or a surprise, usually both, await us at almost every visit. What a number of old garden flowers we find in the Perennial border. The Columbine, Pink, Canterbury Bell, Hollyhock, Sweet William, and a host of other friends, all find a home in this department. Then the Perennials fill a space that but for them would be almost destitute of flowers, for after the Bulbs they give us our earliest spring flowers. The Columbine and Canterbury Bell and Larkspur and Foxglove follow the Hyacinths and Tulips, and keep us well supplied until the Annuals are in their glory. Always have a few Perennials, but in a somewhat retired part of the garden, a pleasant border in some place where you can retire and see a little unadorned beauty. You will enjoy it occasionally much more than the gayest bed on the lawn. The Perennial Climbers are admirable, and when we have so few adapted to our climate, should not be neglected.

## ADLUMIA, Nat. Ord. *Fumariaceæ*.

Adlumia cirrhosa, or Alleghany Vine, is a very pretty native Biennial climber. The principal attraction consists in its delicate pale green, triply pinnate foliage, the twining foot-stalks of which act as tendrils. The flowers are pink and white, not very conspicuous or beautiful, and yet are neat and graceful, and of the form seen in the engraving. The plant neither runs nor bears flowers the first season, but the second will often grow twenty feet. Sow seed in the spring, in a damp, cool place, or keep the ground shaded. Transplant in the autumn, if possible, though the spring will answer. Although strictly a biennial, and therefore flowering but once, most persons would judge it to be a perennial, because in a damp situation, as on the north side of a porch or fence, self-sown seed germinate so freely that plants are always in abundance in every stage of growth, so that some are ready to take the place of the old vines each year. The Adlumia is known as the Wood Fringe, and is really one of the most interesting of our native climbers.

### ADONIS, Nat. Ord. *Ranunculaceæ.*

Adonis vernalis is the handsomest of the family, and is really a desirable border plant, with 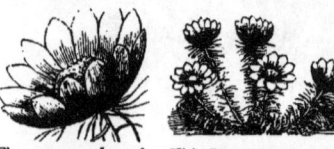 delicate foliage and a large flower, compared to the size of the plant, which is only about a foot in height. The blossoms are yellow, produced in May and June, and on account of this early blooming exceedingly valuable. The Adonis prefers a rather light soil. Seed may be grown in the open ground, and success is almost certain.
Flowers cup-shaped. This flower is now so seldom seen that it will be pronounced new by many.

### ALYSSUM, Nat. Ord. *Cruciferæ.*

Alyssum saxatile compactum is an excellent free-growing Perennial, yet of a compact habit, and with pretty, small, golden yellow flowers, growing in dense clusters. Its popular name is Gold Dust. The Alyssum flowers very early in the season, when flowers are scarce, and this, with its other merits, make it quite valuable. Height of plant about ten inches. This is one of the really valuable plants that we can recommend with pleasure, because we know it will more than meet expectations. The Alyssum is well adapted for rock work, and forms an excellent mass for a bed. Seeds grow readily. Plants can be increased by layering.

### AQUILEGIA, (Columbine,) Nat. Ord. *Ranunculacea.*

The Aquilegia is the old and well prized Columbine, of almost every conceivable color, and singular variations of form. It grows wild in almost every temperate country in the world, and we have always heard it called by children the    Wild Honeysuckle. Like a good many of our Perennials, this flowers early in the spring. The name Columbine was given because the five spurred petals, with incurved heads, have been thought to bear a resemblance to five doves, the sepals representing the wings. Seeds may be sown in the open ground. A fine bed of Aquilegias when in flower is a beautiful exhibition. Our engravings show both the double and single flowers. Plants can be increased by a division of the roots.

### CAMPANULA, Nat. Ord. *Campanulaceæ.*

The perennial Campanula is the well known, popular, large, blue, bell-shaped flower, known every where as the Canterbury Bell. The C. medium is the only variety really entitled to the name, but it is commonly applied to all. Of late there have been many new varieties introduced, and some of them quite valuable. Calycanthema, shown in the engraving, has the calyx very large, and the same color as the corolla. There are also double varieties of every color produced by the Campanula, white, rose, blue and lilac. The double varieties, though curious, are not really so beautiful as the old single bell. They lose that light, transparent grace that is so attractive in a flower. We never yet saw a bell-  shaped flower improved by doubling — at least we do not now remember a case of the kind.

## DIANTHUS, Nat. Ord. *Caryophyllaceæ*.

Under this name we include three of the most magnificent members of the Floral family, the rivals of the Rose for queenly honors, the Carnation, the Picotee and Pink. As long as we can remember, these have been the favorite flowers of the florist, and proud and happy was the man who could produce a perfect flower. The Carnation, *Dianthus caryophillus*, is a grand flower, smooth edged, with the stripes broad and running from the base to the outer edge of the petal, as shown in the engraving at the left. The more clear and defined the stripe the better. The Picotee differs mainly in the coloring, the stripes running around the edge of the petal, as shown in the engraving, that is, when perfect, though there are some very good flowers with narrow and broken stripes running from the base to the outer edge of the petals. The Pink, *D. hortensis*, is smaller, more compact and more mottled than striped, with white ground. Seeds of all may be sown under glass, or in the open ground in the spring, and the second season will flower. Some will prove poor or single, and these can be pulled up as soon as they show their character. Young plants are perfectly hardy, and will endure our winters well, but old plants are much injured generally. A succession of young plants should be procured either from seeds or layers every year. Layering is simply cutting a slit in a young shoot to obstruct the flow of sap, and thus aid in the formation of roots. First cut half way through the shoot, then make a slit lengthwise about an inch. Remove the earth a few inches in depth, and press down the branch so that this slit will open, and then cover with the soil. Roots will form where the cut was made, and thus a new plant will be formed, which can be removed in the autumn or spring. The layering should be done in midsummer. The Pink is more hardy than the others and will not become injured in the winter, unless the plants are very much weakened by old age. The engravings show the Carnation and Picotee on the left of the page, and the Pink on the right. The plant of the Pink is smaller and more compact than the others, and the leaves narrower.

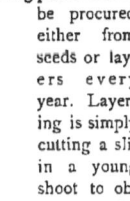

### DELPHINIUM, Nat. Ord. *Ranunculaceæ*.

The perennial Delphiniums, commonly known as Larkspurs, are valuable plants, the foliage clean and pretty, habit strong and good, the flowering branches often four feet in height, the spikes of flowers six inches or more in length, and generally compact. The prevailing color is blue, and of the most intense character imaginable. Some varieties very light, azure blue, others of the darkest indigo shades. White and pink sorts are prized by some, but none are so gorgeous as the bright blues. Sow the seed in the spring, and very strong plants will be produced by autumn, that flower the next spring. Transplant from the seed-bed early in the fall. Roots of old plants may be divided either in the spring or autumn, and thus after good plants are once procured, they may be increased indefinitely. The name Larkspur is given on account of the spur, which resembles the spur of a bird, and forms a prominent feature in the flowers of this family.

### DIGITALIS, (Foxglove,) Nat. Ord. *Scrophulariaceæ*.

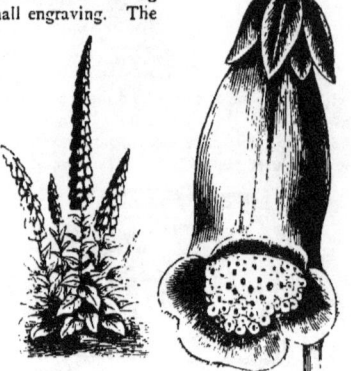

The Digitalis is a stately plant, when well grown, with flower-stems at least three feet in height. The raceme of flowers is at the extremity of the stem, several score of them, and all drooping on one side, and sometimes covering more than half its length, as may be seen in the small engraving. The flowers are of an irregular bell shape, and the engraving shows a flower of full size, marked in the interior with circular dark spots which are interspersed among a number of delicate, light colored hairs. There are several varieties, differing somewhat in form and color, but we have shown the general form, and the colors are white and different shades of purple. The Digitalis is a native of Europe, and the old variety, D. purpurea, may be found on the sides of almost any of the shady country lanes of England. The Digitalis is used in medicine. Its common name is Foxglove. Perfectly hardy, and seeds may be sown in the spring, in the garden, and transplanted as desired. In the autumn large plants can be divided, and thus plants may be increased indefinitely, but it is well to secure a few fresh plants from seed occasionally, as is in this way only new colors and varieties are obtained.

### HEDYSARUM, (French Honeysuckle,) Nat. Ord. *Leguminosæ*.

Pretty much all the species of this genus are handsome flowering plants, producing racemes of attractive, pea-formed flowers. H. corenarium is the best, and there is a scarlet and a white variety. Strange to say, this Hedysarum is called in England and America the French Honeysuckle, though it originated in Italy, and not in France, and bears no kind of resemblance to the Honeysuckle, but more resembles clover, and as the children suck the tubes of clover flowers and call them honeysuckles, perhaps this accounts for the name. It is used in the South of Europe as green feed for cattle. It bears some resemblance to the Scarlet Clover, but is a much bolder and handsomer flower, and really a most desirable Perennial. Every one who secures a few plants will be highly pleased with the investment. Perfectly hardy, and seed may be sown in the open ground.

## HOLLYHOCK, (Althea rosea,) Nat. Ord. *Malvaceæ*.

Every one knows the old Hollyhock, that all the children have played with, and that was so interesting and useful as a trap for bees, when you and I, dear reader, were young. Then it grew tall enough almost for a flag staff, with here and there a single flower about the shape, and half as large as a tea-cup, and every one of them, not appropriated to other uses, turned into a cheese about as big as a cent, which the girls thought made splendid necklaces. This was the old Hollyhock — not very pretty, not very graceful — and yet there were places where the Hollyhock of by-gone days looked well; at least we thought so once, and we have no desire to correct that opinion. But look from the picture we have drawn to the one made by our engraver. Here we have a stately flower, and one showing as much grace as the finest architectural column the skill of man ever devised. No Rip Van Winkle, just awakened from a forty years' sleep, would recognize the modern Hollyhock as akin to any flower he had ever before beheld. Indeed, when made up in bouquets, pretty good judges are often at fault. A good, double, clear, white Hollyhock is a very good substitute for a Camellia or a white Rose, as a center of a bouquet. I do not now think of one as good, except the double white Balsam. In situations suitable for tall flowers, we know of nothing better than the Hollyhock; and yet the improved varieties do not grow very high, from three to four feet being about the average. The Hollyhock is biennial. New plants are obtained from seed and by dividing the roots.

## HONESTY, (Lunaria,) Nat. Ord. *Cruciferæ*.

Lunaria biennis is what is known as Honesty in all our gardens, and by all florists. There are a good many varieties, all, we think, native of Southern and Central Europe, and all tall-growing biennials and perennials. Honesty, the cultivated variety, bears racemes of pretty, single, purple flowers, and our engraving shows the general habit of the plant, as well as the size and form of the flower, a single specimen of which we give. The pod which contains the seeds is the most interesting to many growers, and indeed the plant perhaps is cultivated mainly for its peculiar seed-pouches, which are very large, perhaps two inches in length by one in width, very thin, and silvery white when ripe. These silvery pouches are curious and pretty, and are grown for winter ornaments, for which use they are very desirable. We have endeavored to show the appearance of these curious pods, each raceme of flowers producing about such a cluster as shown in the engraving. The plant is very hardy; two feet in height.

## IPOMOPSIS, Nat. Ord. *Polemoniaceæ*.

The Ipomopsis are very beautiful plants, with long, elegant spikes of rich orange and scarlet flowers, excellent for conservatory and out-door decoration. The foliage is very fine, like that of the Cypress Vine, giving great beauty to the plant, which grows usually from three to four feet in height, and keeps in flower a long time. The plant is a little difficult to keep over the winter, but generally proves quite hardy in a dry place. A wet situation is sure to destroy them in winter, causing decay at the surface of the ground. With this exception, there are few plants of easier culture.

### LINUM, (Flax,) Nat. Ord. *Linaceæ*.

Height one foot.

Every one is acquainted with our common flax, which is a Linum, and has been cultivated for a good many thousand years, certainly since the time when Joseph gained such distinction in Egypt, for we read that Pharaoh clothed him in fine linen; and we are also told in the history of the plagues that occurred in the time of Moses, that the flax was smitten. There are several varieties of ornamental flax well worthy of culture, however, which few people know. The plants are very graceful, the foliage and stems delicate, and the flowers on the light, spray-like plants, seem floating in the air. Seeds may be sown either under glass or in the garden. There are several varieties, white, blue, rose and yellow, and all desirable.

### PAPAVER, (Poppy,) Nat. Ord. *Papaveraceæ*.

There are a few Perennial Poppies that are not only worthy of cultivation, but exceedingly valuable to the gardener. The Oriental Poppy, for instance, which is of the most intense scarlet, with a blackish or purplish blotch at the base of each petal, we have often six inches in diameter. It is a monstrous single flower, and the flower stems generally reach three or four feet in height. There are other varieties somewhat similar in character, but we have never found any better. All the perennial Poppies are perfectly hardy, and seed may be sown in the open ground. Our engravings show the appearance of the plant when in bloom, as well as the form of the flower, of course much reduced in size. The single large perennial Poppies are a great addition to the herbaceous border, and are of great value among shrubbery, as they tend to relieve and lighten up the usual dark and sombre character borders or clumps of shrubbery assume after the early summer. A few plants of annual Poppies, and other free-growing hardy annuals, will give the shrubberies a cheerful and graceful wildness quite charming.

### PENTSTEMON, Nat. Ord. *Scrophulariaceæ*.

The Pentstemon is one of the best of the perennial border plants. The very pretty long-tubed flowers grow in panicles, and are purple, blue, scarlet, rose and white. The Pentstemons are all natives of America, and are very popular in all parts of the world. Our engravings show the habit of the plant, and also a portion of a panicle, with flowers of natural size. Seeds may be sown in May, in a cool, shady place, or under glass. The flowers of different varieties present a great difference in appearance, some with a bold, open mouth and a generous throat, while others are of the form shown in the engraving.

### PEAS, PERENNIAL, (Lathyrus,) Nat. Ord. *Leguminosæ.*

The Perennial Pea, to our fancy, is one of the prettiest climbers that grows, and peculiarly adapted to our climate. When in Europe, we saw it cover-

ing hundreds of humble cottages, causing the otherwise unsightly buildings to bloom with beauty. We determined to grow this fine climber and advise others to do the same. It is perfectly hardy in this climate, dies down to the ground every winter and starts again in the spring, making a rapid growth, and properly trained, reaching ten or more feet in height, and flowering for a long time. The seed does not grow very readily sometimes, but roots can be obtained, and at a very moderate price. The engraving shows something of the habit of the plant, and also the size of the flowers, which grow in large clusters.

### PRIMULA, Nat. Ord. *Primulaceæ.*

The Primulas do not succeed in our climate, either North or South, East or West, in any locality that we are aware of. In the moist, mild climate of England, and particularly of Scotland, the Primula family present a gorgeous array in the early spring. The Polyanthus is the favorite spring flower of English cottage gardens. Indeed, we found Spring Flower to be the common name in many localities for the P. polyanthus. The P. auricula is extensively grown in Europe in conservatories, or, more generally, houses exclusively devoted to the culture of this flower. In this country

all do well in a cold house, but in the open ground succeed best in a Northern border, as the winter's sun is injurious. P. veris is the English Cowslip, and P. vulgaris is the sweet and beautiful English Wild Primrose, that every one who spent his childish days among the green lanes and copices of England, ardently loves. Seed in our country must be sown under glass.

### PYRETHRUM, Nat. Ord. *Compositæ.*

The Pyrethrum, like the Aster, which it resembles, once was a rather poor single flower, and

though somewhat showy, could claim but little beauty. The old Feverfew, with a small, double, yellowish white flower, was for a long time the best of the family, but recently many new varieties have been introduced, mainly from France, double, and of bright colors. They come only partly double from seed, but are well worthy of cultivation. We have found the plants to be entirely hardy in this section. It would be well to sow seed under glass, but we have grown it by sowing seeds in the open ground. A good double Pyrethrum is as desirable as a good Aster, quite as large and as double, and if seed would uniformly or even generally produce double flowers, we would advise every one to introduce it to their gardens; but from the best seed we could ever obtain from the most reliable growers of France, the proportion of good double flowers was very small. We shall continue to try, and hope for better results.

## ROCKET, (Hesperis,) Nat. Ord. *Cruciferæ*.

The Sweet Rocket is a very hardy biennial, bearing clusters of single flowers, about the size shown in the engraving, and very much resembling the Stock, single, and fragrant during the evening. The best colors are purple and white. There are other colors which are not desirable, and a double white, which produces no seed, and which we have not succeeded in naturalizing in America. The plant, with fair culture, will grow eighteen inches in height, is perfectly hardy, and seed will germinate readily in the open ground. The Rocket is thoroughly hardy, but the little pest that makes our Radishes "wormy" is very fond of its root, and sometimes causes the destruction of the plant.

## STOCK, BROMPTON, (Mathiola incana,) Nat. Ord. *Cruciferæ*.

The Brompton Stock is the biennial of the Ten-Weeks Stock. The plant is of a larger growth than the annual, the flowers larger, and the spikes longer and bolder. It would be difficult to find any flower more gorgeous than a good Brompton Stock, as seen growing in the gardens of the mild districts of Europe. We have measured spikes of blossoms nearly a foot in length, with the flowers as compact as possible. In the colder districts, the Brompton Stock is grown in conservatories. Unfortunately this Stock can not endure our winters, but if plants are grown in the open  ground during the summer, in autumn they can be removed to the house, where they will flower well if not kept too hot and dry. In the spring, the plants may be again transferred to the garden, where they will furnish a good many flowers during the early summer.

## SWEET WILLIAM (Dianthus barbatus,) Nat. Ord. *Caryophyllaceæ*.

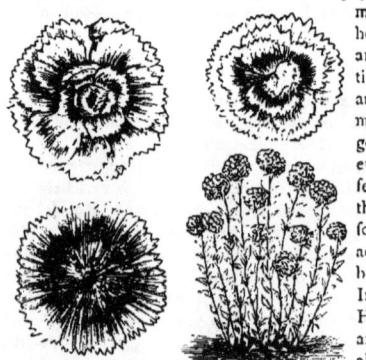

The Sweet William is a very old and popular garden flower, but not now so often as formerly seen in our gardens. Indeed, the system of bedding with Geraniums, and other bright flowers and ornamental foliaged plants, and the introduction of the Phlox and Petunia, and similar valuable annuals that give a constant display during the summer, has almost driven a good many of our really good flowers from the garden. A re-action, however, has commenced, and both amateurs and professional gardeners are beginning to look about for their old favorites, so long neglected and almost forgotten. They are not quite content, however, to accept the old flowers as they were thirty years ago; but are making earnest efforts for their improvement. In this improvement the Sweet William, like the Hollyhock, has largely shared. The best varieties are of exceedingly beautiful colors, very large, and almost perfect in form, with trusses of great size. Treatment as for Carnation. The plants are perfectly hardy, and may be increased by division of the roots. There are very good double varieties, though a single Sweet William is much to be preferred to any double we have ever seen.

TENDER BULBOUS FLOWERS

## VALERIANA, Nat. Ord. *Valerianaceæ.*

The Valerian is a beautiful border plant that we can recommend to all lovers of flowers for the hardy, perennial border. There are a good many species of this genus, a few of them natives of Southern countries, tender, and only suitable for green-house culture, but they are mostly hardy, natives of Switzerland, Austria, the Pyrenees and Scotch Mountains. Nothing can be more beautiful than the chalk cliffs of England when covered with Valerian, as we saw them one glorious July day, a few years since. The improved or garden varieties are beautiful, bearing large corymbs of small flowers, scarlet, white and red, the plant from two to three feet in height. The Valerian will bear shade and moisture.

## WALLFLOWER, (Cheiranthus Cheiri,) Nat. Ord. *Cruciferæ.*

The Wallflower resembles the Brompton Stock in appearance, habit and necessary treatment. In the South of Germany, and in England, in early spring, the gardens are gorgeous with Wallflowers, while the fragrance peculiar to this flower perfumes the air. By growing plants in the ground and transplanting to pots in the autumn, or better, by placing the young plants in pots when taken from the seed-bed, and sinking the pots to the rim in earth, good plants will be secured for winter flowering in the house. Give a cool room, and plenty of water. By placing the pots in a pit or cold cellar, with a little light the plants may be kept alive during the winter, and until time to remove to the garden. For the conservatory the Wallflower is desirable. While the Brompton Stocks are clear white, purple, pink, &c., all the colors of the Wallflower possess more or less of yellow, the richest being deep, velvety, brownish red.

## DICTAMNUS, Nat. Ord. *Rutaceæ.*

The *Dictamnus Fraxinella* is a desirable hardy perennial with racemes of large, showy flowers often a foot in length. There are two varieties, white and pink. The fragrance of these flowers is pleasant to most people, being somewhat aromatic or resinous. The plant attains a height of two or three feet, and the leaves being beautiful in form and color, it is desirable in the border for a summer hedge or screen, and for all decorative purposes, where large flowers are admissable, it is very useful. Seeds germinate freely if sown either in the autumn or spring, and we have never known a plant injured in the winter. Plants can be safely transplanted or shipped at either season.

DICTAMNUS — PLANT AND FLOWER.

# GREENHOUSE

THE names in this department will have a familiar sound to all lovers of house plants. The Heliotrope, the Calceolaria, Gloxinia, Chrysanthemum, Cineraria, Geranium, Fuschia, etc., are associated with our earliest recollections of floriculture. Most persons procure house plants from the green-houses, and when but one or two of a kind are needed this is a good plan. It is also well to purchase of the nearest florist, if good plants can be obtained, because you can then make the selection personally, and your florist needs, and we hope deserves, encouragement. Some, however, have green-houses and desire many plants, and others take pride and pleasure in growing from seed — in watching every day's mysterious growth, from the tiny seed-leaf to the full developed plant, in all its grand display of beauty. To all such we shall be happy to furnish seeds. As the seeds in this department are mostly delicate, it is best to make several sowings at different times. The most experienced gardeners always do this. Most of the varieties known as greenhouse plants will, of course, succeed as well in the dwelling house as the green-house, if we can only secure the conditions necessary to their health, and which the conservatory or green-house furnishes. These are light, warmth, moisture, air, and occasionally a little sunshine. Some may think that they supply all these conditions, and yet the plants do not flourish. The difficulty generally is that we keep our living rooms too warm for plants, and too warm also for our own good. The atmosphere of the living room, also, is too dry. The florist syringes his plants, and throws water on the paths, and all about his houses, so as to obtain a moist atmosphere by its evaporation. In our living rooms we provide no water for evaporation, and the consequence is a dry and unhealthy atmosphere, generally filled with fine dust from the carpets. Keep the plants clean and comfortable, with thermometer not over seventy or seventy-five in the day, and not more than fifty or sixty in the night. Keep the leaves clean. Smooth leaves, like those of the Camellia and Oleander, should be washed with a sponge, but some rough or woolly leaved plants, like the Begonia, dislike wetting of the foliage. This is particularly the case with the Chinese Primulas. The engravings at the right, commencing at top of page, show the Heliotrope, Calceolaria, and Cineraria; on the left, the Clianthus.

66

## TENDER BULBS AND TUBERS.

THE Tender or Summer Bulbs, in this latitude, during August and the early part of September, are truly grand beyond comparison. They may not be equally gorgeous in some places, but our experience and observation is that the Summer Bulbs are delightful almost everywhere. It is no wonder they are becoming so popular in all parts of the civilized world. The Gladiolus takes rank at the very head of the list and the Dahlia is gaining more than its old popularity. The tender bulbs are so certain in their growth that disappointment is hardly possible, and so easily cared for that no one can complain of the trouble. Summer Bulbs should not be planted until frost is over in the spring, and in the autumn must be taken up before hard frosts. They are easily preserved in any place free from frost during the winter. These remarks, and the instructions throughout this chapter, refer to the places where severe frosts occur. In sections where there is little or no frost these tender Bulbs, of course, are perfectly hardy. We cannot give directions for every locality, and our readers must use a little judgment in the matter. Protect the bulbs from frost, and give them the benefit of spring and early summer growth.

### GLADIOLUS.

The Gladiolus is the most beautiful of our Summer Bulbs, with tall spikes of flowers, some two feet or more in height, and often several spikes from the same bulb. The flowers are of almost every desirable color — brilliant scarlet, crimson, creamy white, striped, blotched and spotted in the most curious and interesting manner. Perhaps we have no flower that presents such a gorgeous display of delicate yet brilliant colors in the garden, or on the exhibition tables, or for extensive floral decorations, as the Gladiolus. For many years the French have been the most skillful propagators of this flower, and every season introduced many very beautiful new varieties, grown, of course, from seed, which the rest of the world have been very glad to purchase at extravagant prices—five dollars or more each. There is no country in the world, we think, where the Gladiolus thrives as it does in America — it is subject here to no disease, which is not the case in Europe — and to plant a bulb is to insure a good spike of flowers. It is not strange, therefore, that the Gladiolus is becoming exceedingly popular, and receiving especial attention from florists. In our own grounds we cultivate from five to ten acres of the best named varieties, and several acres of seedlings. Among these seedlings are annually produced some very choice flowers, while the average is very good, quite as fine as ninety per cent. of the best named sorts. The bulb, as it is commonly called, is really a corm, and from this grows the erect stem, terminating in a spike of flowers. The culture is very

simple. Set the bulbs from six to nine inches apart and cover about four inches. If set in rows

they may be six inches apart in the rows, and the rows one foot apart. The planting may be done at different times from the middle of April to the first of June, to secure a long succession of bloom. Keep the earth mellow, and place a neat stake to support the spikes in storms. I have never known a a case where the Gladiolus failed to give the most perfect satisfaction, opening a new field of beauty to those unacquainted with its merits. In the fall, take up the bulbs, let them dry in the air for a few days, then cut off the tops and store the bulbs out of the way of frost, for next season's planting. Look at them occasionally. If kept in a place too moist, they will show signs of moisture and perhaps mildew. If this appears, remove them to a dryer position. If the bulbs shrivel, it shows they are getting too dry; but they do not usually suffer from a dry atmosphere. To prevent disappointment, I would say, I know of no Gladiolus of a bright yellow color, and none of spotless white. Our engravings show two plants in flower, of somewhat different habit; also, a bulb or corm, and a single flower, the two latter about natural size.

## DAHLIAS.

The Dahlia, some twenty or more years ago, was altogether the most popular florist's flower, and Dahlia exhibitions the most noted horticultural contests. The Dahlia for a time lost part of its eclat, but is now not only regaining its lost ground, but bids fair to exceed even its former position in public estimation. We are not surprised at this, for when we look upon a well-formed Dahlia, we are compelled to acknowledge that it is a wonder of beauty and perfection. The Dahlia, when first discovered in Mexico, about 1784, and named after Dr. DAHL, a pupil of Linnæus, was a single flower, and its improvement was accomplished by the patience and skill of European florists. It was first cultivated for its tubers, which were thought to be eatable. It was not until 1814 that it began to excite the attention of florists, and the improvement of the Dahlia has been constant to the present time; for though florists thought this flower had attained the highest point of beauty many years since, every year seedlings are produced and named which are considered as surpassing their predecessors in some point of excellence.

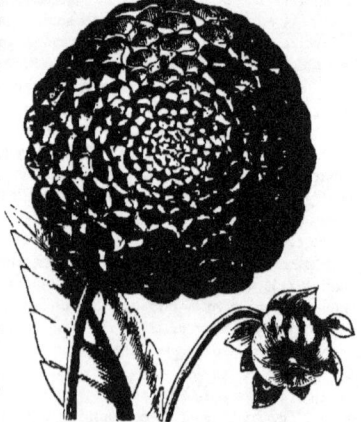

We exhibited seedlings of our own growing in 1874, which such excellent judges as ISAAC BUCHANAN and C. L. ALLEN pronounced superior to any they had before seen. The flower shown is about one-half the size of a large Dahlia, though they differ very much in this respect,

some varieties always producing large and others small flowers, the small or medium being usually the most perfect, and the largest often somewhat coarse. Purchasers of Dahlias usually

SHOW DAHLIA.

obtain the tubers for planting, because they are more safely transported than plants, and the appearance of these tubers will be seen by the little engraving of the Dahlia root. Buds are found at the neck of the tubers and these form the plants. Put the tubers in the ground when the season becomes warm, covering the neck some three inches. If many shoots start, thin them out. There is no necessity for planting the Dahlia early, as it is an autumn flower, and seldom gives good blossoms until the nights are somewhat cool. After flowering, and before hard frosts, take up the bulbs, dry them a little, remove the tops, and store in the cellar until spring, when they can be divided and re-planted. The size of the tuber has no influence on the strength of the plant or the beauty of the flower; all the tuber is needed for is to sustain the young shoot until it can take root and obtain its own support. Florists

usually place the tubers in a hot-bed early in the spring, and as fast as the young shoots get a few inches of growth, take them off and pot them, when, everything being favorable, each one will root and make a good plant. They are often sold in this way, especially new and scarce varieties. The tall growing plants require staking, if growing in exposed situations, or they are often broken by the wind. The Dahlia is divided into three pretty distinct classes, the first being the largest and most important, as follows: *Show Dahlia*, growing from three to four feet in height, and embracing all our finest sorts, fit for exhibiting at horticultural shows, from which the name is derived; the flowers ranging in size from two and a half to four inches in diameter. The *Dwarf or Bedding Dahlia* grows about eighteen inches in height, and makes a thick, compact bush, and covers a good deal of surface. Flowers of the size of Show Dahlias. They are therefore very desirable for bedding and massing. The *Pompon or Bouquet Dahlia* makes a pretty, compact plant, about three feet in height. The leaves are small, and the flowers from one to two inches in diameter. Many expect to find small flowers on their Dwarf Dahlias, and feel disappointed because they are of the ordinary size, not knowing that it is the plant, and not the flower that is dwarfed, and that only the Pompon gives the small flowers. The striped and

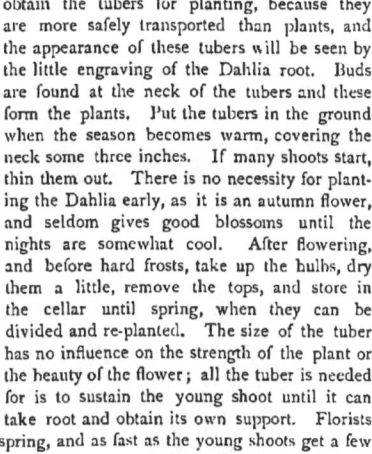

DWARF DAHLIA.

POMPON DAHLIA.

DAHLIA ROOT.

mottled and spotted flowers belonging to the Show section are called *Fancy*, and though not as rich and usually as highly prized as the selfs, or those of one color, are very attractive.

## CANNA.

The Canna is a fine foliage plant, making a good bed alone, but particularly desirable as the center of a group of foliage plants, of which it is one of the very best. Growing from three to four feet. The leaves are sometimes two feet in length, of a beautiful green, some varieties tinted with red. The flowers are on spikes, pretty, but not conspicuous. Roots can be taken up in the autumn and placed in the cellar. They flourish and are vigorous in the dryest and hottest weather. A bed of Cannas presents a very beautiful tropical appearance that is exceedingly pleasant, contrasting delightfully with the ordinary foliage of the garden. In the West Indies a superior kind of arrowroot is made from the fleshy underground stems; the tubers of some species are eaten as a vegetable. The seeds are large, round and black, which gives its common name, Indian Shot. The Canna and the Ricinus we consider the two best foliage plants known for ordinary use in this country, as they will give better satifaction with less trouble and expense than any others we are acquainted with. A good, large bed, entirely of Cannas, and another of Ricinus, will almost make one dream he is luxuriating in the tropics.

## CALADIUM ESCULENTUM.

The Caladium is one of the handsomest of the ornamental-leaved plants. The leaves are often more than a foot in length, nearly as much in breadth, and of a beautiful green, somewhat variegated or mottled. Roots obtained in the spring will make a good growth in the summer, and in the fall should be taken up and stored in the cellar, like Dahlias. The Caladium delights in heat and moisture, and in localities pretty well North it is well to start the root stalks, or rhizomes, which the fleshy bulb-like root is called, in the house a few weeks before it is time to plant in the garden, as in this way a larger and earlier growth is obtained. The Caladium is a native of very warm countries, such as the Sandwich Islands and the West Indies, and as the roots abound in starch, they are eaten by the natives, after being deprived of their acrid properties by some process of cookery, or perhaps filtering, in some such manner as the Indians of California remove the tannin and bitter taste from the acorns, which they do by washing and filtering through the sand, selecting any sandy spot, and scooping out a hollow for the purpose.

## OXALIS.

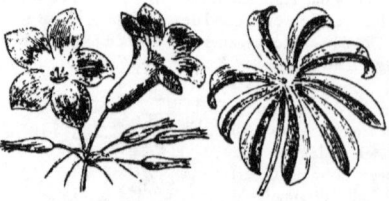

One of the prettiest things we are acquainted with for borders or edgings of beds and walks, is the Oxalis lasiandra. We first saw it in the grounds of an English gardener, and thought it a good thing to take the place of the old box edging, now gone out of use, obtained bulbs, and have cultivated it ever since. It forms a fine rounded edging a foot or so in height, and about the same in breadth. The leaves are in nine divisions, as shown in the engraving, the flower-stems standing well up above the foliage, of a bright, purplish pink, and of the size seen in the illustration. The flowers open in sunny weather, and close in the afternoon. The bulbs are small, and should be planted one or two inches apart in the spring, and every one will produce a good plant. Take up the bulbs and store them away in the fall. We leave a few out each season, with satisfactory results, but cannot recommend the practice in the North, until we are better satisfied of their entire hardiness.

## TUBEROSE.

The Tuberose is a beautiful, pure white, wax-like, very sweet-scented, double flower, growing tall stems three feet in height, each stem bearing a dozen or more flowers. The engravings show a plant, much reduced in size but giving a very good idea of its appearance when in blossom; a flower, and also a tuber, both of natural size. The Tuberose, being a native of the East Indies, delights in great heat, and where summers are short and not very warm, does not always flower before frost destroys the plant. In such latitudes, obtain tubers early and plant them in boxes of earth, and place these boxes in the hottest place in the house, watering very little, where they can remain until the atmosphere and soil is quite warm. Then transplant to the garden. Those who want this beautiful flower in the early winter can plant a few bulbs in pots in July or August, sink them to the rim in earth in the garden, where they can remain until the cool nights of autumn, to be then removed to the house. Those who are favored with warm and long summers, need only plant the tubers in the garden as soon as the weather is warm. The Tuberose flowers but once; but the old tuber forms many small ones, and these, after one year's growth, under favorable circumstances, make flowering bulbs. A dwarf variety, called Pearl, has a shorter flower-stem, usually about eighteen inches. Those who preserve tubers over winter for flowers the next summer, must keep them in a warm room, or the flower stem will rot, and the tubers never flower.

## MADEIRA VINE.

The Madeira Vine is a beautiful climber, with thick, glossy, light green, almost transparent leaves, and climbing to almost any remarkable height, and twining in any desired form. Then it is as useful as beautiful, because it will bear almost any kind of merciless treatment, without saying a word. Plant the tuber out of doors in the spring, and it commences to grow at once, and if in a warm, sheltered place, very rapidly, until its slender branches, covered with pretty leaves, have climbed nearly a score of feet over pillar or porch; and then towards autumn, as though grateful for a chance to live and grow, it sends forth its racemes of little, delicate, white flowers, as sweet almost as Mignonette. In the autumn, cut off the tops, dig up the tubers, and throw them into a cellar, where they will keep sounder and safer than potatoes; or, take up the bulbs carefully, pot them, remove them to the house, and they will bear the heat, dust and smoke of the worst living room imaginable, with perhaps only a pitiful look of remonstrance from their sensitive leaves, while anything like decent usage will cause a smile of satisfaction, from the root to tiniest leaflet. The Madeira Vine is excellent for baskets and vases, furnishing a large amount of pretty, graceful foliage. For screens for windows and other in-door work it is equaled by no climber, except, perhaps, the Ivy, which is almost a salamander.

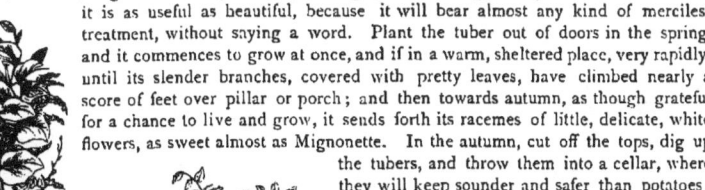

## TIGRIDIA.

The Tigridia, or Mexican Tiger Flower, is one of the most curious and beautiful flowers that this earth produces. T. Pavonia is of the richest scarlet, with a center of golden yellow spotted with black. T. conchiflora, orange, variegated with yellow and spotted with black. The flowers are from three to four inches in diameter, and, though short-lived, are produced in succession during the whole season, so that a little bed is never without flowers. The blossoms appear very early in the morning, and in dull weather will be bright nearly all day, but a few hours of sunshine destroy their beauty. The next morning, however, a new lot appear, and the bed is gay as ever. The flower stems are from twelve to eighteen inches in height, the bulbs are small. Plant about the middle of May in this latitude, and take them up in October, dry for a few days in the air, and then pack them away in dry sand or sawdust in any room free from frost, and out of the reach of mice and rats, as these animals consider them a great luxury.

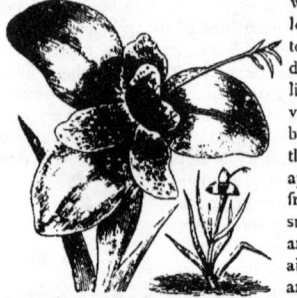

## AMARYLLIS VALOTTA PURPUREA.

This is becoming a very popular plant for summer blooming, and for a pot-plant for the decoration of porches, piazzas, etc., there is nothing prettier. It throws up a strong flower-stem, in August, about eighteen inches in height, bearing from four to eight brilliant, purplish scarlet flowers, two to three inches in diameter, and as these flowers open in succession, the plant continues in blossom a long time, and therefore makes a very durable as well as beautiful ornament. It flowers most surely and freely in a small pot; indeed, a pot a little more than sufficient to hold the bulb is all that is necessary, and this is an advantage, because any of the little ornamental pots may be employed for this bulb, and they are charmingly in keeping with the neat habit of the plant, and the honorable position it is destined to occupy on the entrance porch, or the verandah in front of the parlor windows. Bulbs may be potted any time in the spring, or even as late as June. After flowering, the bulb may remain in the pot until the following spring, and should be kept pretty cool and not over moist. In May next the bulb will probably need more room, and should be re-potted for flowering. In a year or two a number of bulbs will form, giving several flower stems.

## ERYTHRINA CRISTA-GALLI.

The Erythrina is a fine, robust plant, with broad leaves and large red flowers, somewhat pea-formed, an inch or so in length, and growing in long racemes, sometimes ten or twelve inches in length. There is great substance in the flower, giving it a leathery appearance. The roots are thick and fleshy, but not exactly tuberous, and may be kept in a pit or cellar during the winter. Plants put out in the spring will flower during the summer, and before hard frosts should be taken up, the main branches cut back to within four or five inches of the root, and then stowed away in winter quarters until spring. It is a very fine plant, and those who have never grown it will derive a good deal of pleasure from its culture. It is a native of Brazil, and in the more Southern States and Pacific coast would prove hardy. In giving direction for culture we are apt to furnish those suited to our latitude, forgetting the great extent and diversified climate of our country, though we have endeavored to be particular on this point. Readers, however, are always ready to take advantage of any climatic favors that will save trouble.

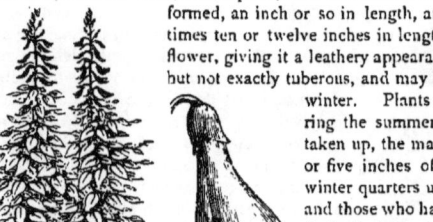

## TRITOMA.

The Tritoma uvaria is a stately, vigorous plant, sending up its strong flower stems four or five feet in height, surmounted by a spike of curious red and orange, pendant flowers, a foot in length, very striking, and by its supposed resemblance to that domestic implement, generally known as the Red Hot Poker. The Tritoma flowers late in the summer, usually commencing in August in this latitude, and continuing until winter, and is admirably adapted for forming large beds or groups, the numerous flame-colored racemes forming a stately object. The Tritoma was supposed to be tender, and for some years we removed plants to the greenhouse or pit in the autumn, but lately we have allowed nearly our whole stock to remain in the open ground during the winter, and without the loss of a plant. There are several varieties advertised in Europe, and we have imported and grown all, but the difference is very slight.

## CALLA.

This is the well-known Egyptian Lily, or Lily of the Nile. Its large white flowers are indispensable in the winter, its foliage is broad and good, and it will prosper under very adverse circumstances, if water is provided in abundance. It is also an excellent plant for aquariums — none better, either placed in the center bedded in a little earth and sand, which may be covered with stones, or planted in a pot which can be placed in the aquarium, and so covered with pieces of rock as to be entirely concealed. In the spring, the plant may be planted in the garden, where it can remain until autumn, when it should be repotted for winter flowering. It will not appear to advantage in the garden, nor is it designed to do so, the object being to place it where it will be no trouble and at the same time gain strength for winter blooming. In California the Calla makes a wonderful growth, and is perfectly hardy, as, of course it is in the South.

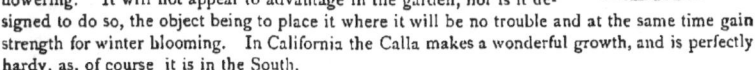

## HARDY PLANTS, BULBS, &c.

Hardy Bulbs are those that, like the Lilies, endure the winter in the garden without injury, and when once planted will continue to grow and increase for a number of years. They are, and always will continue, popular, on account of their great beauty, and because they require so little labor. The work of planting once well done is over for a life time. There is no taking up and storing and re-planting — no danger of loss from frost, or rotting from improper storing. Occasionally, when the increase has been so great that the plants crowd each other, they can be taken up, divided and re-planted, and if the increase has been too great for the space desired to be appropriated to them, flower-loving neighbors will be glad of the surplus. No plant, or class of plants, however, possess all good qualities, and those in this department do not generally keep in flower a long time, like some of our best annuals and tender bedding plants.

### ANEMONE JAPONICA ALBA.

Anemone Japonica alba is the best hardy, white blooming, autumn flowering plant we have.

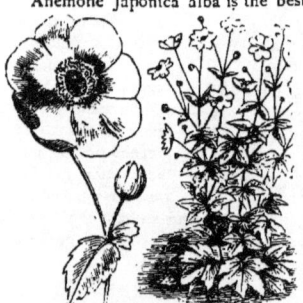

The Anemone, during the summer, is a plain looking plant, with dark green foliage, one that would attract no attention; but in the latter part of summer flower stems begin to appear, and when some eighteen inches in height the white flowers commence to open; and if the nights are rather cool and dewy, the advancement of the plant to perfection is rapid. It soon bears from a score to a hundred of its clear white flowers, and is an object to delight every lover of flowers, especially as it continues to improve until destroyed by frost, thus giving a mass of white blooms when every other white flower is gone, except the Ten-Weeks Stock, Candytuft and Alyssum. The flowers are more than an inch in diameter. The plant is perfectly hardy every where, we judge, never having lost one, and increases so rapidly that a small plant soon makes a conspicuous clump. Although perhaps not to be recommended for cutting, as it does not carry very well, for large floral decorations it is quite valuable.

### DAY LILY.

The pretty Funkia, commonly called Day Lily, we believe, because one of its beautiful flowers opens every day, is truly a very desirable autumn flower that every one should possess, and everybody will be pleased with.

The plant has light, broad foliage, prettily veined. The buds form in a cluster on a stem six inches or more in length, as shown in the engraving, but usually only one opens each day. The flowers are of the purest white imaginable, trumpet-shaped, about five inches in length. The blue variety, shown in the engraving at right of page, has smaller flowers, but larger clusters, makes a taller growth, and though not so pretty nor so popular as the white, is a meritorious autumn flowering plant.

## LILIES.

THE LILY is loved in every land. It is the queen of flowers, and only the Rose can dispute its regal honors. We find it in the humid vale, the arid desert, and on the lofty mountain top. With few exceptions, Lilies succeed in our gardens admirably, are subject to no diseases, and continue to increase in strength and beauty for many years. From six to a dozen of the best varieties will give a good collection, better far than is seen even in most of our best gardens. The past twenty years has added to our garden Lilies the best we now possess, such as *Lancifolium*, of several varieties, *Auratum, Washingtonianum, Bloomerianum*, &c. Some of the newer varieties have been affected with a strange disease, or perhaps did not take kindly to our climate and soil, or may have been seriously injured by a long journey. Whatever may have been the cause, the Auratum certainly was not reliable for a number of years after its introduction. Some, having every appearance of soundness, when planted would make a vigorous start, and then, without apparent cause, perhaps as the buds were about to open, show signs of disease, the leaves drooping, and an examination showing a decaying bulb. Others would flower beautifully the first season, and decay the second or even the third. We have lost thousands of Auratum bulbs in this way. We have now mature, good sized bulbs, raised in our grounds — beds of many thousands, with the foliage very much improved, and very little, if any, sign of disease. The Auratum is so grand that we must have it, though we occasionally lose a bulb or two; and as we now grow them with every appearance of soundness, the difficulty, whatever its cause, we hope is entirely overcome.

LILIUM LANCIFOLIUM.

The California Lilies we have not before dared to describe, although we have cultivated them several years, because sometimes we have received several species under one name, and at other times, what seemed to be one variety, with a good many more names than it was entitled to. Our management, also, seemed to be defective, so we visited California to see the Lilies and consult with her most conscientious florists and most experienced botanists. We think we now understand the characteristics of the California Lilies, and their habits, so that we can describe them understandingly; but the most important lesson we learned was the necessity of deep planting. We are quite certain we dug Lily bulbs in California fully eighteen inches below the surface, and are satisfied that much of our losses with the Auratum and the Pacific Lilies was the result of shallow planting, though we are well aware that this was not the entire cause. We would advise all who plant the Auratum, or any of the California Lilies, to set them deep. Indeed, all Lilies require deep planting.

The collection of Lilies is now so large and so good that no lover of flowers can afford to ignore this interesting and elegant family, and no garden can be considered complete without a good collection. We will describe a few of the best.

LILIUM CHALCEDONICUM.

*Lilium lancifolium.* Among the many truly valuable flowers that have been introduced into this country and Europe from Japan and China, during the past twenty years, we know of

none that excel the beautiful, delicate, yet brilliant Japan Lilies — *Lilium lancifolium*. In addition to their beauty, these Lilies are exceedingly fragrant and as hardy as any of our common varieties. Strong bulbs send up flowering stems from three to four or five feet in height, and begin to bloom about the middle of summer. Each flowering stem will have from two to a dozen flowers, according to strength of bulb. No description can do anything like justice to these flowers, or show the beautiful frost-like white of the surface, glistening like diamonds, or the rubies that stand out on the surface. *L. Chalcedonicum* is one of the Martagon or Turk's Cap Lilies, being much reflexed, as can be seen in the engraving. The flower is small, about the size of our common Can-

LILIUM AURATUM.

adense, but it is the most brilliant flower of the family — a scarlet so bright that no painting can do it justice, as it is impossible to procure a color sufficiently intense. We have endeavored to portray this Lily in our Chromo B, where it will be found quite correct, except in coloring. The Chalcedonicum is a native of Palestine, and is, no doubt, the flower referred to by our SAVIOR as the Lily of the field arrayed in glory far exceeding even the glory of Israel's most voluptuous monarch. In addition to the brilliant color, the flower has the appearance of being freshly varnished. Plant pretty deep, and it is well to give a little mulching the first summer. A few flowers only will be given the first season, if any, but the improvement will be marked and satisfactory every season.

*L. auratum* is the great Lily of Japan, often called Golden-Banded Lily. This is the King of Lilies. The flower is from ten to twelve inches in diameter, composed of six very delicate white ivory parts, each being thickly studded with spots of crimson, and having a

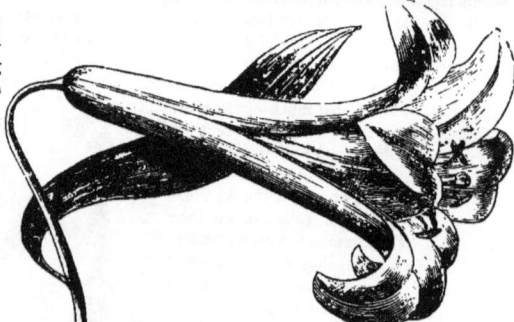

LILIUM JAPONICUM LONGIFLORUM.

golden band through its center. As the bulbs acquire age and strength, the flowers attain a very large size, and upward of a dozen are produced on a single stem. As before observed, I find Auratums grown on my own grounds are fine and healthy, showing every sign of strength and

vigor. Plant in as dry a place as possible, and at least six inches in depth. The bulbs should remain in the ground several years without removal, if possible. If good bulbs are planted, they will generally bloom the first summer, and continue to improve every year.

LILIUM CANDIDUM.

*Japonicum longiflorum* is trumpet-shaped, four inches or more in length, and of pearly whiteness. It is perfectly hardy and healthy. The plant seldom exceeds eighteen inches in height. Bulbs small. It is destined to become a universal favorite. The Longiflorum bears forcing well, and therefore can be grown in the house where it will invariably give perfect satisfaction. Indeed it is one of those beautiful and useful flowers that we cannot praise too highly. There are two Lilies very similar, though larger and somewhat scarce. Eximium has flowers about an inch or two longer, and the plant is somewhat taller. Takesima produces flowers about the same size as Eximium, but the plant is quite distinct, the flower stalk being purplish.

*Lilium candidum* is our common white Lily, and we have none more beautiful. It is hardy everywhere, and constantly improves, throwing out new bulbs, so that after a few years a clump is formed several feet in diameter and from four to five feet in height, giving a perfect mass of beautiful, white, fragrant blossoms. For floral decorations no flower excels this beautiful white Lily, and we advise everybody to grow a clump of these flowers in some corner of the garden, especially for cutting for decorative purposes. Was this Lily newly discovered it would be very much prized, and every one would desire to possess it, regardless of cost, but being old it is too much neglected. For this reason we urge upon our readers the claims of one of our oldest and best friends.

*L. speciosum album*, by some florists called Præcox, is a new white Lily from Japan, of the Lancifolium style, and is far superior in purity of color, size of flower and vigor of plant, to the old Lancifolium album. In habit, the plant is as robust as Rubrum, but shorter, the flowers are as large, but more reflexed, while they are of the purest white, the flower stem and band in center of petals being pea-green. Leaves and stems a very light, almost transparent green. We have had this variety in cultivation several years, but our stock was so small that we could not offer it for sale until recently.

*L. excelsum* is a very delicate flower, being creamy or light buff, and exceedingly fragrant. The plant is vigorous, blooms abundantly, and is one of the tallest of the family. This is the only true buff Lily we know of, and it is a real beauty, a strong bulb throwing up a stem more than four feet in height, and bearing a score or more of flowers, of a creamy buff, almost salmon, reflexed, and about three inches in diameter.

*L. Washingtonianum* is one of the best of the California and Oregon Lilies, pure waxy white, glossy as though freshly varnished, and spotted with fine purple spots. The flowers, though perfectly white when they open, change to pink, becoming darker each day, so that flowers are seen on the same plant of every shade from white

LILIUM WASHINGTONIANUM.

to deep purplish pink. We have this Lily in flower, growing from four to five feet in height, and bearing over twenty flowers each. Flowers two inches in length and the same in breadth. The engravings show a flower just opened, and also the habit of the plant, both, as in all our Lily engravings,' much reduced. Having spent the summer of 1874 in California, mainly for the purpose of examining the Lilies of the country, and learning all we could of their habits and true names, we feel prepared to offer the Lilies of the Pacific coast to our customers with confidence. The Washingtonianum we have flowered for a number of years, and we think our bulbs are sound and healthy, though we would say to all to whom money is an object, and failure would prove a disappointment, procure but one or two of these new California Lilies, just for trial. If they succeed you will be delighted, and if any fail the loss will not be serious. Set the bulbs down not less than six inches.

LILIUM HUMBOLDTII.

The *Bloomerianum*, or *Humboldtii*, is a pretty yellowish Lily, with large brown spots, a native of California, and which we found growing mostly in shady places and near the banks of running streams. It is a very desirable Lily. About four feet in height. It was named Bloomerianum after a worthy Botanist of California, our late friend BLOOMER, by that enterprising and whole-souled collector, Dr. KELLOGG, with whom we have spent many pleasant hours; but by some it is thought to have been previously discovered by ROEZL, and named in honor of Baron HUMBOLDT. Plant this and all California Lilies deep, certainly not less than six inches, and we think this variety might well be grown in partial shade. A good mulching the first season after planting is very desirable, not only for this variety, but for all the Lilies. We are apt to think because a plant is a native of a warm, dry country, that it can endure any amount of heat, but we often find that such plants, in a natural state, grow in shady nooks and ravines and on mountain sides, constantly watered by cool springs.

LILIUM PARDALINUM.

The *Pardalinum* is a California Lily, very much like our Canadense and Superbum, but of clearer yellow and brighter red. It is a very good small Lily, growing in large clusters, and very handsome. The lower half of each petal is yellow, spotted with brown, the upper half red, almost crimson, giving the flower a very marked appearance. The foliage is lanceolate, that is, very narrow, lance-shaped leaves, and we have never seen a plant or bulb, or even leaf, that was not entirely healthful.

*Lilium parvum* is a small California Lily, and one of the prettiest very small varieties we are acquainted with. The engraving at the left shows the size of the flower, which is dark yellow, ornamented with small reddish dots. The small engraving will give something of an idea of the habit of the plant. It does not usually exceed eighteen inches in height. It seems to be perfectly healthy, and we do not remember having seen one sickly plant in a bed of several thousands.

LILIUM PARVUM—FLOWER.    PLANT.

Although we have had most of the new California Lilies on trial for a number of years, we have been rather slow in introducing them to the notice of our readers, for reasons previously stated. There is great pleasure in testing comparatively untried plants and bulbs, somewhat the same kind of feeling we experience in traveling a new road or visiting a strange country. We would deprive no one of this pleasurable excitement, yet we cannot forget the fact that many of our friends have but little money with which to indulge their love for the beautiful, and we feel exceedingly anxious that this little should be invested to the best possible advantage.

To three Lilies that are favorites with us we wish to call special attention. They are *Thunbergianum atrosanguineum grandiflorum*, *Thunbergianum atrosanguineum fulgens* and *Thunbergianum citrinum*. They are all grand flowers, bearing immense numbers of blossoms, continuing a good season in bloom, healthy and vigorous, and increase rapidly in numbers; certainly an array of good qualities that should recommend them to general culture, and yet they are not seen in our gardens.

LILIUM THUNBERGIANUM.        PLANTS.

*Thunbergianum atrosanguineum grandiflorum* is a very robust plant, growing only about thirty inches in height. The leaves are narrow, dark in color, thickly set, and no Lily we are acquainted with makes a more vigorous, healthy growth. The flowers are about four inches across, and are borne in immense clusters. The one from which our little engraving was taken had twenty open flowers and as many buds. The color is a very deep red—the darkest of all the red Lilies.

*Thunbergianum atrosanguineum fulgens* is like the preceding in habit, a few inches shorter, the clusters of flowers not quite so large, while the color is a curious mottling or different shades of red.

*Thunbergianum citrinum* grows only about eighteen inches in height. The flowers are generally larger than either of the two preceding varieties, and the color we hardly know how to describe. It is something between a cream and salmon, and one of the best of the light colored Lilies. The engravings of the plants show the comparative difference in height between the Citrinum and Atrosanguineum.

PLANT.        TIGER LILY.

The flower shows the form of both, but much reduced in size.

Our last engraving shows the old Tiger Lily, that everybody knows. It is still as good as some of the varieties we have tried, and which are claimed to be improvements upon this old fashioned flower.

Our native *Canadense* or *superbum* is a goodly Lily, improves by cultivation, and deserves an honorable place in every collection of Lilies.

## CHINESE PÆONIES.

The Chinese Pæonies are so valuable on account of their large size, beautiful coloring and delightful fragrance, and so entirely hardy and vigorous, that I am anxious all my customers should have at least a *White* and a *Pink* Pæony. Fragrans is one of the best Pink varieties, but there are few exhibitions that present such a wonderful combination of colors as a bed of Pæonies. The Paeonies are perfectly hardy, never suffering injury by cold, and will succeed in any ground, unless so wet that the water will lay on the surface in the winter and spring. They may be planted either in the autumn or spring, and are transported with greater safety than almost any plant — not one in a hundred failing. They are also easily increased by division of the roots. A little extra attention in the way of manure will induce a vigorous and rapid growth. We do not know of anything that injures the Pæony except starving in a poor soil and standing water during the cold season.

PÆONY FLOWER.

For large floral decorations few of our flowers can surpass the Pæonies. They seem designed for a grand display, without anything cheap or gaudy in their appearance. The large engraving shows a flower about one-half natural size, though it must be understood there is a good deal of difference in the formation of flowers of different varieties. The small cuts give a pretty good idea of the form and habit of both plant and roots, the drawings being taken from a full grown and vigorous plant the second season after planting.

PÆONY PLANT.

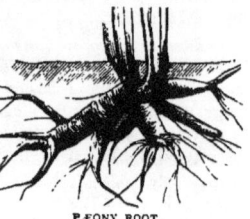

PÆONY ROOT.

Such a growth must not be expected the first season, nor should flowers be looked for or desired. Secure first a good strong plant, and then flowers will come in abundance. Those who are so impatient that they will plant only those things that flower the first season will never be very successful florists. Time passes swiftly, and plants grow while we work and sleep and travel.

## VIOLETS.

The little sweet Violet is a plant that we need not describe very particularly, for it has not only made itself known, but universally loved by its sweetness. A single flower will perfume a bouquet, or a room, with its delightful aroma. It is also perfectly hardy and flowers freely very early in the spring. The color is blue, and our engraving shows pretty faithfully the habit of the plant and the size and appearance of the flower.

Plants may be set out either in the spring or autumn, and can be increased by division when they attain a large size. The Violet flowers well in the house in winter if not kept too hot and dry.

## PERENNIAL PHLOX.

Very few plants give such universal satisfaction as the Perennial Phloxes. In the first place they are perfectly hardy, and will come out of any winter in good healthy condition without the  loss of a plant. Then we send them out with perfect confidence that they will reach their destination in just as good condition as they leave us. The flowers, when plants get strong, are immense bunches of bloom, from the purest white to crimson. Plants will keep increasing in size, and may be divided at the roots every year or two. Half-a-dozen well established plants, and of well selected colors, is a treasure for the garden that every lover of flowers must appreciate. The Perennial Phlox is one of those hardy, useful and beautiful flowers whose culture we are anxious to increase, because the expense and trouble is but little, and the result more than satisfactory. The flower resembles that of the annual Phlox, but the clusters are large, sometimes forming majestic heads of bloom. We have endeavored to show the appearance of the plant when in bloom in the little engraving, but we fear without much success. When in flower it is two feet or more in height. Seed does not germinate very readily, unless sown as soon as fully ripe, or before.

## DICENTRA SPECTABILIS.

There are several varieties of the Dicentra, natives of America, and very pretty plants, one is known commonly as Squirrel Corn, and another as Dutchman's Breeches; but the best of all is D. spectabilis, from Northern China, sometimes called Bleeding Heart, from the heart-like form of the flower, and its beautiful color. We well recollect the first time we saw this flower, soon after its introduction from China, and that we then thought it the most delicate and graceful flower we had ever seen. It was then considered tender, and cultivated in conservatories. It, however, soon proved its right to be classed among our hardy plants, where it has held for twenty years an honored position. The flowers are heart-shaped, deep pink, a dozen or more being borne on a graceful, drooping raceme, a foot or more in length. The Dicentra is also excellent for flowering in the house, and furnishes in winter very agreeable foliage, as well as beautiful flowers, and both quite freely.  Plants may be taken up and potted in the autumn.

## IVY PLANTS.

For a climbing plant in the garden to do duty as a screen for an old wall or building, or to  adorn either when new, we know of nothing in the world equal to the Ivy—it is so connected in our minds with ruined castles and brilliant poesy that it seems to throw an atmosphere of grace and beauty around every object subject to its transforming and beautifying influence. Unfortunately it does not prove quite hardy in some Northern sections of our country, when exposed on walls, not that it is injured by the cold, but by our warm winter sunshine. On the North or West side of a building it usually does well, receiving less sun than in other exposures. Wherever the Ivy does well we advise every one to grow a few; and as the best substitute, we recommend our beautiful Virginia Creeper, which is much more highly prized in Europe than in America. For in-door winter decoration the Ivy is unequalled, as it can be trained in any desired form, one style being shown in the engraving, and will bear more hardships and bad usage than any plant we are acquainted with. Strong roots with branches from one to five feet in length should be planted.

## LILY OF THE VALLEY.

The Lily of the Valley is one of those delicate, sweet little flowers that not only easily win our love, but keep it forever. No one would tire of the little Mignonette or the Lily of the Valley any quicker than he could of spring and sunshine, and singing birds. The Lily of the Valley is as hardy as any plant can possibly be, and when planted in the open ground will increase pretty rapidly; but florists and everybody wanted this pretty flower in winter, so the celebrated bulb growers of Holland grow and send to us tens of thousands of little buds, with roots attached, like the engraving, only a little larger, and these are called "pips," and sold at about a dollar a dozen. These are put four or five or half-a-dozen in a pot, and in about four or five weeks will flower. They will flower in damp moss, and can be handled in almost any way desired. The pips are not injured by frost, and can be sent out any time in the winter. When received, a part can be kept in damp moss or sawdust, cool and dormant; thus by making several plantings, flowers can be secured almost all winter. In the spring transfer to the garden.

---

## PLANTS INSTEAD OF SEEDS.

In addition to the plants already noticed, there are a few that we have described in our list of plants to be grown from seed, that some people prefer to obtain in a more speedy way, and therefore like to procure plants that will flower the first season. This is the case with the GARDEN PINKS, CARNATIONS and PICOTEES. Good plants of either, set out in the spring, will flower freely during the summer, and will also furnish layers for new plants. Plants of the DAISY, also, can be obtained, either spring or autumn, and generally with flowers and buds, for the Daisy gives its best flowers in fall and spring, and does not object to removal. The HOLLYHOCK, too, many are so anxious to obtain that they prefer plants to seeds. In the north, plant only in the spring; but we say to all, when you purchase a Hollyhock plant, obtain a few seeds at the same time, and the next autumn you will have plenty of plants without purchasing. Almost every one prefers plants of that beautiful grass, ERIANTHUS RAVENNÆ, but we say as of the Hollyhock, obtain seeds also. That useful Climber, the PERENNIAL PEA, grows rapidly from strong roots.

# HOLLAND BULBS

All our readers, no doubt, have heard of HOLLAND BULBS, but, perhaps, few would be able to give a list entitled to the name, and we do not know that we could make a very correct one. These Holland Bulbs did not originate in that country, but the good Hollanders have almost monopolized their culture for so many years, doubtless to their own profit and the good of the world, that the name has been conceded, by general consent, to a class of Bulbs of which the Hyacinth, Tulip and Crocus are the leading members. With few minor exceptions these Bulbs require to be planted in the autumn, and are admirably adapted for winter culture in the house. In many sections of our country the winters are long, unpleasant, and, of course, tedious. For full half the year no flower, not even a green leaf, is found to cheer the long gloom. While all is cold and sterile without, with a little care and skill, and at a trifling expense, we can make our homes cheerful, have buds and blossoms and emerald leaves every day from November until May, make our own little summers, and thus rob winter of half its tediousness. We shall endeavor to show how this can be done.

## THEIR CULTURE.

Those who wish a show of bulbous flowers in the spring must MAKE THEIR SELECTION, PRE-

FLOWERING BULBS IN WATER.

PARE THE GROUND and PLANT IN THE AUTUMN. It is useless to wake up to the importance of this subject and order Bulbs just as other people's plants are coming into flower. Any fair garden soil will grow Bulbs well; but it must be drained, so that water will not lie on the surface for any length of time, or the Bulbs will be likely to rot. After planting, and before winter sets in, cover the beds with a good dressing of leaves—say five or six inches in depth, or more. Over these throw a little brush, or earth, or manure, to prevent blowing off. If the leaves cannot be obtained readily, coarse manure will answer. In the spring, rake off the covering, taking off about half at first, and then waiting a week before removing the remainder. Nothing more is required except to destroy the weeds as fast as they appear.

As a general rule, beds should be made so narrow that the weeds can be destroyed and the ground kept mellow without walking among the plants. Any breaking or wounding of the leaves causes injury to the Bulb, but the flowers can be cut at pleasure, and all should be removed as soon as they fade.

It is in the HOUSE, in the winter, that Bulbs afford the greatest pleasure. A few dozen Hyacinths, Tulips, Crocuses, &c., will furnish useful recreation for months. From the planting of the Bulbs until the last flower has faded, there is continued excitement. The unfolding of each leaf and bud is watched with the most pleasurable and unabated interest by all members of the family. By the exercise of a little taste a great deal of pleasure can be derived from the cultivation of Bulbs in water, and at very little cost. The simplest and cheapest form of a Hyacinth glass is shown at D. A form preferred by some is seen at B. The Duc Van Thol Tulips may be grown in ornamental pots, like A, or in baskets or boxes of any form. A very satisfactory arrangement is to obtain a common shallow box, and ornament it with sticks of bark, as in the engraving on next page, and fill it with sandy earth, mixed with moss finely broken up. Then plant a row or two of Crocuses on the outside, and fill up with Tulips, Narcissus, Hyacinths, &c., making a miniature bulb garden. After planting, the whole can be covered with moss, such as is found on logs in damp woods. The plants will find their way through the moss.

DUC VAN THOL TULIPS.

Another very good plan is to have a box, similar to the one described, as a kind of little nursery, or reserve. Fill it almost entirely with broken up moss, with a very little sandy soil. Plant this with Crocuses, Hyacinths, &c., and keep it in any convenient, pretty cool room, where it will not freeze. As fast as the plants come into flower you can take them up and place them in glasses of water, and thus keep up a supply for the parlor or sitting room for a long time. If preferred, these Bulbs, when in flower, can be placed in pots or baskets filled with damp moss. In fact, they can be used in almost any way desired, and will be found to produce the greatest saisfaction, furnishing flowers for a long time. If placed in moss, it must be kept constantly moist or the flowers will suffer. Bulbs, when flowered in the house, should be kept in as moderately cool a room as possible. If placed in a living room, which is kept at the usual temperature of such rooms, from 70 to 75 degrees, they will bloom too early, and the flowers will soon fade. A good arrangement is to keep them in a parlor, or some spare room, not frequently used, and which is usually kept pretty cool. They will then mature slowly and keep in perfection a long time. A few may be brought into the sitting-room, placed on the dining table occasionally, or may be even taken to church, for special occasions, where floral decorations may be needed, and returned to their places as soon as possible. In this way a bulb can be made to do long service. Nearly all failures, I think, result from keeping plants in too dry an atmosphere and too high a temperature, supposing, of course, that sound Bulbs are used.

MINIATURE BULB GARDEN.

TIME OF BLOOMING.—We are often asked when Hyacinths will bloom; can we have flowers by Christmas? The request often accompanying orders is, send me the early kinds, so that I can soon have flowers. Now, the truth is, there is but a week or two of difference between the time of flowering of the early and late sorts, and none except the little White Roman will bloom by the holidays, with, perhaps, an exceptional case. The Hyacinth needs a long season of rest, and does not become anxious to grow until about the first of December, and this desire increases as time advances. A Hyacinth planted the first of November will go along moderately, and will take nearly three months in blooming. The same

Bulb, if kept out of the ground, in a cold and moist place, so that vitality is not weakened, and planted in January, will flower in thirty or forty days. The Hollanders informed us that the best way to force early flowers is to pot the bulbs as early as possible, sink the pots in the earth in the garden, so that the bulbs will be covered several inches, and there let them remain a couple of weeks or more. Then remove to the green-house or room where they are to flower, giving warmth, air and moisture pretty freely.

SUPPORT FOR HYACINTHS.—When in flower, the tall Hyacinths need some support for the flower stem, and various contrivances of wire, &c., have been devised, but we have seen nothing so simple and effective as we show in the engraving. It is made of hard wood and fastened to the neck of the glass by a string. Any one, in a few minutes, with a sharp knife, can make this support. A brass or other wire can also be attached to the glass very readily.

BULBS IN THE GARDEN.—Nothing makes a prettier bed in the garden than Hyacinths and Tulips. For a ribbon bed composed of three or more colors, we know of nothing that excels the Tulip.

CARE OF BULBS AFTER FLOWERING.—When Bulbs have been flowered in water, they should, as soon as the flowers begin to fade, be removed and planted in earth, where they will get a little nourishment for the future good of the Bulb. Even then the Bulb is much weakened, and it is useless to try to flower Bulbs in water twice, though they will answer for the garden.

All Bulbs with annual roots, which includes pretty much all but the Lilies, can be taken up, as soon as the leaves become ripe and brown, and be stowed away without the least injury to the flowers of the next season, because the roots will die if the Bulbs are allowed to remain in the ground. After taking them up, allow them to dry in the shade for a few days. Then remove the tops, roots and rough skin, and put them away in paper bags, properly labelled, in a cool place in the house until planting time in the Autumn. Look at them occasionally during the summer to see that they are receiving no injury. If

HYACINTH SUPPORT the beds are needed for other plants, so as to have a continuous show of flowers, the plants can be set when young between the rows of Bulbs, and before the space is needed by the new crop the Bulbs will have ripened their leaves, and will receive no injury from the new occupants, and the old Bulbs can remain in the ground. They may, however, be removed as soon as flowering is over and replanted in some corner of the garden, there to remain until ripe, or until time for planting in the beds again in Autumn. Hyacinths gradually deteriorate in this country, but Tulips and almost all other Bulbs retain their good character and increase in number.

## HYACINTHS.

THE HYACINTH is the most beautiful and fragrant and popular of the Bulbous flowers, and seems particularly designed for house culture. It is cultivated in every Northern country in the world, where it does more than any other flower to make winter cheerful. A very small pot will answer for the Hyacinth, but some prefer to plant three or four in a large pot, and this makes a very pretty ornament. Fill the pot with sandy, porous soil. Make a space in the soil for the bulb, so that it will be about half below the earth, then press the bulb down so that it will just show its upper surface above the soil, then water, giving all the earth will hold. The pots can now be set away in a cool, dark cellar for several weeks, where they will make roots, but the top will advance but little. By removing a few at a time into a warm, light room, something of a succession can be kept up. When we speak of a warm room for bulbs we do not mean 75 or 80 degrees, but less than 70, if possible.

When placed in glasses for winter flowering the base of the bulb should just touch the water; it will soon evaporate so that the water is a little below the base of the bulb, and this is as it should be. Set them away in a cool place, as recommended for Hyacinths in pots. As soon as flower buds appear, sprinkling the leaves and buds is of benefit, and give plenty of light and air, and as moist an atmosphere as possible. No Hyacinth can do itself justice if flowered in a room ranging from seventy-five to eighty degrees, and dry as well as hot.

A good plan is to keep a stand containing the stock of Hyacinths in a parlor or hall, which is kept most of the time at a low temperature. From this room they can be taken as needed

— one or two of each color — to the sitting, or the dining-room, for special occasions, but always returned to their cool quarters for the night. By this method they not only flower well, but keep in bloom a long time. Change the water occasionally, if it becomes discolored. The choice named varieties grow best in glasses and pots, and single are more reliable than double sorts for house-culture, while they are in every respect as desirable. Some of the double sorts do well in the house, but the selection of varieties should be left to those who have some knowledge of their habits.

Hyacinths should be planted in the garden in September, October or November. For beds of early flowers on the lawn, nothing excels the Hyacinth. Where beds are small and so near together that they can all be seen at once, it is well to fill each one with a separate color. Plant Hyacinths in the garden from three to four inches below the surface of the soil, and in ground likely to be much affected by freezing and thawing, be sure to give a good covering before severe frosts. Hyacinth flowers may be cut freely, without injury to the bulbs. Indeed, all flower stalks should be removed as soon as the flowers begin to fade. In about five or six weeks after flowering, and when the leaves are becoming yellow, the bulbs may be taken up, dried, and packed away in paper bags or boxes, for planting again in the fall. If the beds are needed for other flowers, as is generally the case, the bulbs may be removed in about two weeks after the flowers have faded. In this case, after removing the flower stems, if this has not been done before, place the bulbs on a dry bed in the garden, and cover them with a little earth, leaving the leaves exposed. Here they can remain until the leaves have ripened, when they are ready to be packed away for fall planting, or can remain where they are until needed.

SINGLE HYACINTH.

DOUBLE HYACINTH.

Hyacinths will usually commence flowering in this latitude the latter part of April, and by choosing the *Early* and *Late* varieties, a good show of blossoms can be secured for about three weeks if the weather is not too hot and dry. The *Late* varieties are mostly *double*, and are from one to two weeks later than the *Early* sorts. The *Low* sorts throw up a stem five or six inches in height, and the trusses are usually globular and compact. The *Tall* sorts have a flower stem from six to ten inches or more in height, and the trusses are usually more loose. The *Roman Hyacinth* is a very early flowering, white variety, that comes into bloom about the Holidays, and therefore is very popular with florists for cut flowers. The spikes are small, the flowers somewhat scattering, but each bulb gives several spikes, usually.

Hyacinths differ in habit very much, some varieties throwing up a strong flower stalk, with a bold and rather loose truss, while others have but a short stem with a compact, almost globular truss. The stronger growing kinds generally have larger bells, while those of a more dwarf habit present small bells in immense numbers. The low growing kinds often throw up two or more flower stems. The bright red colors are all low, with a compact truss, and disposed to throw up several flower stalks. Our artist has attempted to show the habit, but without much success, as he has only given us the tall or erect habit of double and single. The center plant is the little Roman White.

The Hyacinth in a wild state is usually blue, though sometimes a pink variety is found, and always single. It is a native of the East, abounding in parts of Turkey and Syria. It has been, however, cultivated for nearly two hundred years in England. For a long time white, blue and pink were the only colors, and the rich, deep red and the yellow are of somewhat recent introduction. Of the latter color we have not much yet to boast, for we do not know of any clear, bright yellow Hyacinth. To

ROMAN HYACINTH.

HYACINTH PLANTS.

the Hollanders we are indebted for nearly all the improvement made in this beautiful flower. Could we present to our readers a colored plate of Hyacinths now before us, made some forty years ago, they would then realize how great this improvement has been. The florists of Holland have almost entirely monopolized the culture of Hyacinths, and their skill is only equaled by their success; though, doubtless, a remarkable soil and climate have much to do in securing to the good people of Holland the exclusive culture of this most popular of our winter flowers.

Hyacinth growers like a single, clean stem, and it would not be orthodox to say that anything else is desirable, but "really and truly," some of the prettiest objects we have ever seen have been Hyacinths, which, against all rule and order, have thrown up four or five flower stems, forming a mass of bloom truly gorgeous. Our engraving shows one with nine spikes of flowers, grown by J. FISHBACK, Esq., of Jacksonville, Illinois. May all of our readers meet with merited success in the culture of this beautiful flower, though, of course, we cannot all draw such prizes. However, with care and forethought, there is no reason why one should fail to any great extent. There will, of course, be occasional failures, as there is in all the business and pleasures of life; but no one should be satisfied with general failure, nor expect uninterrupted success.

HYACINTH WITH NINE FLOWER STEMS.

## TULIPS.

The Tulip is so perfectly hardy, flourishes so well under the most ordinary care, and is so varied and brilliant, that it never fails to give the greatest satisfaction. I sell but very few bulbs with so much pleasure as the Tulips, because I feel sure they will be more than satisfactory. The Tulip is dashing and showy, of the most brilliant and varied and delicate coloring, and desirable even as single specimens, but it is when grown in masses that the finest effect is produced. Nothing in the floral world can equal the dazzling brilliancy and gorgeousness of a bed of good Tulips. The early varieties are excellent for house culture.

DUC VAN THOL TULIP.

Any good garden soil will do for the Tulip. A very rich soil is not necessary, though well rotted manure, rotted sods, or leaf-mold may be applied when the earth is poor. See that the drainage is good before planting. Plant in October and November. Make the soil fine and deep. Set the *Early* flowering kinds five inches apart, and the *Late* varieties six inches. Cover three inches deep. After Tulips have done flowering they can be taken up and planted close together in any corner of the garden until it is time to replant in the beds in the autumn, or Verbenas or other bedding plants can be set out between the rows, and before they cover the ground the leaves of the Tulips will be sufficiently ripe to be removed, and the ground raked off.

Tulips are divided into two general classes, Early and Late, and these again into several others. The earliest Tulips flower in this latitude the latter part of April, and by a proper selection of early and late sorts a good display can be kept up for more than a month, if the weather proves tolerably cool and moist.

**Early Tulips.** — The *earliest* of the early class is the Duc Van Thol, single and double. They are in bloom here in April. The single varieties are of fine colors — white, yellow, scarlet, crimson, etc., growing about six inches in height, and make brilliant, dazzling beds. They are also excellent for flowering in the house during the winter, three or four in a pot. The double variety is about the same height, red, bordered with yellow. We recommend those not acquainted with them to try a few Duc Van Thols for winter flowering in pots, or boxes, or baskets. Let the soil be very sandy, and if mixed with a little moss, all the better.

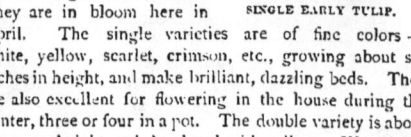

SINGLE EARLY TULIP.

The Tournesol follows the Duc Van Thol, with very large, *double flowers*, keeping in bloom a long time, and very desirable in all respects. Two varieties, orange and red, and very fine yellow. Good for pot culture in winter.

Following the Tournesol, is a large class of Single Early Tulips, containing very many splendid varieties. They flower early, before the sun becomes very hot, and hence continue in perfection longer than later kinds. These can always be depended upon for a brilliant and enduring bed. No class of Tulips will give greater satisfaction. These, like the two preceding kinds, will give great satisfaction grown in pots in the house. For bedding in masses, and especially for the formation of ribbon beds, these Single Early Tulips are unsurpassed.

DOUBLE TULIP.

**Double Tulips.**—The DOUBLE TULIPS are becoming more popular every year, and this popularity is not undeserved. Some are beautifully formed, with delicate shades and stripes; others are as large and brilliant as the old Pæony; while others of equal size are fine yellow, rose, white, etc. The list of named varieties, possessing more or less distinctness, is quite large.

**Parrot Tulips.** — The PARROT TULIPS are exceedingly brilliant. The petals are long, loose and fringed. Most varieties have three or four colors, as crimson, yellow, orange and green; and the effect of such a mingling of bright colors may be imagined. Those who plant the Parrots, and are unacquainted with them, will be surprised at their gay appearance.

**Late Tulips.** — Of the LATE TULIPS there are many varieties, the distinction between each more or less clearly defined. These are the great favorites with florists the world over, and

PARROT TULIP.      TULIP BULB.

are truly magnificent, with tall, stately stems, usually eighteen inches in height, and large, well-formed, highly colored cups. The Late Tulips are divided into *Bizarres, Byblooms* and *Roses.* The *Bizarres* have yellow ground, marked with any other color. *Byblooms* have white ground, marked with purple and violet. *Roses* have white ground, marked or variegated with rose, scarlet, crimson or cherry. I have some two hundred named varieties of this class, but many do not differ very materially from others of a different name, though all are exceedingly fine.

The engraving shows the general appearance of the Tulip Bulb, though the varieties differ a good deal in form. A full sized bulb, when planted in the autumn, blossoms the coming spring. The bulb planted decays, flowering but once, and gives place to one or more new bulbs, that will bloom the next spring. These may be taken up or allowed to remain in the ground. As the new bulb has no roots, removal does not injure flowering in the least, though unless

DUC VAN THOL.    SINGLE EARLY.      DOUBLE.      LATE SHOW.      PARROT.

replanted pretty early in the autumn, those that are allowed to remain in the ground flower a few days earlier. This is true of Hyacinths and all bulbs that are taken up and dried.

We give the accompanying small sketches of Tulips when in flower, to show the habits of the different classes. They are as correct as we can give in so small a space, though different varieties in the same class often show quite a difference in habit.

We have endeavored to give pretty full descriptions of the Tulip, and simple directions for culture, and if further information is needed on any point, we shall be happy to furnish the desired facts in the FLORAL GUIDE, where we answer all inquiries. The large engravings showing the cut flowers are about one-half the natural size.

## CROCUS.

THE CROCUSES are very interesting flowers, delicate and tasteful in form, and varied and gay in color. They begin to throw up their leaves before the frost is fairly gone, and in sheltered situations in this latitude will flower in March, though early in April is their season of greatest beauty. For several weeks, and until the flowering of the Hyacinth, through the most changeable and unpleasant of the spring weather, the garden depends upon the Crocus almost alone for its brightness.

Crocuses must be planted in the autumn. Set the bulbs about three inches apart and cover with not less than two inches of earth. Before winter sets in, cover the bed with a little straw, coarse manure, or other litter, to prevent the bulbs being thrown out by the frost. The Crocus will flower well in the house in winter—half a dozen or more in a little pot—or in baskets of moss, or in any other way that good taste may suggest. The bulbs may be set so close as almost to touch each other.

There is really but one objection to its use in the house, and that is the brief existence of the bloom. However, the Crocus is so cheap and flowers so soon after planting, that it will always prove interesting and remain popular. For general purposes the unnamed are quite as good as the named, and as they are bought by the hundred for less than two cents each, cannot be considered an expensive luxury. The Yellow are the most vigorous in growth. A few Crocuses scattered over the lawn is a pretty sight.

CROCUS.

## COLCHICUM.

The COLCHICUM, or Autumn Crocus, is a curious and interesting flower. The leaves appear in the spring, and the flowers in the autumn, and the seed the next midsummer. This singular habit makes the flower very interesting both to the Botanist and Florist. The bulbs are perfectly hardy, and we have never known one injured by the winter. Each bulb gives quite a cluster of flowers, generally six or eight, and so persistent is it in its determination to flower, that if taken up early in the autumn, before time for flowering, and placed in a pot or basket, it will bloom just as well as if left in the ground. Indeed, if placed upon a bracket or shelf, without either soil or moisture, the pretty pinkish flowers will appear just the same as though it had retained its natural position in the ground. *C. autumnalis* is a delicate pink; *C. Agrippina* of a deeper color and checkered. A few of either variety will afford great satisfaction, and to those who have never grown the Colchicum we would say, try them, and obtain the cheapest, if money is of any particular consequence.

COLCHICUM.

## SNOW-DROP.

THE first flower of spring is the delicate SNOW-DROP, white as snow. Its appearance about the first of March is a joyful surprise. The bulbs are quite small; the leaves and flowers about six inches in height. Plant in the fall, in beds or masses of a dozen or more, about two inches apart, and about the same depth. They are very desirable for growing in pots, etc., in the house in winter. A dozen may be planted in quite a small pot or saucer. A few planted on the lawn produces a fine effect early in the spring, and mowing will not destroy the bulbs, for the leaves will ripen so early that they will be pretty well matured before the grass will need cutting. Perfectly hardy, and bulbs can remain several years without removal.

SNOW-DROP.

The SNOW FLAKE, (*Leucojum*,) is sometimes called the Large Snow-Drop, from its resemblance to this delicate flower. It is much larger, and more robust in habit. Flowers white, with bright green spots. Once planted, it manages to take care of itself pretty effectually, and flowers very freely in summer. It is not as desirable as the Snow-Drop.

## NARCISSUS.

The Narcissus is a very fine class of early blooming flowers, including the well known Daffodil and Jonquil. Most of the varieties are hardy, and should be planted in the autumn, like the Hyacinth, but may remain in the ground a number of years, after which they will become so matted together as to make a division of the roots necessary.

SINGLE NARCISSUS.   DOUBLE NARCISSUS.

The *Single Narcissus* is extremely hardy and popular as a border flower, and the central cup being of a different color from the six petals, makes the flower exceedingly attractive. Some have the petals of a light yellow and the cup orange; others have the petals white and the cup yellow; while the Poet's Narcissus (*Narcissus poeticus*,) sometimes called Pheasant's Eye, is snowy white, the cup cream color, with a delicate fringed edge of red, which gives its latter name. The *Double* varieties are very desirable. The common Daffodil is well known under that name, though not so well by its true one, *Van Sion*.

The most beautiful class of the Narcissus family, however, is the *Polyanthus Narcissus*. The flowers are produced in clusters or trusses of from half a dozen to three times this number. Like the others, they show every shade of color, from the purest imaginable white to deep orange.

The *Polyanthus Narcissus* is not quite hardy in this climate, unless planted in a sandy soil, and well covered before winter, and then often fails; further South it does well. For flowering in pots in the house the Polyanthus Narcissus is unsurpassed, and nothing can be more satisfactory for this purpose. The Jonquils are also desirable for winter flowering. Three or four may be grown in a small pot. Try them in the house this winter; you will find nothing sweeter. The *Polyanthus Narcissus* will also flower well in glasses of water, like the Hyacinth, and it is desirable to grow a few in this way, yet nothing looks so natural and nice as a good healthy plant in a neat pot of earth, and no other method leaves the bulb in a sound, healthy condition for the next season.

TRUMPET NARCISSUS.   POLYANTHUS NARCISSUS.

## SCILLAS.

SCILLA.

The Scilla is the brightest and prettiest and hardiest of the early spring flowers. When the Crocuses are in bloom the little modest *S. Siberica* and *S. campanulata* may be seen throwing up a little cluster of flowers of the most intense blue imaginable. The flower stem is only about four inches, and is just the pretty flower that everybody craves for the button hole. The plant flowers without showing a leaf. After the flowers are gone the leaves appear, and these should not be injured. Many, after the flower has disappeared, remove the leaves so as to make room for other plants, but this course injures the bulbs unless the leaves are pretty well matured. No bulb is more hardy or more competent to take care of itself. The bulbs are quite small, as is also the plant, and, like all small bulbous rooted plants, look best and are less likely to be destroyed if grown in little masses—a dozen or so in a group. When small bulbous roots are scattered over the garden singly, they are almost certain to be destroyed especially where help in cleaning up the garden is occasionally employed.

## CROWN IMPERIAL.

Early in the spring, before the frost is fairly out of the ground, the strong flower stem of the Crown Imperial begins to appear, and gradually it ascends, the most brilliant green of the garden, the true herald of spring, upward and upward, until it stands erect full three feet in height, its glossy emerald leaves waving in the breeze, and often bending beneath the untimely snow. Nearly at the top of this column appears the flowery crown of bell-shaped flowers, and above these a tuft of leaves, all forming a pretty crown from which its name is derived. Although the Crown Imperial is so pretty in early spring, its fragrance is not at all desirable. The flower stem, when removed, leaves an open space in the center of the bulb, which sometimes causes those inexperienced to consider the bulb injured. There are several varieties, differing mainly in the color of the flowers, as yellow, scarlet, red, orange, &c. The bulbs should be planted four or five inches deep and about a foot apart. They will not usually flower the first year after planting. This is one of those hardy and useful plants about which there is no mystery or difficulty. Once put in the ground, and having obtained a fair start, it will continue to grow and increase from year to year, until the children become men and women, and often decorate the graves of those who first planted them, scores of years before.

CROWN IMPERIAL.

## SMILAX.

This plant, a native of the Cape of Good Hope, has now become one of the essentials of the florist and amateur. It is extensively used in decorating parlors and reception rooms and for decorating the hair, and for trimming party dresses, for which purpose it is not only admirably adapted, being an extremely graceful vine, with glossy green leaves, but surpasses anything with which we are acquainted. With a little care it can be grown successfully as a house plant. The vine does not require the full sun, but will grow well in a partially shaded situation. It can be trained on a small thread across the window or around pictures. Grown from both seeds and bulbs.

SMILAX.

Pot the bulbs as soon as received, watering but little until you see signs of growth. They grow very rapidly, and should always have strings to twine on. Give plenty of fresh air, but be careful and not let a direct draft of cold air blow upon the vines, as they are very tender when young. Give them a warm place, and they will amply repay all care. When growth is complete the foliage will turn yellow. Then gradually withhold water, and allow the bulbs to dry. They then can be put away in some dry, cool place. After they have been in this dormant state six or eight weeks they will begin to show signs of life, and then are ready for another season's growth.

## ANEMONE.

ALL will admit, who have ever seen the ANEMONE in bloom, that it is a most beautiful flower. Double and single are both desirable — the single the most brilliant. The Anemone has not been grown generally, because it has been thought too tender to bear our winters. The bulbs may be kept until spring, and if planted early will flower well. Although we cannot recommend the Anemones for fall planting in the North with the same confidence we do more hardy things, they are well worthy of trial, and those who succeed will be delighted. The roots look like dried ginger, and customers must not think they are worthless because "dry as sticks."

Plant the roots five or six inches apart, and cover about three inches deep. They flower after the Hyacinth, and continue a long time in bloom. As soon as the leaves begin to turn yellow, the roots may be taken up, dried in the shade, and packed away.

DOUBLE ANEMONE.     SINGLE ANEMONE.

## RANUNCULUS.

THE RANUNCULUS is not considered hardy generally, but with good dry soil, with drainage so that the surface water may run off easily, tolerable success may be obtained. Desirable for culture in the house. The bulbs are very curious, tooth-like, and may be kept out of ground almost any length of time, and will then grow as well as when freshly taken up. They can, therefore, be kept until the spring, and if then planted early, in a pretty cool place, like the north side of a fence or hedge, the result will be usually quite satisfactory. Our fierce summer suns are not favorable to the full development of this flower, as it delights in a cool, moist atmosphere. This fact should be remembered in house culture. No success may be looked for in a hot, dry room. This is one of those beautiful flowers that will never be common in America. Many, however, delight to show their skill in managing difficult things, and there is abundance of pleasure in this work. Nothing affords satisfaction like conquering success.

RANUNCULUS PLANT.     R. FLOWER.

## IRIS.

The IRIS, or Flowering Flag, as it is called, or *Fleur de lis* of the French, is a well known family of hardy border flowers. They are natives of damp spots in all four quarters of the globe, but were adopted for garden culture more than three hundred years ago. In that time they have become very much improved, and some varieties are exceedingly beautiful. *Susiana major* is five inches across, and of the richest colors and most singular markings. The *pavonia* is small, but beautifully marked, almost looking like a butterfly. This, however, is not hardy, and is suitable for winter flowering in the house. The others are perfectly hardy, needing scarcely ordinary care. The *I. Persica*, also, is admirable for winter flowering. A few years ago, in almost every garden a clump of the Iris was to be found, but being common varieties they have been abandoned.

IRIS PLANT.     IRIS FLOWER.

## OXALIS.

An interesting class of small bulbs, desirable for winter-flowering in pots, producing an abundance of bloom. They should be potted as early as convenient, and in nice sandy loam, with good drainage. Most of the varieties have small bulbs, and should be planted from three to five bulbs in a pot; *versicolor* is particularly small. When through flowering, and the foliage begins to turn yellow, let them dry off gradually. When perfectly dry, knock them out of the pots, separate, and plant on fresh soil, keeping them in a dry place. About August or September they will commence growing again. Then bring them to the light and air, and commence watering. In this way the bulbs will keep sound all summer, and will increase rapidly. The leaves, as will be seen by the engraving, resemble in form the Clover leaf; indeed, the celebrated Irish Shamrock is an Oxalis. As the leaves are on long, slender stalks, and consequently droop, it can be readily understood how well the Oxalis is adapted to hanging baskets and other similar purposes. Generally, both leaves and flowers are abundant, so that a few plants present a very cheerful aspect during the whole winter. There are varieties that will not blossom in the winter, and these are mostly desirable for borders, edgings, &c., and the one figured on page 70 is particularly desirable for this work, and is becoming very popular as a summer border plant; but it is the winter flowering sorts, so desirable for pot culture, and particularly for basket work, to which we desire to call especial attention. Our little engraving shows a plant in bloom, but the different varieties vary very much in habit, and the plants make a more vigorous growth and fill a larger space than the size of the bulb would seem to indicate. We have plants now, almost globular in form, and measuring from a foot to eighteen inches in diameter.

OXALIS.

## CYCLAMEN.

This pretty flower is too little known. It is a native of Europe and Asia, some varieties being very abundant in Switzerland and Italy. It is of the easiest culture. Pot in October or November, in rich loam; mix about a spoonful of soot with the same, which will add brilliancy and size to the flowers. Bits of charcoal, broken fine, will serve the same purpose. Use a small pot, and place the crown of the bulb just above the surface of the soil. Keep the plants cool till the leaves are well grown. When the flower buds begin to rise on the foot stalks remove to a sunny shelf, where they will soon show bloom. Place as near the glass as possible. After the blooming season (which generally lasts two or three months,) is over, gradually withhold water, and let the leaves dry down. The plant seeds freely, but it is not a good plan to allow it to ripen the seed, as it hurts the blooming qualities of the bulb. Seedlings bloom when two years old. To keep the bulbs through the summer, bury them in the open border. Take them up about the middle of September, and they will be found plump and fresh. It is particularly adapted for window culture,

CYCLAMEN PERSICUM.

and will give more flowers with less trouble than almost any plant we are acquainted with. The colors are usually white, tipped at the base with rich rosy purple. In all the species both leaves and flowers spring directly from a solid tuberous rootstalk, as shown in the engraving. The leaves are heart-shaped, while the flowers are of one petal, but deeply divided into five segments. After flowering the flower stalk coils itself up in a spiral form, with the seed vessel in the center, and bends itself toward the ground, in which position the seeds are ripened.

## IXIAS.

The Ixias are not destitute of beauty; indeed, some of them have strong claims to our regard on account of their good looks, but there are few flowers that attract more attention by their curious forms and strange coloring. Some of them, and, indeed, nearly all, showing three or more colors. They make a nice addition and give variety to the larger bulbs, as Hyacinths, &c., more commonly used in house culture, and seldom fail to please. Several may be planted in a small pot, and the treatment is the same as we have recommended for other bulbs in pots. The Ixias are all natives of the Cape of Good Hope and portions of South Africa. The bulbs exude a viscid gum when cut, and hence the name, from a Greek word which means *to fix*. Our engraving shows the form of flower and habit of plant, though there is a greater difference in the form and color of Ixias than with almost any other class of plants. The variety we figure is *Viridiflora*, and the prevailing color is green, the center being purple and pink, but the Ixias are of almost all imaginable diverse colors.

IXIA FLOWER.

IXIA PLANT

## OTHER WINTER DECORATIONS.

In this department, so fruitful of subjects for winter flowers, it may be well to call attention to the EVERLASTINGS, or IMMORTELLES, and GRASSES, so desirable for WINTER DECORATIONS. Many of them, like the Acroclinium and Helichrysum, are grown in this country, and they will be found described on pages 53, 54 and 55; but large quantities are imported from Europe, especially of the Gnaphalium, which is generally known as the Immortelle. The natural color is yellow, but they are bleached white, and dyed of almost any color, by the ingenuity of French growers.

The Everlastings, with the *Feather* and other Grasses, make up nicely in bouquets and Floral Baskets. For making ornamental letters, by attaching them to pasteboard forms, the little Everlastings are excellent. With a little skill and taste and a good deal of patience, great things can be accomplished in this way. The Grasses and Everlastings are sold by the bunch, pound or hundred by most florists, and are in great demand about the Holidays for decorative purposes. Our engravings give some idea of this work.

# VEGETABLES

THE Vegetable Department is, to many of our readers, exceedingly interesting, and should be to all; for while we have no sympathy with those who say they "see more beauty in a Cabbage or hill of Potatoes than in the finest flower that ever grew," we do most heartily agree with those who take pride and pleasure in the culture of choice vegetables, and their improvement, and who are ready to say, with DIOCLETIAN, "were you to come to my garden, and see the vegetables I raise with my own hands, you would no longer talk to me of empire." As much skill is required to produce an improved vegetable as a new and valuable flower, and perhaps as much as is needed to govern a nation; and the pleasure of success, we doubt not, is quite as great. The improvement in our vegetables for the past score of years has been great; indeed, we notice desirable progress almost every season, and more particularly in the purity of the seeds. To keep varieties pure, and true to name, requires a constant struggle, about which the nurserymen and florist who propagate by budding and grafting, and by cuttings and divisions of roots, know nothing, and of which gardeners usually have but little appreciation.

## ASPARAGUS.

This now popular vegetable is so well known that most persons who have had experience in vegetable gardening are pretty well acquainted with its habits. The Asparagus is a salt water plant, indigenous to various parts of the coast of Europe and Asia, growing in salt water marshes. It has escaped from our gardens, and is now found in some places on the American coast, and is sometimes observed in meadows. The plant is perennial, and grows some five feet in height, with a branching stem, fine cylindrical leaves, small greenish flowers, and red berries containing black seed. The seed may be sown either in the spring or autumn, in drills, about one inch deep, and the rows wide enough apart to admit of hoeing — about a foot. An ounce of seed is sufficient for a drill thirty feet in length. Keep the soil mellow and free from weeds during the summer, and in the fall or succeeding spring the plants may be set out in beds, about a foot apart each way. The beds should be narrow, so as to permit of cutting to the center without stepping upon them. The plants may remain in the seed-bed until two years old, if desired. Before winter, cover the transplanted beds with about four inches of manure. A good many varieties are advertised, with but little difference. As Asparagus plants are all grown from seed, it will be seen that there is great opportunity for variation.

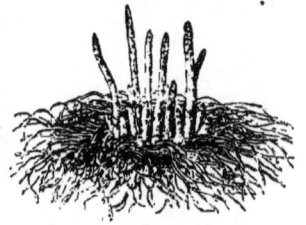

Salt is an excellent manure for Asparagus, and an efficient assistant to the cultivator, keeping down the weeds with very little labor. When grown in large quantities for market, Asparagus

is often planted a foot apart in the rows, and the rows three feet apart, and sometimes three feet apart each way. Cut for use the third year after planting, and if the shoots appear pretty strong, a little may be cut the second year. The part used is the young shoots when about five or six inches in height, and when the bud is close and firm, and these should be cut a little below the surface, with a sloping cut. It is not best to continue the cutting late in the season, unless the shoots are very robust. Always give the bed a good dressing of manure in the fall, first removing the dead brush of the past season. As an Asparagus bed will last longer than the maker, it should be well made, and there should be no haste in cutting. Those who do not wish the trouble and delay of growing Asparagus from seed, can obtain plants either one or two years old at a very moderate price. Secure a good, rich, deep, mellow soil, and set the plants with the roots spread out naturally, just as a good gardener would arrange the roots of any tree or plant, and so deep that the crown will be two to three inches below the surface. In removing weeds, be careful not to injure the crowns. In the spring remove them only by hand. The engravings show a bunch of Asparagus as usually exposed for sale, a root of Asparagus with the young shoots well started, some of them almost ready for cutting, and a branch of the plant at seeding time. The roots, if procured in the spring, and in good condition, will show the buds or young shoots an inch or two in length.

## BEANS.

Beans are usually divided into two general classes, Dwarf and Pole Beans. The Dwarfs are earlier and more hardy, as a general rule, than the running sorts. The Dwarfs are generally used for string-beans when the pods are tender, and the climbers only for shelling. We have endeavored in the engraving to show the habit of both. Beans like a dry and rather light soil, though they will do well in any garden soil if not set out too early in the spring. Nothing is gained by planting until the ground is tolerably dry and warm. The Dwarf varieties grow from twelve to eighteen inches in height, need no support, and are planted either in drills or hills. The drills should be not less than a foot apart,

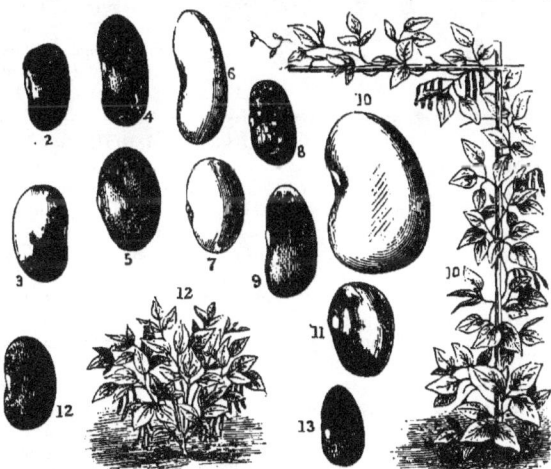

two inches deep, and the seed set in the drills from two to three inches apart. The usual method in hills is to allow about four plants to a hill, and the hills two by three feet apart. Rows are best for the garden. A quart of ordinary sized Beans is about fifteen hundred, and will sow two hundred and fifty feet of rows, or one hundred and fifty hills. Hoe well, but only when dry. Running Beans should not be planted quite as early as the Dwarfs. The usual way of planting is in hills, about three feet apart, with the pole in the center of the hill. A very good way is to grow the running varieties in drills, using the tallest pea brush that can be secured conveniently. When the plants reach the top of the brush, pinch off the ends. The effect will be to cause greater fruitfulness below. In a stiff soil, especially, the Lima comes up better if planted carefully

with the eye down, the hill a little elevated. There are endless varieties of Dwarf Beans; as nothing of the vegetable family is more inclined to sport. We have endeavored to show the appearance of a few of the best sorts, when ripe. Figure 2 is Refugee; 3, Early China; 4, Early Mohawk; 6, White Kidney; 7, White Marrowfat; 8, Early Valentine; 9, Early Rachel; 13, Wax, or Butter — all Dwarfs. Fig. 5, London Horticultural; 10, Large Lima; 11, Concord; 12, Giant Wax — all Runners. The Scarlet Runner is the popular Snap Bean of England, and the Dwarfs are only used early in the season, before the Runners can be obtained.

## BORECOLE, or KALE.

The Borecoles, or as they are usually called, Kales, are not much grown in America, though quite popular in many parts of Europe. They do not form heads like the Cabbage, but furnish abundance of curly leaves, those of some varieties being quite ornamental, their general character being shown in the engraving. The Kales are more hardy than the Cabbage, and will endure considerable frost without injury, so they are often allowed to remain in the ground until spring, except in very severe climates, and are thus in use during the winter. When cut frozen, they are immediately placed in cold water. In northern countries, they are taken up and stored in a cold pit or cellar, and those not needed for winter use are re-planted in spring, and make a new and tender growth. The small variety, called *German Greens*, is usually sown in the autumn, and cut in spring and sold in the markets by measure, somewhat like Spinach. The culture is the same as for Cabbage. While we do not anticipate the very general culture of Kale in America, as in in many sections of Europe, we think it well to call the attention of our readers to this somewhat noted member of the Cabbage tribe.

## BRUSSELS SPROUTS.

Brussels Sprouts is a very respectable member of the Cabbage family, and very nearly related to the Kales. It has a strong stem, sometimes not less than four feet in height, though there is a dwarf variety that never reaches more than half this height. A loose head of Cabbage surmounts the stem, and thus a circulation of sap is secured to the extremity, while below, commencing a few inches from the ground line, are numerous small heads like miniature Cabbages, so thick as almost to conceal the stem, and presenting the appearance we have endeavored to show in the engraving. These heads are very tender and of good flavor. The culture is the same as for Cabbage. If early plants are raised in a hot-bed, they will perfect themselves in September, in the north, and a later sowing should be made in the open ground, that will be in perfection about the time winter commences. These should be taken up and stored in a cool cellar, like the Cauliflower, with the roots in earth where they will remain fit for use during the winter. Where the winters are not very severe, they may remain in the ground to be cut as needed, and in such places the Brussels Sprouts are of the greatest value. In severe climates — climates of great extremes of heat and cold — the Brussels Sprouts, and some other members of the cabbage family, will never be very successfully grown nor become very popular; and yet, there are some in every section who will think us over-cautious, and we would not be surprised to receive a package of "Sprouts" from the most unlikely place in the world, just to prove that we are mistaken. The ability and perseverance of some persons will conquer all difficulties, and this is our response, in advance.

## BEETS.

The Beet is a favorite vegetable, and is exceedingly valuable, being in use almost from the time the seed-leaf appears above ground until we are looking for its appearance the next year. The seeds are in little groups or clusters of calyxes, as seen in the little engraving, so that each rounded cluster which we call a seed, really contains from two to four true seeds. The consequence is that the plants come up much thicker than necessary, and must be thinned out. There is nothing in the way of "greens" as good as these young Beets, and the thinnings of the beds can be used as needed, from the time the young plants are two or three inches in length until they are large enough for ordinary use. To preserve the roots in fine condition during the winter, take them up carefully before hard frosts, and pack them in a cool cellar, and cover with earth. For spring use they may be pitted in the ground. The seed germinate more surely and rapidly if put in warm water and allowed to soak for twenty-four hours. The soil should be rich, mellow, and deep. Plant in drills, about two inches deep, and the rows about twelve or fifteen inches apart. Set the seeds in the drills about two inches apart. An ounce of seed will sow about seventy-five feet of drill, and five pounds are sufficient for an acre. The varieties of Beets are very numerous, and quite diversified in form and appearance, from the little round, table, turnip-formed varieties, to the large, coarse sorts, sometimes three feet in length, and fit only for cattle. Figure 1 shows the Large Red Mangel, one of the best for feeding to stock; fig. 2, the Early Blood Turnip, a very smooth, pretty variety; fig. 3, the Pine Apple, a comparatively new and good dark variety; fig. 4, Bassano, an old favorite, juicy sort, tender and light colored; fig. 5, Dewing's Turnip, a week earlier than Blood Turnip, lighter fleshed, and an excellent variety; fig. 6, Carter's Orange Globe Mangel, thought in England to be the best round variety; fig. 7, the old and excellent Long Blood Red. The *Swiss Chard*, of which we show the leaves, is a variety of Beet cultivated for the broad leaf-stalks, which are cooked and served like Asparagus. Plants should stand a foot or more apart in the rows, and the rows three feet, for field culture.

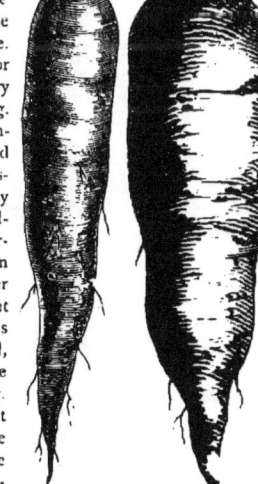

## CABBAGE.

The Cabbage requires a deep, rich soil and thorough working. If these requirements are met and good seed obtained, there is no difficulty in obtaining fine, solid heads. For early use, the

plants should be started in a hot-bed or cold-frame; but seed for winter Cabbage should be sown in a seed-bed, early in the spring. Some gardeners prefer to grow plants for early spring Cabbage in a frame in the autumn, protecting them with boards or matting during the winter, but without good care plants saved in this way often prove a loss. In a mild climate, plants may not only be started in the autumn, but transplanted, and will make considerable growth during the winter season. Some varieties seem to do best if the seed is sown in the hills where they

are to remain; and this is particularly the case with the Marblehead varieties. Sow two or three seeds where each plant is desired, and then pull up all but the strongest. The large varieties require to be planted about three feet apart; the small, early sorts, from a foot to eighteen inches.

Always give Cabbage a deep, rich soil, and keep it mellow with plenty of manure. For early winter use, store a few in a cool cellar. The main crop will be better kept out of doors, set in a trench closely, head down, and covered with straw and earth. There is almost an endless variety of Cabbage, and nearly all extensive growers have their favorite sorts. Some kinds seem to succeed best in certain localities. The Winningstadt, for instance, which we have shown in figure 2, seems peculiarly adapted to the South. The Jersey Wakefield is now, no doubt, the most popular early Cabbage (see fig. 1). Early Schweinfurth (fig. 3), is a very large Cabbage, and matures early, but we have never been able to grow solid heads. Marblehead Mammoth is a large solid Cabbage, but requires a very rich soil, early planting and good culture (fig. 4). Fig. 6 is the popular Premium Flat Dutch, which is the old Flat Dutch somewhat improved, and of American growth. Stone Mason Marblehead is represented by fig. 7, and is an excellent winter Cabbage. Fig. 8 is the Drumhead Savoy, a very tender, sweet Cabbage, very hardy, and improved by a little frost. Figs. 5 and 10 are the Filderkraut, one of the solidest and best Cabbages we are acquainted with; always heads, and as solid as any one can wish. We give two engravings of this fine variety, as the first was drawn from a specimen taken from our grounds when not fully matured. There are several varieties of Pickling Cabbage, but the highest colored and best is one we introduced several years since from Europe, known as Chappell's Red Pickling, (fig. 9).

COLLARDS, or what is now known as Collards, are merely young Cabbage plants. The usual plan is to sow the seed in drills about half an inch deep, and a foot apart. When these plants are a few inches in height, they are pulled. In the South, sowings can be made through the winter every few weeks. A variety very popular at the South, and thought to be much better than any of the common cabbages, is called *Creole Collards.*

## CAULIFLOWER.

The most delicate and delicious of all the Cabbage family, is the Cauliflower. It is more delicate and tender than the Cabbage, and therefore requires a more generous treatment. It delights in a rich soil and abundance of water, which it would be well to apply artificially in a dry season. After seeing the splendid cauliflower growing around Erfurt, in Prussia, and observing the pains taken in its culture, I did not wonder that we fail in our hot, dry climate. Cauliflower there is grown in low, swampy ground, which is thrown up in wide ridges. The plants are set on the ridges, and between these are ditches of water. Every dry day the water is bailed from these ditches upon the growing plants, and the result is cauliflower of enormous size, compact, and almost as white as snow. The engraving will give a

101

pretty good idea of these cauliflower gardens, and the process of watering. In the ditches water cress is grown, both for cutting and seed. Still, we must say that we have never seen or heard

of finer Cauliflower than is sometimes grown in the South and West. The flower buds form a solid mass of great beauty and delicacy, called the "curd," and its appearance is shown in the engraving. This is rendered more delicate by being protected from the sun. Break off one or two of the leaves, and place them upon the flower. Gardeners sometimes sow seed in the autumn, for early Cauliflower, and keep the plants over in frames; but by sowing the early varieties in the spring, in a hot-bed or cold-frame, or even in an open border, they can be obtained in pretty good season. For late Cauliflower, sow seed in a cool, moist place, on the north side of a building or tight fence, in this latitude, about the first of May, and they will not be troubled with the little black beetle, so destructive to everything of the Cabbage tribe when young. Do not allow the plants to become crowded in the seed-bed. Transplant in moist weather, or shade the newly set plants. In the autumn, plants which have not fully formed the "flower," or "curd," may be taken up and placed in a light cellar, with earth at the roots, and they will generally form good heads; or they may be hung up by the stems, head down, in a cool cellar, and will do well.

A favorite European vegetable, BROCOLI, resembles the Cauliflower; indeed, it is hardly possible to distinguish the two. The Brocoli, however, is the most hardy, and in portions of Europe where the seasons are mild, remains in the ground all the winter, furnishing good heads most of the cold season. Of course, in many sections of our country Brocoli would not suffer in winter, but it dislikes severe summer heat more than cold; and to succeed, it would be necessary to grow late plants, and set them out after the extreme heat of summer is past.

## CRESS.

The Cresses are excellent and healthful salad plants, of a warm, pungent taste, and are much relished by almost every one, especially in the spring season. When young and tender the whole plants are eaten, but when older, the leaves only. Cress is often used with lettuce, and other salad plants, and the Curled is very good for garnishing. Sow the seed in a hot-bed or in a sheltered spot in the garden, quite thick, in shallow drills. In a short time it will be fit for cutting. Sow a little every week. The Water Cress is a great luxury to most people, and cheaply obtained by those who live near fresh water. Scatter a little seed in moist places on the edges of ponds or brooks, and in the eddies of streams, and in a few years the shallow water will be stocked with plants. The engraving with the large leaves shows a branch of Water Cress, and with the small leaves a plant of Curled Cress.

## CORN SALAD.

Corn Salad is a favorite salad plant in some portions of Europe, and is much cultivated in America by those who have become familiar with its use across the sea. Its name is derived from the fact that it is found abundantly growing in wheat fields. Sown in August, and protected by leaves or straw during the winter, it can be used in the spring very early. Sown in April or May, it is very soon fit for use. The leaves are sometimes boiled and served as spinach. It is very hardy. Sow as for lettuce, in rows, covering seed only about a quarter of an inch. Thin out the plants so that they will be three or four inches apart.

## CARROTS.

The Carrot should always be furnished with a good, deep, rich soil, and as free from stones and lumps as possible; and if a rather light loam, it is better than if compact and heavy. It is waste of time and labor to try to grow roots of any kind on a poor or unprepared soil. Seed should be got in early, so as to have the benefit of a portion of the spring rains. We knew a part of a field to be sown, when a long rain interrupting the operator, it was not resumed until after the soil had become pretty dry, and no showers coming very soon, the first half sown produced an abundant crop, while the last was almost a failure. Sow in drills about an inch deep,

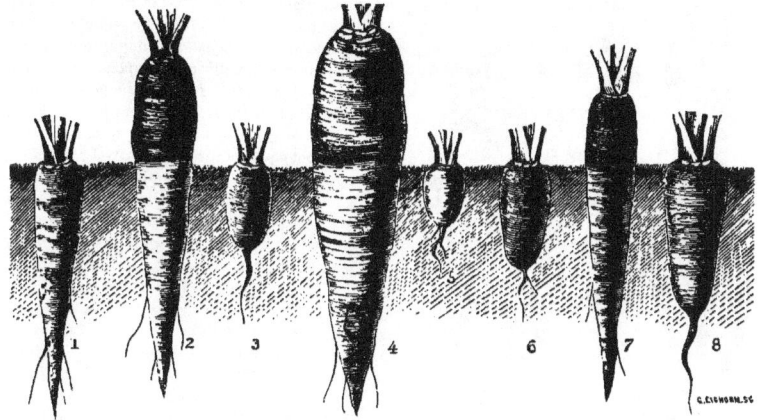

the drills about a foot apart; and at thinning, the plants should be left at from four to ten inches apart in the rows, according to kind. The Short Horn may be allowed to grow very thickly, almost in clusters. To keep roots for table use, place them in sand in the cellar; but for feeding, they will keep well in a cellar, without covering, or buried in the ground, and any desired for spring use may be pitted out of the way of frost. An ounce of seed will sow about one hundred feet of drill, and two pounds is the usual quantity per acre. For field culture, of course, the rows must be sufficiently distant to admit of running the cultivator between them. The Carrot is mostly used in America for soups, and for this the smaller and finer varieties are grown. The Carrot is very nutritious and is relished by all animals. The engraving shows the comparative size and habit of growth of most of the leading varieties. Figure 1, Long Orange; 2, Orange Belgian Green-Top; 3, Early French Short-Horn; 4, White Belgian Green-Top; 5, Early Very Short Scarlet; 6, Half-Long Scarlet Stump-Rooted; 7, Altringham; 8, Half-Long Scarlet.

## CHICORY.

Chicory is used in Europe as a salad plant. Seed is sown in the spring, in drills half an inch deep, in a good, mellow soil; and the after culture is the same as for Carrots. In the autumn, the plants will be ready for blanching. This is generally done by placing a box over them, or by tying the tops of the leaves loosely together, and drawing the earth well up the plant. The greatest value of Chicory is as a substitute for coffee. It has a root something like a parsnip. They are washed clean, cut into pieces that will dry readily, kiln-dried, and then they are ready to roast and grind for coffee. The prepared root is brought from Europe, for the adulteration of coffee. An ounce of seed will sow about one hundred feet of drill, and from two to three pounds are required for an acre. The second season the Chicory sends up a flower stem three or four feet, bearing pretty, bright blue flowers, which we have shown about half size in the engraving. It is so hardy there is danger it may become a troublesome weed, as it flourishes on the road-sides and in meadows in many places.

## CELERY.

Celery is a luxury that few would like to dispense with, and fortunately there is no necessity for such a sacrifice, as every one who has control of a few feet of ground, with a little skill and industry, can grow a winter's supply. To obtain good Celery, it is necessary that the plants should be strong and well grown. Sow the seeds in a hot-bed or cold frame. When the plants are about three inches in height, transplant to a nicely prepared bed in the border, setting them about four or five inches apart. When some eight inches high, and good stocky plants, set them in the trenches — about the middle of July is early enough. Too many make trenches by digging out the top soil, and only putting a few inches of mold at the bottom, and never obtain good Celery. The trenches should contain at least eighteen inches of good soil and well rotted manure, in about equal portions. Take off all suckers and straggling leaves at the time of transplanting. Earth up a little during the summer, keeping the leaf stalks close together, so that the soil cannot get between them; and during September and October earth up well for blanching. Those who grow Celery for market extensively do not use trenches, but make the soil deep and rich, and plant in rows, earthing up with the plow. The time to take up Celery is just before hard frost. Dig a trench about the width of a spade and a few inches deeper than the height of the Celery. The place selected must be high ground, where no water will be at the bottom, and where surface water will not drain into the trench. Take up the Celery with any dirt that may happen to adhere to the roots. Set the stalks close together, and close to the sides of the trench, but do not press them in. After the trench is filled, place pieces of board or scantling across it at intervals of five or six feet, one of these pieces being shown in the engraving. On these place boards, five or six feet long, covering the entire trench. Then cover the boards with a good body of straw or leaves, with boards or earth on top to keep it from blowing away. The work is then completed. When Celery is needed, take up a length of short boards, and remove enough Celery to the cellar to last a few days, and place it in the coolest part, covered with earth. Replace the boards and covering as before. The dwarf Celeries are generally the most solid, sweetest, and really the most profitable. The pink sorts are very pretty as a table ornament, and as good as the white, though there seems to be a foolish prejudice against the colored varieties in this country. The engravings show the general appearance of a well grown Celery stalk, also of a variety called Boston Market, of a straggling habit. We also show the Turnip-rooted Celery, the bulbous root only being eatable.

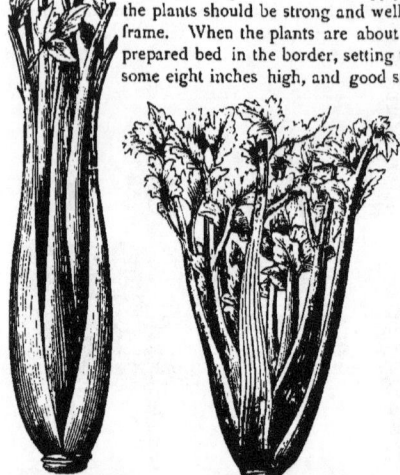

## CORN.

We need not consume time or space in speaking of the value of good Sweet Corn, nor of its culture. Every sensible person knows the former, and every sane one the latter — at least so it seems to us. A few remarks about varieties is all that will be necessary. The earliest good Sweet Corn we are acquainted with is the Minnesota (fig. 1); following in about ten or twelve

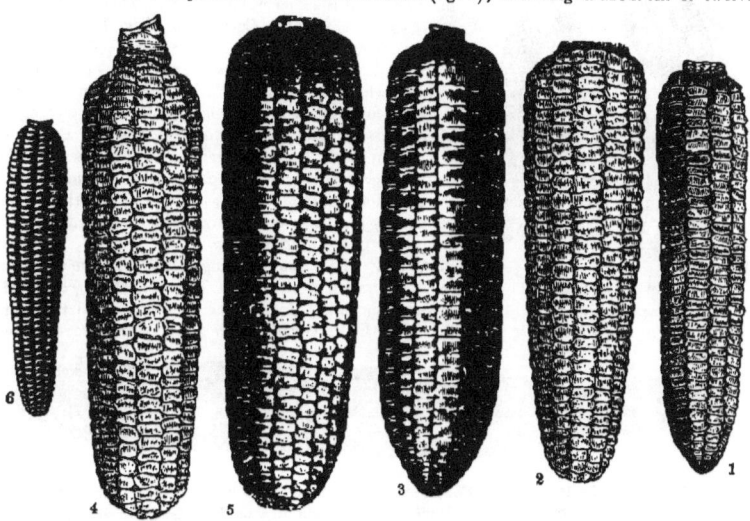

days, is Russell's Prolific (fig. 2); Moore's Early Concord (fig. 3) is in eating a week or so after Russell's, and Crosby's Early (fig. 4) is in eating about the same time, perhaps a day or two earlier. It is very thick, twelve or sixteen-rowed. Stowell's Evergreen (fig. 5) is a magnificent late variety, keeping in eating until frost, almost. There are many varieties of Parching Corn; one of them is shown in fig. 6, called the White Parching.

## CUCUMBERS.

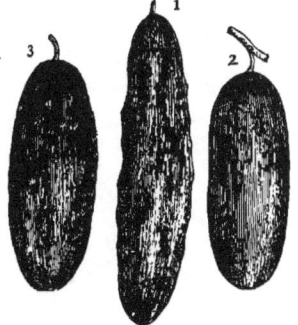

The hardiest varieties — in fact, all the American or common sorts — will produce a medium and late crop, if the seed is sown in the open ground in well prepared hills, as soon as the soil becomes sufficiently warm. In this latitude it is useless to plant in the open ground until nearly the first of June. Make rich hills of well rotted manure, two feet in diameter — a large shovelful of manure, at least, to each hill — and plant a dozen or more seeds, covering half an inch deep. When all danger from insects is over, pull up all but three or four of the strongest plants. The middle of June is early enough to plant for pickling. Make the hills about six feet apart. For early Cucumbers, the hot-bed is necessary; but the simplest and surest way to produce a tolerably early crop of the best kinds is, where it is designed to place a hill, dig a hole about eighteen inches deep and three feet across; into this put a barrow of fresh manure, and cover with a small box-like frame, on the top of which place a couple of lights of glass. When the plants grow, keep the earth drawn up to the stems. Water, and give air as needed; and if the sun appears too strong, give the glass a coat of whitewash. By the time the plants fill the frame, it will be warm enough to let them out, and the box can be

removed; but if it should continue cold, raise the box by setting a block under each corner, and let the plants run under. The Fourth of July is the time we always remove the boxes or frames. Always pick the fruit as soon as large enough, as allowing any to remain to ripen injures the fruiting of the vine. One pound of seed is sufficient for an acre. There are not very many varieties of hardy Cucumbers. Fig. 1 is Improved Long Green, the largest of American sorts, and one of the best; fig. 2, Early Frame, a good variety for table, and for pickling when small; fig. 3, Early White Spine, an excellent sort for table, a great favorite, and forces well; fig. 4, Early Russian, small, very productive, and the earliest of all; fig. 5, Early Green Cluster, next in earliness to the Russian, generally grows in pairs, quite productive and esteemed for pickles. There are very many foreign varieties of very great size and beauty, and of excellent quality, and their general appearance is shown in the annexed engraving. They range in length from eighteen inches to more than two feet, and, when well grown, as straight as an arrow. They are called *frame* varieties, because much cultivated in frames or under glass. Some of the hardiest do well in America, if coaxed a little early in the season under boxes covered with glass, as recommended for

our hardy sorts. The Long Green Southgate and the Stockwood we have found the best for the garden in this latitude, but in the South we have no doubt all would succeed admirably. Some persons think because these foreign sorts are large, that they are coarse and scarcely eatable. This is a mistake. They are fine-grained and very solid, having very few seeds, sometimes not more than half-a-dozen perfect seeds in a fruit. Seed, therefore, is always scarce and dear.

## EGG PLANT.

A tender plant, requiring starting in the hot-bed pretty early to mature its fruit in the Northern States. The seed may be sown with tomato seed; but more care is necessary at transplanting, to prevent the plants being chilled by the change, as they seldom fully recover. Hand-glasses are useful for covering at the time of transplanting. Those who have no hot-bed can sow a few seeds in boxes in the house. There are various modes of cooking, but the most common is to cut in slices, boil in salt and water, and then fry in batter or butter.

There are several varieties, but the largest and best of all is the Improved New York Purple, an engraving of which we give. The Early Long Purple is the earliest, and valuable on that account, and about eight or nine inches in length. There is an early round variety called Round Purple, and there are several very pretty sorts more ornamental than useful.

### KOHL RABI.

Intermediate between the Cabbage and the Turnip we have this singular vegetable. The stem, just above the surface of the ground, swells into a bulb something like a Turnip, as shown in the engraving. Above this are the leaves, somewhat resembling those of the Ruta Baga. The bulbs are served like Turnips, and are very delicate and tender when young, possessing the flavor of both Turnip and Cabbage, to some extent. In Europe they are extensively grown for stock, and are thought to keep better than the Turnip, and impart no unpleasant taste to milk. Seed sown for a general crop, in the spring, like the Turnip, in drills; or may be transplanted like Cabbage. For winter table use, sow middle of June. One advantage claimed for the Kohl Rabi is that it suffers less from severe drouth than the Turnip, and therefore a crop is almost certain. This being so, it must be well adapted to culture in many sections of our country.

### LETTUCE.

Lettuce is divided into two classes; the *Cabbage*, with round head and broad, spreading leaves; and the *Cos*, with long head and upright, narrow leaves. The Cabbage varieties are the most tender and buttery, and the Cos the most crisp and refreshing. In Europe, the Cos varieties are used very generally. They are the most liked by dealers, because they will carry better and keep longer in good condition than the Cabbage sorts. There are several varieties with loose, curled leaves, having the habit of the Cabbage, though not forming solid heads, and are very pretty for garnishing, but otherwise not equal to the plain sorts. Seed sown in the autumn will come in quite early in the spring, but not early enough to satisfy the universal relish for early salad. The hot-bed, therefore, must be started quite early. Give but little heat, and plenty

of air and water on fine days. Sow a couple of rows thick, in the front of the frame, to be used when young—say two inches in height. Let the plants in the rest of the bed be about three inches apart, and, as they become thick, remove every alternate one. Keep doing so, as required, and the last will be as large as Cabbages. Sow in the open ground as early as possible; or, if you have plants from fall sowing, transplant them to a rich soil, giving plenty of room and hoe well. We give engravings showing the appearance of the Cabbage, Cos and Curled varieties.

### MARTYNIA.

The Martynia is a hardy annual plant of robust growth, and some of the varieties are somewhat grown as flowering plants, as will be seen by reference to page 33. M. proboscidea produces its curious seed-pods, shown in the engraving, quite abundantly, and these, when tender, are prized by a good many for pickling. They should be gathered before getting fibrous or "stringy." A little experience will soon make the matter of selecting easy.

## MELON.

Those who have their homes a little further South than Rochester, in Maryland, Delaware, Virginia, and in most of our Western and all Southern States, enjoy a luxury in the Melon crop of which many Northern people have but little idea. We once very much astonished some kind friends in England because we preferred well ripened English Gooseberries to some Melons that had been procured for our special benefit; but which, though softer, were not much richer than

Pumpkins. The Melon, being a plant of tropical origin, reaches perfection only in a warm temperature, though by a little care in securing a warm, sandy soil, a sheltered, sunny position, and a little skill in starting plants early, fair crops are grown in what would be considered unfavorable localities. In this latitude we must give the Melon every possible advantage to secure earliness and thorough ripening. The same culture as recommended for Cucumbers will insure success. The striped bug is the great enemy of the Melon and other vines, and the best safeguard is gauze protectors of any simple form that can be easily and cheaply made. There are two distinct species of Melon in cultivation, the Musk Melon and the Water Melon. Our engravings show a few of the leading varieties. MUSK MELON — Fig. 1, Nutmeg; 2, White Japanese; 3, Casaba; 4, Prolific Nutmeg. WATER MELON — Fig. 5, Black Spanish; 6, Mountain Sweet; 7, Citron, for preserves.

## MUSTARD.

Young Mustard is used as a salad early in the spring, with Cress, Lettuce, and other salad plants. It can be grown in hot-beds as early as desired, and in the spring, being very hardy, can be sown as soon as the soil is free from frost. Sow in shallow drills, and cut when a few inches in height. It grows very rapidly; but little will be needed, and several sowings should be made at intervals. For a crop of seed sow in early spring, in rows, thin out the plants to six inches apart, making the rows about eighteen inches apart for garden culture, and for field far enough for the cultivator. The Chinese is the best for Salad, and the Black-seeded is usually preferred for commerce, being stronger than the White; but the White is chosen by many on account of its mildness, and is the kind recommended for medicinal purposes.

## ONIONS.

The Onion must have a clean and very rich soil, or it will not do well enough to pay for the trouble. Use well rotted manure freely, and be sure to get the seed in as early as possible in the spring, no matter if it is ever so cold and unpleasant, for if Onions do not get a good growth before hot, dry weather, the crop is sure to be a failure; then thin out early, and keep the soil mellow and clear of weeds, and if your seed is good, you will have a large crop

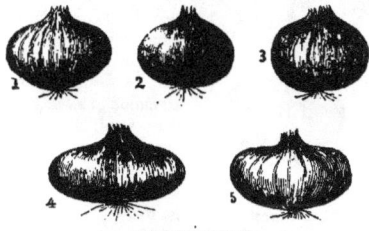

AMERICAN ONIONS.

of Onions. On no other conditions can you hope for success. The Onion is very sensitive, and it won't do to slight it in the least. Sow in shallow drills, not less than a foot apart. When the young Onions are three or four inches high, thin so that they will stand about two inches or more apart, according to kind. Disturb the roots of Onions as little as possible, either in thinning or hoeing, and never hoe earth toward them to cover, or hill, as we do most other things. Four pounds of seed are sufficient for an acre. American Onions are quite different from those of Europe; they are generally smaller, with a finer neck, bulb much more freely, are stronger, less sweet, and much better keepers. Our little engraving shows the leading native sorts reduced to quite one-sixth natural size. Figure 1, Wethersfield Red; fig. 2, Early Red; 3, Danvers Yellow; 4, Large Yellow; 5, White Portugal, which is a foreign sort so hybridized or acclimated as to become a native.

As before intimated, while the European varieties of Onions lack a great many of the good qualities belonging to the "native Americans," they possess some peculiar to themselves, and which certainly entitle them to favorable notice. They are mild, sweet, and large. It is no strange sight to see peasants eat for their dinner, with brown bread alone, and with apparent relish, an onion that would weigh a pound. These foreign Onions seem to succeed pretty well in the South. We thought it best to give engravings of a few of the leading sorts. Fig. 6 represents the Large Strasburg; 7, Large Oval Madeira; 8, Large Round Madeira; 9, White Lisbon; 10, Silver-Skinned, the favorite sort for pickles.

For several years past there has been a good deal of excitement among the seedsmen and gardeners of Europe, respecting some new Italian Onions of monstrous size, and very mild, superior flavor. Being in Europe when these Onions were attracting considerable attention, we saw some of them weighing as much as four pounds, and had the best of evidence of their fine flavor. We obtained seed and sent it all over the country, particularly to the South, for trial. The reports were generally favorable. The larger kinds, and they are the best, are wonderful in size, beautiful in appearance, sweet, and of pleasant flavor, and excellent for summer, autumn and early winter use. The engravings represent the principal kinds, very much reduced, but show the comparative size and form. Fig. 11, New Giant Rocca, of Naples, one of the best; 12,

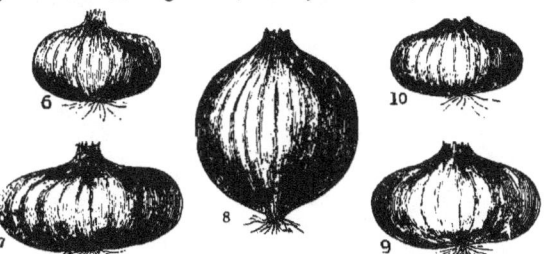

FOREIGN ONIONS.

Blood Red Italian Tripoli; 13, Large White Flat Italian Tripoli, one of the best; 14, Marzajola, very early, but not as large or showy as the others.

To those in the North who would secure a good crop of these Onions—and in fact, to all who have difficulty in growing a crop from seed early—we advise the following plan: Sow the seed thickly in rows in a hot-bed early. When severe weather is over and the glass is wanted for other purposes, it will not be needed for the Onions, as they are pretty hardy.

Keep the weeds down, and about the time for sowing Onion seed, transplant these Onions to the open ground, giving them a rich soil and plenty of room. Every one will form a large bulb, and very early. The hot-bed work and transplanting will be some trouble, but the troublesome hoeing and hand-weeding and thinning of young Onions will be avoided, which all Onion growers know is no small labor. We hope many of our readers will try a few in this way, at least, as we have pursued this course of culture for some years with the most gratifying results. It is doubtless known to most of our readers that it has been considered difficult to grow Onions from seed at the South, because the warm weather checks their growth before bulbs are formed. The hot-bed plan suggested we think will remedy this evil, but the one usually pursued is to plant what is called ONION SETS. These are small Onions, about the size of large peas. The seed is sown in the spring in broad rows, in a poor soil, and very thick, where they have not space to make a fair growth. About twenty-eight pounds of seed are sown to the acre. The result is a large quantity of stunted Onions, that are taken up in July and dried thoroughly on the ground. They are then stored away to be sold for planting the following spring. These, when planted in the spring, produce good Onions, and are used extensively in the South. It is, of course, a good deal of labor to raise a bushel of these little Onions, and they generally sell at high prices, from $10 to $15 a bushel.

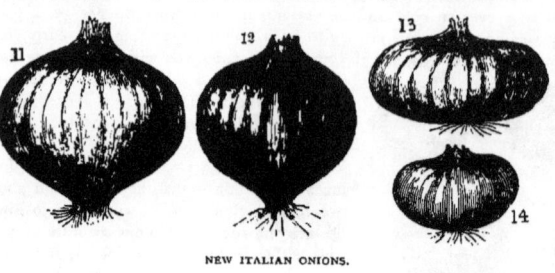

NEW ITALIAN ONIONS.

POTATO ONION.

Another Onion very largely grown by those who cannot succeed with seed, or who want early green Onions, is the ENGLISH POTATO ONION, which is the best underground variety. A large Onion produces, the first season, under ground, a large cluster of Onions, like that shown in the engraving, but the size is reduced. Many of them, with good culture, will be half the size of ordinary Onions. These are put out in the spring, and very early they are ready for use as summer Onions, and are a great favorite with market gardeners. It is this sort that is usually sold in bunches in the markets. Those that are allowed to remain in the ground during the summer make very large bulbs, to be sold or re-planted the next spring for small Onions. They are rather poor keepers, and the practice here is to spread them on the floor of a barn-loft and cover with straw, where they will freeze and keep frozen all the winter. They will then be in pretty good condition, but if kept in a warm place they must be turned every day, or they will rot, as they will if subjected to frequent freezing and thawing. If they were good keepers they would be very popular. The price is always high, generally about $5 a bushel.

TOP ONIONS.

Another variety not so good or so popular as Potato Onion, is the TOP ONION. When large Onions of this sort are planted, each one sends up a strong stem, just like the seed-stem of the common Onion, but instead of bearing on its top a number of seeds it produces a cluster of small Onions, just as we show in the engraving. Next spring these small Onions are planted, and each one produces a full sized Onion. They can be eaten during the summer, and are often sold in bunches, or they can be kept for winter use for spring planting. Each of these large Onions, of course, produces a cluster of small ones after a season's growth. Onion culture has become such an important interest, throughout our country, and in fact, throughout the civilized world, that we thought it important to give pretty thorough information on this subject.

## OKRA.

This vegetable is a native of the West Indies, though now grown in almost all warm countries. Its green seed-pods are used in soups, to which they give a jelly-like consistency, as they abound in mucilage, like all of the Mallow family. It is considered very nutritious, and exceedingly grateful to stomachs not over-strong. The common name South is Gumbo. It is of the easiest possible culture, and bears well. North it would be best to sow the seeds in hot-beds, and transplant, except in favored localities. There are two varieties generally grown, known as dwarf and tall. The Okra is a vigorous, large plant, requiring a good deal of room, and the large kind should be planted not less than three feet apart, and the dwarf about eighteen inches. In mild climates it is only necessary to sow the seed in the open ground, about two inches deep, and then merely keep the ground clean and mellow, as for a hill of corn. We have grown good Okra here by sowing in the open ground early in May, in a warm exposure and soil.

## PARSLEY.

Parsley is a hardy biennial plant, and therefore is in use two seasons, but about the middle of the second summer it goes to seed, so that sowings must be made every second year. Parsley seed germinates very slowly; it should be started in a hot-bed, if possible. For outdoor sowing always prepare the seed by placing in quite hot water and allowing it to soak for twenty-four hours, in a warm place. When the plants are a few inches in height, set them in rows, three or four inches apart. Parsley makes a pretty edging for the walks of the vegetable garden. As but little generally is needed, if sown in the garden in rows, it will be only necessary to thin out and destroy the surplus plants. Parsley is a universal favorite for soups, and for garnishing there is nothing so good as some of the best kinds. Indeed, it has been recommended and used for bouquets; but one poor gardener tried it only once, for he was coolly informed by the lady that she wished a bouquet for the parlor, and not herbs for the kitchen.

## PUMPKINS.

The Pumpkin is now but little used, except for agricultural purposes, the Squashes being so much sweeter and drier and finer grained. No good gardener, we think, would tolerate a pumpkin in the garden, nor would any sensible cook allow one in the kitchen. Those monster kinds that we see occasionally at our fairs are the worst of all. The farmer, however, finds the Pumpkin a very serviceable addition to his fall feed, and probably as long as Maize is grown in America the golden Pumpkin will gild our corn-fields in the beautiful Indian summer days of autumn. After all, a good many will think what we say of the Pumpkin all nonsense, and perhaps it is. We shall not certainly disagree about so small a matter as a Pumpkin, and some persons will always defend the good old-fashioned pumpkin pie, against all innovators.

## PARSNIPS.

The Parsnip flourishes best, and gives the longest, largest, smoothest roots in a very deep, rich soil—one that has been made rich with manure the previous year. Manure, especially if fresh, makes the roots somewhat ill-shaped. Sow as early in the spring as the ground can be made ready, in drills, from twelve to eighteen inches apart, and about an inch deep. Thin the plants to five or six inches apart. An ounce of seed will sow one hundred and fifty feet of drill very thickly. Six pounds of seed is the usual quantity sown on an acre. The part of the crop required for spring use can remain in the ground during the winter. If a portion is covered heavily with leaves, they can be dug at any time. A few can be stored in a pit or cellar. For feeding cattle, no root is superior to the Parsnip. In the Island of Guernsey, a few years ago, and perhaps the same state of things still exists, pigs and cattle were almost or entirely fattened on this root. We have always thought that American farmers did not realize the value of this root. In field culture it would be advisable to make the rows wider apart, so as to admit the cultivator one way. Although from the ease with which corn is grown, particularly in the Western States, it has been thought that there is no great necessity for the culture of roots in this country, we have no doubt that their more general growth would be of material advantage in many ways, especially in the older sections of the country. Animals always thrive better, and are more healthy on a somewhat mixed diet in which roots form an important part. This fact our best farmers are fast learning. As the Parsnip is not injured by frost it seems well adapted to general culture. Every one who visits any of the agricultural exhibitions of Canada, must notice the great attention given to root culture in that country, as shown by the quantity and quality of those exhibited. There are several varieties of Parsnips, but we have found little difference, and the old Hollow Crown seems as good as any. Roots that are allowed to remain in the ground during the winter are better flavored than those dug in the fall. As the roots go very deep, and seem to have an unusually firm hold of the soil, if they are carelessly dug more than half will be broken, which is a great injury to the crop.

## PEPPERS.

There are perennial shrubby or woody Peppers, and very beautiful plants they are when seen growing in their tropical homes. What we cultivate is an annual species, from India. The pod or fruit is in demand in every kitchen, and very large quantities are grown to supply our large cities and the manufacturers of pickles, and it is used somewhat freely in medicine. Sow the seeds early under glass, if possible, and transplant only when the weather has become steadily mild. If no hot-bed is to be had, prepare a seed-bed in a warm place in the garden, and sow, in the Middle and Northern States, in May, and transplant when the plants are about three inches in height. As usually only a few plants are needed, it is well to sow the seeds where the plants are to remain, and thin them out to about a foot apart. The fruit is often used green, but will be ripe in September. There are several varieties, ranging in height from one to three feet, while the fruit varies from the Little Cayenne to the great French Monstrous, six inches in length. Fig. 1 shows Long Red; 2, Cayenne; 3, Tomato-formed; 4, Monstrous, or Grossum. The Large Bell, and several other large sorts, differ little from the Tomato-formed, but larger. The Sweet Mountain, or Mammoth, is very large, mild, with thick flesh, and is pickled, stuffed like mangoes. The engraving shows Cayenne of natural size; all others are very much reduced.

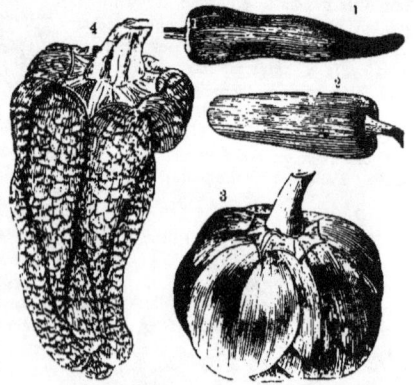

## PEAS.

The Pea is very hardy, and will endure a great amount of cold, either in or above the ground; and as we all want "green peas" as early as possible in the season, they should be put in as early as the soil can be got ready — the sooner the better. Peas are divided by seedsmen and gardeners into three classes, *Early, Second Early* and *Late*. The earliest are mostly small, round, smooth and hardy, the tallest not growing more than from two to three feet in height. Of late years some very fine dwarf, sweet, wrinkled sorts, like Little Gem, have been added to this class, of very great merit. The *Second Early* contain a list of excellent wrinkled varieties, like Eugenie. The *Late* are large, mostly wrinkled, and formerly were nearly all tall, like the Champion of England, but very many excellent dwarfs have been added to the list, like Yorkshire Hero. If the *Earliest* sorts are planted about the first of April, in this latitude, they will be fit to gather in June, often quite early in the month. The *Second* will come in about the Fourth of July. By sowing two or three varieties of *Early*, and the same of *Second* and *Late*, as soon as practicable in the spring, a supply will be had from early in June to late in July, with only one sowing. After this Sweet Corn will be in demand. Sow in drills not less than four inches deep, pretty thickly — about a pint to forty feet. The drills should not be nearer than two feet, except for the lowest sorts. Those growing three feet high, or more, should not be nearer than three or four feet. As they are early off the ground, Cabbage can be planted between the rows, or the space can be used for Celery trenches. All varieties growing three feet or more in height should have brush for their support. The large, fine wrinkled varieties are not as hardy as the small sorts, and if planted very early, should have a dry soil, or they are liable to rot. Keep well hoed up and stick early. When grown extensively for market, Peas do well sown on ridges made by the plow, two rows on each ridge, and not sticked, the pea vines drooping into the furrows. In response to the inquiry so often made, why we cannot sow Peas late, and thus have them in eating all through the summer, and why Peas are "buggy," we will say that the Pea delights in a cool, moist climate, and suffers in warm, dry weather. Those planted late will most likely be attacked with mildew, and never give half a crop. The Pea, when grown in a tolerably mild climate, is troubled with a weevil, the egg being laid in the pea when it is very small, through the pod. The way to obtain sound Peas for seed, is to grow them where the weevil does not exist.

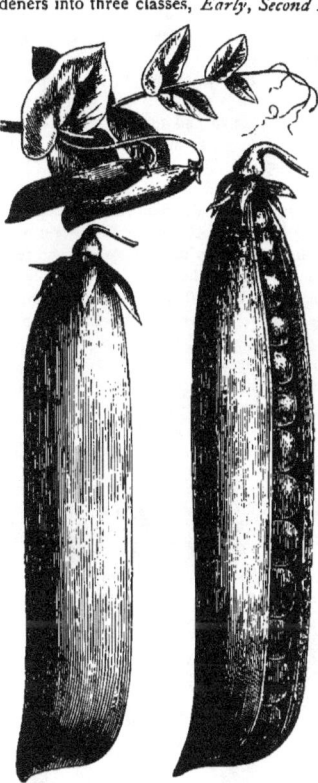

## RHUBARB.

The Rhubarb, or Pie-Plant, is usually grown from divisions of the roots, for every portion which has an eye will form a plant. Occasionally persons prefer to grow from seeds. It will take two years to obtain a strong plant from seed, but a package of seeds in two years will give enough plants to stock a neighborhood. Give a good, rich, deep, mellow soil, both to seeds and plants. In the spring, two weeks before frost is gone, cover two of the finest roots with barrels. Then throw over the roots and around the barrels leaves, straw or manure, and the earliest and tenderest stalks will be the result.

## RADISHES.

Radishes are divided into two classes, *Spring* and *Winter*, or as denominated in some of the books, *Summer* and *Autumn*. The Spring varieties are much smaller than the Winter, tender, arrive at maturity in a very brief time, and very soon become over-grown and worthless. The winter sorts mature more slowly, are large, very solid, and with proper care keep a long time.

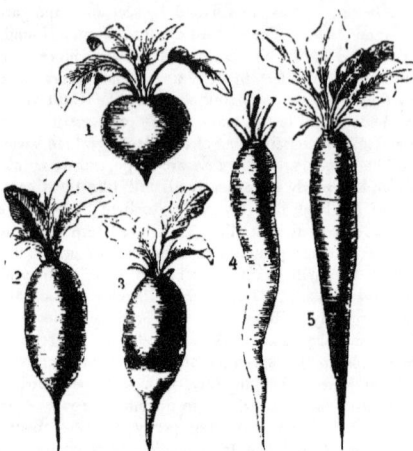

The SPRING RADISH must make a rapid growth to be fit for use; it will then be crisp and tender, and of mild flavor. If grown slowly, it will be hard, fibrous, and disagreeably pungent. For early use, seed should be sown in the hot-bed, in drills four or five inches apart and half an inch deep. Thin out the young plants so that they will stand two inches apart in the rows. Give plenty of light and air, or they will become drawn —that is, slender and worthless. For out-door beds, select a warm, sunny location, with a sandy soil. A little new earth from the woods, as a top-dressing, before the seeds are sown, will be of great service. A top-dressing of soot, or even coal ashes, will be of much benefit, as we have found by long experience. The great point is to get the plants to grow rapidly after the seed-leaf appears above ground, so as to be out of the way of the black beetle that proves so troublesome when they are young, puncturing every leaf. Sow soot, ashes, or dust over them frequently, as the beetle dislikes gritty food. Our engraving shows a few of the leading varieties, fig. 1 representing Red Turnip; 2, Rose Olive-Shaped; 3, Scarlet Olive-Shaped, with white tip; 4, Long White Naples, an excellent variety for growing late in the season; 5, Long Scarlet Short-Top.

The WINTER RADISH should be sown in July or August, about the time of Turnip sowing. They may be kept in a cool cellar and covered with earth for winter use. Put them in cold water for an hour before using. The engraving represents the principal varieties of winter Radishes — indeed, all worthy of culture. These Radishes are every year becoming more popular, and particularly so since the introduction of the newer Chinese varieties; though for that matter we are indebted to China for all our Radishes. Fig. 6 is the California Mammoth White Winter, a splendid variety which we saw in San Francisco, more than a foot in length, and as crisp and tender as one could desire; it was brought to California by Chinese emigrants. Fig. 7, Chinese White Winter; 8, Black Round Spanish; 9, Chinese Rose Winter.

## SALSIFY, or OYSTER PLANT.

A delicious vegetable. Cut into small pieces; it makes a fine soup, like that from oysters. It is also par-boiled, grated fine, made into small balls, dipped into batter, and fried. Culture same as for Carrots and Parsnips.

## SQUASHES.

The Squashes are an interesting and useful class of vegetables; interesting because presenting such a variety of forms; of their usefulness we need not say a word. The Squashes are of tropical origin, and therefore it is useless to plant them until the soil is quite warm, and all danger of frost or cold nights is over; and as they make a very rapid growth there is no necessity of haste in getting the seed in the ground. We usually divide the Squashes into two classes, Summer and Winter. The SUMMER SQUASHES are eaten when the rind and flesh are tender, about midsummer. The best of this class are the Crook-Neck and Scollop, and these are what are called bush varieties, and do not run. The WINTER

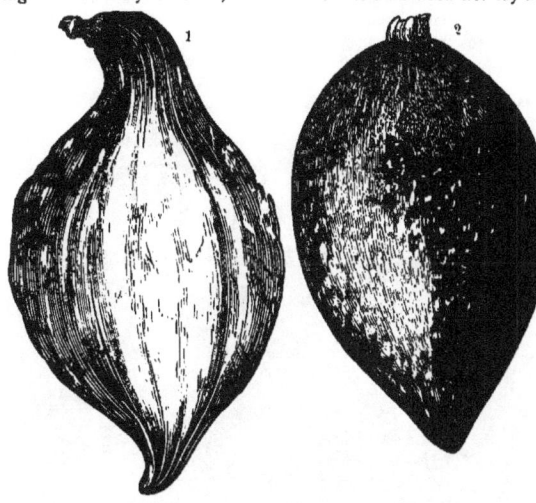

SQUASHES are allowed to ripen thoroughly before gathering, and are then stored away for winter use. A good, cool cellar will preserve these winter Squashes until May, if well ripened. The winter varieties are all runners, we believe. The best winter Squash is the Hubbard, fig. 1, and if pure and well ripened, and decently cooked, it is almost as good as a Sweet Potato. Fig. 2 represents the Marblehead, another excellent winter Squash, but we think hardly equal to the Hubbard. Fig. 3, Scollop, or Pie-formed, a good sort, and liked by market gardeners, because the rind is somewhat hard, and it bears shipping well. Fig. 4 is the excellent

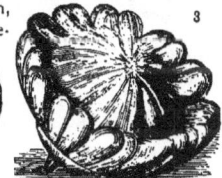

summer Crook-Neck, one of the best, if not the best, of the whole race of Summer Squashes. Squashes are good feeders, and like a rich soil; it is best to manure in the hill. Sow a dozen seeds in each hill, and when danger from "bugs" is over pull up all but three or four. A mellow, warm soil is best. For bush sorts, make hills three or four feet apart, and for the running kinds twice this distance.

## SPINACH.

To grow Spinach in perfection, the soil must be rich. Sow in the autumn for spring use, in good drained soil, in drills a foot apart. As soon as the plants are well up, thin them to about three inches apart in the rows. Covering with a little straw or leaves before winter is useful but not necessary. For summer use, sow as early as possible in the spring. There are two popular varieties, the principal distinction being that one has a round seed, and the other with sharp points, and called prickly. These we have shown in the engraving.

## TOMATOES.

The Tomato is more generally used in America than in any country in the world. The amount consumed seems wonderful, especially when we consider how brief the time since its first introduction as an article of diet. Almost every one likes it, and most persons regard it as a great luxury; but the Tomato is so slow perfecting its fruit that it is quite after the middle of summer, and at the end of most people's patience, before the ripened fruit can be enjoyed. To

obtain early varieties, therefore, is the great desire of all, and it is no strange thing to have varieties advertised as two weeks earlier than any other kind, that are entirely worthless in all respects, not even having the merit of earliness. We are satisfied that Hubbard's Curled Leaf is the earliest Tomato grown, and this is its only merit, for it is small and far from being smooth. The plant is small and will bear close planting, the leaves curling as if wilted. Gen. Grant is an excellent early Tomato, about ten or twelve days later than the Curled Leaf, but Hathaway's Excelsior is as early as Gen. Grant, and the best Tomato we are acquainted with. It received a certificate of merit from the Royal Horticultural Society of England, is pronounced by the press of Europe the best variety produced, and is everywhere popular. It is smooth, solid, of good flavor, excellent color and productive. Pinching off a portion of the side branches, and stopping others beyond where the fruit is formed, hastens the ripening very much. To obtain plants early, sow seed in the hot-bed early in March. In about five weeks they should be transplanted to another hot-bed, setting them four or five inches apart. Here they should remain, having all the air possible, and becoming hardened, until about the middle of May, when they may be put out in the ground; that is, if there is no danger of frost. Very good plants can be grown in boxes in the house, starting them even in the kitchen. Those, of course, who live in a southern clime will be spared a good deal of this care. The soil for early Tomatoes should not be too rich, and a warm, sheltered location selected, if possible. The Tomato may be made very pretty by training on a fence or trellis, like a grape-vine. No plant will better bear trimming. We have tested hundreds of varieties of Tomatoes in our grounds during the past ten years. Every season we put on trial every new kind we can obtain from any source, and feel quite competent to speak on the subject. Still, we can judge well of the influence of soil and climate only as we receive reports from our friends in different sections of the country.

The engraving, fig. 1, represents the Cherry Tomato, useful only for pickling; 2, Persian Yellow; 3, Hathaway; 4, Gen. Grant; 5, Early Smooth Red; 6, Curled Leaf. All are, of course, very much reduced in size, though very well representing the form and characteristics of each.

## TURNIPS.

There are two quite distinct species of Turnips grown, one called the *English Turnip*, and the other the *Swede*, or *Ruta Baga Turnip*. As they require somewhat different treatment, serious mistakes are sometimes made on that point. In ordering seeds, care should be taken to state which kind is desired. The English Turnip, if designed for early use, should be sown soon as the ground can be prepared in the spring, so as to have the benefit of early showers, for the Turnip will not grow in dry, hot weather. For the main crop, for fall and winter use, sow in August, and the plants will have the benefit of the autumn rains. If the weather should prove dry, the crop will be light. The soil for Turnips should be rich and mellow. Sow in drills, from twelve to eighteen inches apart, and half an inch deep. When the plants are a few inches in height, and strong enough to resist the attack of insects, thin them out to some five or six inches apart in the drills. Two pounds of seed are sufficient for an acre.

ENGLISH TURNIPS.

Fig. 1 represents the Strap-Leaved Purple-Top; 2, Orange Jelly; 3, Yellow Malta; 5, Jersey Navet; 7, White Norfolk.

The SWEDE, or RUTA BAGA TURNIPS are large, very solid, perhaps the most solid vegetable that grows. The flesh of nearly all the varieties are yellow. They do not grow as rapidly as the English Turnips, and should be sown as early as the first of June. The rows should be about eighteen inches apart, and the plants in the rows not less than ten inches.

SWEDE TURNIPS.

The engravings show, fig. 4, Carter's Imperial Purple-Top; fig. 6, Green-Top. We do not suppose that a warm, dry climate will ever be considered favorable to Turnip culture, and yet we never saw better crops in the most favored districts of England than we have seen in America. It is only in exceptionally dry seasons that our crop fails, with good culture. A soil rich in phosphates is necessary for a large crop, hence all bone manures are exceedingly valuable. With proper Turnip food and a moist season success is almost certain. There is then only one enemy to be conquered. The little black flea, or Turnip beetle, is very destructive when the plants are in the seed-leaf, but with a fair season and a rich soil the plants are soon in the rough leaf, when they are troubled no longer. Some good farmers sow twice the usual quantity of seed, and in this way save plenty from the little enemy, and this, we have no doubt, is the safest and most economical way, for it is better to feed them on plants that we do not need than on those upon which the crop depends.

## LEEK.

The Leek is a vegetable not much grown in America, except by market gardeners in the neighborhood of large cities. It is of the Onion family, and partakes alike of its flavor and fragrance, but never forms a rounded bulb. The Leek has the appearance of what is known as "scallions" among Onions. The long, thick neck or tunicated bulb, when well grown and blanched, is white for several inches, and nearly to the leaves, and this is used for flavoring soups, and is sometimes served as Asparagus. The seed is generally sown in the spring in a seed-bed, and the young plants transplanted about the first of July, or after an early crop of Lettuce or Peas have been taken from the ground. The Leek requires earthing up so as to let as much of the stem blanch as possible. Some growers plant in shallow trenches. It is not necessary to transplant, as the seed can be sown in rows and thinned out, as for Onions, and then earthed up. The Leek requires a rich, clean soil. In mild climates the Leek may be allowed to remain in the ground all winter, to be gathered as needed; but in cold climates they are taken up and stored, like Celery, for winter and spring use. The Leek will bear 20 degrees of frost without injury. At transplanting set the plants rather deep. The demand for this seed has been so small that we have several times omitted it from our list. The engraving shows the appearance of the Leek with the top removed, ready for bunching for market. Six or eight are usually put in a bunch.

## ENDIVE.

Endive is another plant but little inquired for in this country, and yet it is an excellent autumn and winter salad. It is naturally very bitter, but this is much lessened by blanching. The Endive is thought to be a native of China. For growing, select a cool, moist situation, such as would answer for growing Lettuce in the summer. Sow the seed late in the spring, or even as late as July, in shallow drills, and when the plants are strong thin out so that they will stand about a foot apart. Towards fall gather up the plant in a conical form, and tie near the top. The outside, coarse leaves will keep the plant in shape and blanch those inside near the heart. Sometimes a little earth is drawn toward the plant. Plants not needed for autumn use can be taken up and planted in a bed of earth in the cellar, the tops being tied up, and the roots only in the earth. In this way they will keep until spring. Be sure that the plants are dry when they are tied up or stored in the cellar.

---

[Vick's Flower and Vegetable Garden is published by JAMES VICK, Rochester, N. Y. Price, in paper covers, 35 cents; bound in handsome cloth covers, 65 cents. At this price it will be sent by mail, *postage paid*, to any part of the world.

Every year, on the first of December, we publish a Priced Catalogue of Seeds, giving the prices of everything for the Winter and Spring. We will send this free to all who write for it, enclosing the postage, TWO CENTS.

Vick's Floral Guide is a Quarterly Magazine, beautifully printed and illustrated. Price, only 25 cents a year. To every one who trades with us to the amount of One Dollar it is sent free. *Two Dollars* for a club of *Five*. Any person having paid for the GUIDE, and afterward ordering seeds, can deduct the money sent for the GUIDE.]

## SWEET AND POT HERBS.

A few fragrant, or, as they are sometimes called, Sweet or Pot Herbs, constitute a little treasury upon which the house-keeper will find occasion to make almost constant drafts, and these will be honored from early summer until autumn. A good reserve can also be stored in some closet or store room for winter use. As a general rule it is best to cut herbs when in flower and dry in the shade, and they dry more evenly and in better shape if tied up in small

BORAGE. THYME. SUMMER SAVORY. ROSEMARY.

bunches and hung in the shade. For soups and dressing for poultry these herbs are a necessity in the estimation of most persons, while as domestic medicines several kinds are held in high repute. The *Sage* and its uses, of course, every one is acquainted with. The Broad-leaved English is the best. *Thyme*, is of universal cultivation, as is also *Summer Savory*. *Rosemary* is a very fragrant herb, and is everywhere popular. *Borage* is a beautiful plant, with azure blue flowers, pretty enough for any flower garden. It is much used in Europe for flavoring Claret and other wines. We give a list of the herbs generally cultivated and prized, either by the cook or the nurse.

| | | | |
|---|---|---|---|
| Anise, | Cumin, | Marjoram, Sweet, | Savory, Winter, |
| Balm, | Dill, | Rosemary, | Thyme, Broad-Leaved |
| Basil, Sweet, | Fennel, Large Sweet, | Rue, | English, |
| Borage, | Horehound, | Saffron, | Thyme, Summer, |
| Caraway, | Hyssop, | Sage, | Thyme, Winter, |
| Coriander, | Lavender, | Savory, Summer, | Wormwood. |

A very small space in the garden will give all the herbs needed in any family. The culture is very simple, and the best way is to make a little seed-bed in the early spring, and set the

LAVENDER. HYSSOP. SWEET MARJORAM. SWEET BASIL.

plants out as soon as large enough in a bed. The trouble, therefore, is trifling, while the expense is comparatively nothing, as a paper of either can be obtained for five cents, and will contain more seeds than any one will be likely to need. In a mild climate some kinds will live over the winter, but they are so easily grown from seed that saving old plants is not of much consequence.

# Contents.

| | |
|---|---|
| SUCCESS IN FLOWER CULTURE, | 2 |
| THE LAWN AND GARDEN, | 8 |
| CLASSIFICATION OF FLOWERS, | 11 |
| ANNUALS, | 18 |
|     Climbers, | 48 |
|     Everlastings, | 53 |
|     Ornamental Grasses, | 56 |
| PERENNIALS, | 57 |
| BULBS AND PLANTS, | 67 |
|     Tender Bulbs and Plants, | 67 |
|     Hardy Bulbs and Plants, | 74 |
| HOLLAND BULBS, | 83 |
| VEGETABLES, | 96 |

## Description of Colored Plates.

### NUMBER ONE.—GROUP OF ANNUAL FLOWERS.

1. *Striped Petunia.* 2. *Pansy.* 3. *Japan Cockscomb.* 4. *Nemophila.* 5. *Camellia Balsam.* 6. *Double Portulaca.* 7. *Varieties of Phlox Drummondii.* 8. *Ten Weeks Stock.*

### NUMBER TWO.—BOUQUET OF PERENNIAL FLOWERS.

1. *Everlasting Pea.* 2. *Carnations.* 3. *Adonis autumnalis.* 4. *Pentstemon.* 5. *Sweet William.* 6-7. *Larkspur.* 8-9. *Digitalis.* 10. *Aquilegia.*

### NUMBER THREE.—TENDER BULBOUS FLOWERS.

1. *Gladioli.* 2. *Tiger Flower.* 3. *Dahlia.* 4. *Tuberose.* 5. *Tritoma.*

### NUMBER FOUR.—HARDY BULBOUS FLOWERS.

1. *Peony.* 2. *Dicentra.* 3. *Auratum Lily.* 4. *Rubrum Lily.* 5. *Thunbergianum atrosanguineum grandiflorum Lily.* 6. *Thunbergianum citrinum Lily.* 7. *Longiflorum Lily.* 8. *Martagon Purple Lily.* 9. *Martagon Yellow Lily.* 10. *Canadense Lily.* 11. *Blue Day Lily.* 12. *Lily of the Valley.*

IN this PRICED CATALOGUE will be found almost every variety of SEEDS and BULBS worthy of culture, and of the very choicest quality. These we keep on hand, and can supply them to our customers at all seasonable times. The prices are as low as good, reliable articles can be furnished by any one, while the quality of what we furnish we feel quite sure will gratify all. We do not propose to sound our own praise, as our customers and their gardens do this more effectually than we could do, had we the disposition to engage in this unnecessary and ungracious work. All that we desire to say is that we have spared neither time, nor expense, nor labor, either of body or mind, to obtain the best the world produces — just such as we would be willing to plant in our own grounds or furnish to Gen. GRANT or Queen VICTORIA, or to the poor widow or little child who send us their little savings for the purchase of a few seeds.

The different CLASSES of Flowers are arranged under appropriate headings, such as ANNUALS, PERENNIALS, EVERLASTINGS, CLIMBERS, VEGETABLES, &c., so that there will be no difficulty in finding anything that may be desired. Reference is made to the page in VICK'S FLOWER AND VEGETABLE GARDEN, where full descriptions of each article are to be found, and the mode of culture explained. Our FLOWER AND VEGETABLE GARDEN we think the most beautiful and useful and popular standard work on the subject in the world, and so cheap as to be within the means of everybody, as we furnish it at 35 cents in paper covers, and 65 cents in cloth.

In addition to the valuable matter of this work, it contains hundreds of Illustrations and FOUR COLORED PLATES, a group of *Annuals* and *Bouquets of Perennials, Hardy Bulbs* and *Tender Bulbs.*

By these methods we furnish the facts necessary to successful culture; at least, we design to do so, but questions continually arise that cannot be anticipated or answered in a book. Some thing fails to grow in a very unaccountable manner, destructive and unknown insects appear in a very unexpected season, and at a very unseasonable time; information is needed at once by some inexperienced cultivator, and, of course, there is no time for delay — so we publish a QUARTERLY, in which we answer all these questions, and without much delay. We call it VICK'S FLORAL GUIDE, and furnish it for 25 cents a year. To all customers who trade with us to the amount of One Dollar or more we give it for a year free, and those who pay for the GUIDE and afterward order seeds can deduct the money sent for the GUIDE from their remittance for Seeds or Bulbs.

## ANNUALS

Under this heading, ANNUALS, we give not only the true Annuals, but all those flowers that blossom the first season they are planted. On the lines with the headings, in large type, will be found figures which refer to the page in VICK'S FLOWER AND VEGETABLE GARDEN, in which the flower or vegetable mentioned will be found fully described, and its character more plainly shown by the aid of illustrations. All necessary directions for culture, &c., will be found in this work. For instance, the first article mentioned is "*Abronia, page* 14." On page 14 of the FLOWER AND VEGETABLE GARDEN will be found a history of this flower, its native home, &c. The same descriptions will be found in No. 1 of FLORAL GUIDE of last year.

The figures on the right of the column show the price of each package of seed, for instance a package of Adonis is five cents. These packages contain from one hundred to five hundred seeds, though of new or scarce seeds the quantity is far less.

### ABRONIA, page 14.
umbellata, rosy lilac; white eye, . . . . . . 10
arenaria, yellow, . . . . . . . . . . . . . 20

### ADONIS, page 14.
æstivalis, summer; scarlet; 1 foot, . . . . . . 5
autumnalis, autumn; blood red; 1 foot, . . 5

### AGERATUM, page 14.
conspicuum, white and blue; 18 inches high, . 5
Mexicanum, blue; 1 foot, . . . . . . . . . . 5
Mexicanum albiflorum, white-flowered; 1 foot, 5
Mexicanum albiflorum nanum, dwarf white;
 6 inches, . . . . . . . . . . . . . . . . 5
Lasseauxii, dwarf, compact plant; flowers pink, 10
cælestinum (Phalacræa) Tom Thumb, light
 blue; 8 inches high, and of compact habit, . . 5

### AGROSTEMMA, page 15.
New Scarlet, bright, . . . . . . . . . . . . 5
Cæli Rosa, deep rose color, . . . . . . . . . 5
elegans picta, center dark crimson, white margin, 5
cardinalis, bright red, . . . . . . . . . . . 5

### ALONSOA, page 15.
Warszewiczii, flowers small, bright scarlet,
 forming a very pretty spike; 18 inches high;
 set plants 8 or 10 inches apart, . . . . . . . 5
grandiflora, large-flowered, scarlet; 2 feet, . . 5

### ALYSSUM, page 15.
Sweet, hardy annual; flowers small and sweet,
 in clusters; 6 inches, . . . . . . . . . . . 5
Wierczbeckii, hardy perennial; flowers yellow;
 blooms first season; 1 foot, . . . . . . . . 5

### AMARANTHUS, page 16.
salicifolius, a beautiful Amaranth, both in habit
 and color; plant pyramidal, 2 feet in height;
 leaves long, narrow and wavy, . . . . . . . 10
bicolor, crimson and green foliage; 2 feet, . . . 5
bicolor ruber, a new bedding plant, the lower
 half of the leaf a fiery red scarlet, the upper half
 maroon, sometimes tipped with yellow, . . . 5
tricolor, red, yellow and green foliage; 2 feet, . .
melancholicus ruber, of compact habit, with
 striking blood red foliage; 18 inches, . . . . . 5
caudatus, (Love Lies Bleeding) long drooping "chains" of flowers; pretty for decorating, 5
cruentus, (Prince's Feather,) flowers somewhat similar to *A. caudatus*, but in erect masses, 5

### ANAGALLIS, page 16.
Napoleon III, rich maroon color; new, . . . . 10
Eugenie, fine, velvety blue, . . . . . . . . . 10
sanguinea, showy, bright red; new, . . . . . 10
superba, red, blue, scarlet, lilac; separate or
 mixed, each packet, . . . . . . . . . . . . 10
Garibaldi, crimson; exceedingly beautiful; new, 10
Memoria dell' Etna, bright red; new, . . . . 10

### ANTIRRHINUM, page 17.
Brilliant, scarlet and yellow, with white throat;
 very showy, . . . . . . . . . . . . . . . . 5
Firefly, orange and scarlet, with white throat, . 5
Galathe, crimson, throat white; large, . . . . 5
White-flowered, white; not showy, but good
 for variety, . . . . . . . . . . . . . . . . 5
papillionaceum, blood red, throat pure white, . 5
caryophylloides, irregularly striped, . . . . . 5
Striped Dwarf, six inches high, . . . . . . . 5
Best and brightest varieties mixed, . . . . . 5

### ARGEMONE, page 17.
grandiflora, white petals, yellow stamens, four
 inches in diameter, . . . . . . . . . . . . 5
Mexicana, flowers bright yellow, . . . . . . . 5
Hunnemanni, carmine and yellow, . . . . . . 5

### ASPERULA, page 17.
azurea setosa, a profuse blooming hardy annual
 of dwarf habit, with clusters of small, light blue,
 sweet-scented flowers; desirable for small bouquets, . . . . . . . . . . . . . . . . . . 5

### ASTER, pages 18 and 19.
Truffaut's Pæony-flowered Perfection, large,
 beautiful flowers, petals long; a little reflexed;
 2 feet in height; mixed colors, . . . . . . . 15
Truffauc's Pæony-flowered Perfection, same
 as above, with twelve separate colors, and very
 true to color; each color, . . . . . . . . . . 15
La Superbe, large flowers, 4 inches in diameter,
 20 inches in height; three colors mixed, . . . 20
La Superbe, three separate colors — rose, sky
 blue and white — each color, . . . . . . . . 20
New Rose, 2 feet in height; robust; large, double flowers, the outer petals finely imbricated
 and of great substance; one of the very best
 Asters; several colors mixed, . . . . . . . . 15
New Rose, eight separate colors — white, crimson, violet, etc., each color, . . . . . . . . 15

Aster, Tall Chrysanthemum-flowered, large flowers; 18 inches in height, .......... 10
Imbrique Pompon, very perfect; almost a globe, and beautifully imbricated; mixed colors. . . 10
Imbrique Pompon, twelve separate colors— white, blue, crimson, etc.; each color, . . . 15
Cocardeau, or New Crown, double flowers, the central petals being of pure white, sometimes small and quilled, surrounded with large, flat petals of a bright color, as crimson, violet, scarlet, etc.; 18 inches, . . . . . . . . . . . . . 10
Cocardeau, or New Crown, carmine, violet, blue, deep scarlet, violet brown, etc., each with white center; each variety, . . . . . . . . 10
New Pæony - flowered Globe, a new variety, and the earliest of the Asters—at least two weeks earlier than *Truffaut's Pæonyflowered;* flowers very large; plant branching and strong; does not require support, . . . . . . . . . . 10
Pyramidal-flowered German, late, branching, good habit; needs no tying, . . . . . . . . . 10
New Victoria, flowers large; habit pyramidal; 2 feet high; flowers freely; mixed colors, . . 15
Giant Pæony, Brilliant Rose, a hybrid between *Giant Emperor* and *Truffaut's Pæonyflowered Perfection;* flowers large and perfect, 25
Washington, a new Aster recently introduced from Germany, and has the largest flowers of the family. We grew and exhibited them last year five inches in diameter, and perfect; the plant is robust and perfectly healthy; mixed colors, . . . . . . . . . . . . . . . . . . . . . . 25
Goliath, another large new variety, but not as large or as good as Washington. The plant is not healthy, and we cannot recommend it; it is no better than the old *Giant Emperor* for America, and has the same faults, . . . . . . . . 10
New Chrysanthemum - flowered Dwarf, a desirable class, 1 foot in height; late, and desirable on this account, as well as for its great beauty; mixed colors, . . . . . . . . . . . . . 15
Chrysanthemum - flowered Dwarf, Snowy White, a superb snow white variety, changing from white to azure blue as the plants become old; every flower usually perfect, . . . . . . 15
Newest Dwarf Bouquet. Each plant looks like a little bouquet of flowers set in the ground; fine for edging or filling small beds; about 12 different colors mixed, . . . . . . . . . . . . . 15
Dwarf Pyramidal Bouquet, 10 inches high; abundance of flowers; very early, . . . . . . 15
Dwarf Pyramidal Bouquet, Blood Red, a novelty of 1870, which has proved quite distinct and true; very brilliant in color, free blooming, and uniform in habit; excellent for outside row of bed or border, . . . . . . . . . . . . . . . . . 20
New Schiller, a late, dwarf, bouquet Aster, of peculiar habit and great beauty; 15 inches high, with great quantity of bloom; finest mixed, . . 10
Hedge - Hog, or Needle, petals long, quilled, and sharply pointed; very curious; two feet; mixed colors, . . . . . . . . . . . . . . . . . . . 15
Original Chinese, plant tall; flowers large and loose; distinct in appearance, and of bright colors; resembling the first imported Asters, . 10

BALSAM, page 20.
Camellia-flowered, French, double, perfect in form; mixed colors, . . . . . . . . . . . . . 15
Camellia-flowered, French, ten colors, each in separate package: each color, . . . . . . . 15

Balsam, Camellia - flowered Spotted, German, double; spotted with white; mixed colors, . . 15
Rose-flowered, French; double; mixed colors, 15
Rose-flowered, French; ten colors, each in separate packages: each color, . . . . . . . . 15
Dwarf Camellia - flowered Spotted, German, 8 or 10 inches in height; splendid for a border or outside row of a bed, . . . . . . . . . . 15
Extra Double Dwarf, very double; 6 inches, . 15
Half Dwarf, 18 inches in height, . . . . . . . 15
Carnation, double; striped like the Carnation, 15
Solferino, white, striped and spotted with red, . 15
Common Double, occasionally only semi-double, 10

BARTONIA, page 21.
aurea, is a very showy, half-hardy annual, with large, yellow flowers. Plant prostrate in habit, 5

BRACHYCOME, page 21.
Iberidifolia, (Swan River Daisy,) blue and white, separate or mixed, . . . . . . . . . . 10

BROWALLIA, page 21.
Cerviakowski, blue, with white center, . . . . 10
elata alba, white, . . . . . . . . . . . . . . . 10
elata grandiflora, blue, . . . . . . . . . . . . 10

CACALIA, page 22.
coccinea, scarlet, . . . . . . . . . . . . . . . 5
coccinea flore-luteo, yellow, . . . . . . . . . 5

CALANDRINIA, page 22.
grandiflora, reddish lilac; 1 foot, . . . . . . . 5
speciosa, dark purple; very showy; 4 inches, . 5
speciosa alba, white; very free bloomer, . . . 5
umbellata, rosy purple; perennial, but flowering first season, . . . . . . . . . . . . . . 10

CALENDULA, page 22.
officinalis Le Proust, new; uniformly double; nankeen, edged with brown, . . . . . . . . . 10

CALLIOPSIS, page 22.
coronata, yellow disc, encircled with crimson spots, . . . . . . . . . . . . . . . . . . . . . 5
Drummondii, yellow, crimson center, . . . . . 5
bicolor, yellow, crimson center, . . . . . . . . 5
bicolor nigra speciosa, rich, velvety crimson, 5
bicolor nana marmorata, dwarf; reddish-brown, marbled with yellow, . . . . . . . . . 5
cardaminifolia hybrida, yellow; habit compact; blooms profusely the whole season, . . 5
cardaminifolia hybrida atrosanguinea, compact habit; rich, dark bloom, . . . . . . . . 5
tinctoria, quilled; very singular, . . . . . . . 5
Burridgi, (*Cosmidium Burridgeanum*,) the most beautiful and distinct of the family; flowers with a rich, crimson bronze center, and orange yellow border, . . . . . . . . . . . . 5
Mixed colors of every shade, . . . . . . . . . 5

CALLIRHOE, page 23.
pedata, purplish crimson, with white edge; 2 feet, 10
pedata nana, flowers rich velvet crimson, with white eye; 1 foot, . . . . . . . . . . . . . . 10
involucrata, with large purplish crimson flowers; native of the Western prairies, . . . . . 10

CAMPANULA, page 23.
speculum rosea, rose-colored, . . . . . . . . 5
speculum flore-albo, white, . . . . . . . . . . 5
speculum grandiflorum, purple, . . . . . . . . 5
speculum, mixed colors, . . . . . . . . . . . 5
Lorei, blue and white, . . . . . . . . . . . . . 5

**CANNA, page 23.**
Indica Indian Shot, rubra, red; 2 feet, . . . 10
Warszewiczii, red; foliage striped; 3 feet, . . 10
compacta elegantissima, large; reddish yellow; free-flowering; 2 feet, . . . . . . . . . 10
Selowii, scarlet; profuse blooming, . . . . . 10
Nepalensis, superb yellow flowers, . . . . . 10
Mixed varieties, . . . . . . . . . . . . . 10
For good roots we put the price at low rates, this year, to encourage every one to plant, . . . 25

**CANDYTUFT, page 24.**
Purple, . . . . . . . . . . . . . . . . . 5
White, . . . . . . . . . . . . . . . . . 5
Rocket, pure white, in long spikes. . . . . . 5
Lilac, bluish-lilac, . . . . . . . . . . . . . 5
Sweet-scented, pure white; slightly fragrant, . 5
Rose, rosy lilac. . . . . . . . . . . . . . 5
Dunnett's Extra Dark Crimson, . . . . . . . 5
All the above colors mixed, . . . . . . . . 5
New Carmine, a beautiful bright rose. . . . 25

**CASSIA, page 24.**
chamæcrista, a good annual, with light green foliage, like the Sensitive Plant, and with bright golden flowers, . . . . . . . . . . . . . 10

**CATCHFLY, page 24.**
Silene Armeria, (Lobel's Catchfly,) red, white and rose; either separate or mixed, . . 5

**CELOSIA CRISTATA, page 25.**
Crimson Dwarf, . . . . . . . . . . . . . . 10
Rose Dwarf, . . . . . . . . . . . . . . . 10
Yellow Dwarf, . . . . . . . . . . . . . . 10
Violet Dwarf, . . . . . . . . . . . . . . . 10
Scarlet Giant, . . . . . . . . . . . . . . 10
Tall Violet, . . . . . . . . . . . . . . . . 10
Tall Rose, . . . . . . . . . . . . . . . . 10
Tall Sulphur, . . . . . . . . . . . . . . . 10
Japonica, or New Japan Cockscomb, an entirely new and distinct and very beautiful variety of Cockscomb, received from Japan; the best of the family, . . . . . . . . . . . . 15
variegata, showing a mixture of red and yellow, and hardly worth culture; very late, and does best South, . . . . . . . . . . . . . . . . 10
Dwarf varieties mixed, . . . . . . . . . . . 10
Tall varieties mixed, . . . . . . . . . . . . 10
Celosia pyramidalis coccinea, spikes large and showy; scarlet; 3 feet, . . . . . . . . . . 10
Celosia spicata rosea, a very pretty plant, with spikes of rose-colored flowers that keep well for winter ornaments, if picked early; free-bloomer, 10

**CENTAUREA, page 26.**
Cyanus, known as Bachelor's Button and Corn Bottle, various colors mixed, . . . . . . . . 5
depressa, blue, red center; large, . . . . . . 5
depressa rosea, rosy purple, . . . . . . . . 5
moschata, (Blue Sweet Sultan,) . . . . . . . 5
moschata alba, (White Sweet Sultan,) . . . . 5
moschata atropurpurea, (Purple Sw't Sultan,) 5
suaveolens, (Yellow Sweet Sultan,) . . . . . 5
All above kinds mixed, . . . . . . . . . . 5
Americana, very large flowers; lilac purple; strong plant, . . . . . . . . . . . . . . . 10
Americana alba, clear white; very large; novelty, 10
Americana, white, lilac and purple, mixed, . . 10

**CENTRANTHUS, page 26.**
macrosiphon, pale rose; 2 feet, . . . . . . 5
macrosiphon flore-albo, white, . . . . . . . 5

Centranthus macrosiphon flore-carneo, flesh, 5
macrosiphon nanus, dwarf, . . . . . . . . . 5
macrosiphon bicolor, flowers pink and white, 5

**CHAMÆPEUCE, page 26.**
diacantha, an elegant Thistle-like plant, with sharp spines and beautiful variegated foliage; hardy; yellow flowers, . . . . . . . . . . 10

**CLEOME, page 26.**
speciosissima, rosy, . . . . . . . . . . . . 10
integrifolia, . . . . . . . . . . . . . . . 10

**CLARKIA, page 27.**
Double varieties mixed, . . . . . . . . . . 5
Single varieties mixed, . . . . . . . . . . 5

**COLLINSIA, page 27.**
multicolor marmorata, white and rose, marbled; 1 foot, . . . . . . . . . . . . . . . 5
bicolor, purple and white, . . . . . . . . . 5

**CONVOLVULUS MINOR, page 27.**
splendens, violet, with white center, . . . . 5
monstrosus, spreading; dark purple flowers, . 5
subcœruleus, light blue flowers, . . . . . . . 5
New Dark, very dark and good, . . . . . . 5
Striped, fine, . . . . . . . . . . . . . . . 5
lilacinus, fine lilac, . . . . . . . . . . . . 5
White, very pretty for contrast, . . . . . . 5
All the above mixed, . . . . . . . . . . . 5

**CREPIS, page 27.**
barbata, light yellow and bright purple, . . . 5
rubra, pink, . . . . . . . . . . . . . . . 5
flore-albo, white, . . . . . . . . . . . . . 5
Mixed, . . . . . . . . . . . . . . . . . 5

**DATURA, page 28.**
Wrightii, is one of the best, with trumpet-shaped flowers from seven to nine inches long, white, faintly tinted with lilac, sweet-scented, . . . 10
humilis flava flore-pleno, a splendid plant, with large, yellow, double flowers; sweet-scented; start early under glass, . . . . . . . 10
fastuosa alba plena, fine, double white, . . 10

**DELPHINIUM, page 28.**
Ajacis hyacinthiflorum, (Double Dwarf Rocket,) mixed colors, . . . . . . . . . . 5
elatior flore-pleno, (Tall Rocket,) large plant; very showy, . . . . . . . . . . . . . . . 5
Consolida flore-pleno, (Stock-flowered,) double, branching; large, showy flowers, fine for cutting; mixed colors, . . . . . . . . . . . 5
Consolida flore-pleno tricolor, double, striped, branching, . . . . . . . . . . . . . . . 5
Consolida flore-pleno candelabrum, 1 foot in height; peculiar habit; flowering late, . . . 10
cardiopetalum, 18 inches; makes a good hedge, 5
imperiale, fine, compact plant, brilliant colors; mixed, . . . . . . . . . . . . . . . . . 10
Bismarck, red striped; very excellent, in habit between *imperialis* and *candelabrum*, . . . 25

**DIDISCUS, page 28.**
cœruleus, an annual, with sky blue flowers; 2 feet in height, . . . . . . . . . . . . . 10

**DIANTHUS, page 29.**
Chinensis, best double varieties mixed, . . . 10
imperialis, (Double Imperial Pink,) mixed colors, . . . . . . . . . . . . . . . . . 10
imperialis rubrus striatus, double, white, striped with red, . . . . . . . . . . . . . 10
imperialis purpureus striatus, double, white, striped with purple, . . . . . . . . . . . 10

Dianthus imperialis flore-albo pl., double;
white, . . . . . . . . . . . . . . . . . . . . . 10
Imperialis flore-pleno atrosanguineus, blood
red; double, . . . . . . . . . . . . . . . . . 10
Heddewigii, large flower, three inches in diameter, beautiful, rich colors, often finely marked
and marbled, . . . . . . . . . . . . . . . . . 10
Heddewigii flore-pleno, often double, but
sometimes only semi-double, . . . . . . . . . 10
Heddewigii fl.-pl. atropurpureus, large, dark
red, double flowers, . . . . . . . . . . . . . 10
laciniatus, flowers very large, sometimes three
inches in diameter; petals very deeply fringed
and beautifully colored, . . . . . . . . . . . 10
laciniatus flore-pleno, magnificent double flowers, very large; petals deeply serrated; splendid colors. Seeds saved only from finest flowers, 20
Mixed seed of the last five varieties, . . . . . . 10
Heddewigii diadematus fl.-pl.,(Diadem Pink,)
Of the most brilliant markings and dazzling
colors, but unfortunately not always true, . . . 15
Gardnerianus, double and sweet-scented, . . . 20
hybridus, mixed colors, . . . . . . . . . . . 10
Best dwarf varieties mixed, . . . . . . . . . 15

## DOUBLE DAISY, page 29.
Bellis perennis, best German seed, . . . . . . 20

## ERYSIMUM, page 30.
Perowskianum, deep orange flowers, . . . . . 5
Arkansanum, sulphur yellow, . . . . . . . . 5

## ESCHSCHOLTZIA, page 30.
Californica, bright yellow, darker in center, . . 5
crocea, orange, darker in center, . . . . . . . 5
crocea alba, white, . . . . . . . . . . . . . 5
crocea striata, flowers orange, striped with
lemon; new, . . . . . . . . . . . . . . . . 5
crocea rosea, a new variety; face of petals light
pink, and the back being darker, the effect is
quite good, . . . . . . . . . . . . . . . . . 5
tenuifolia, flowers small, pale yellow, resembling
the Primrose; plant only 6 inches in height, . . 5
dentata sulphurea, and E. dentata aurantiaca, two curious new varieties; each petal has
its edge lapped over on itself, with a mark of deeper color running from its center; each variety, 5

## EUPHORBIA, page 30.
marginata, a charming ornamental-leaved annual; edges of leaves snowy white, . . . . . . 10

## EUTOCA, page 30.
viscida, dark blue; pretty, . . . . . . . . . . 5
Wrangeliana, lilac; 6 inches, . . . . . . . . 5
multiflora, flowers more freely than the others, 5

## FENZLIA, page 31.
dianthiflora, free-flowering little plant; flowers
reddish-lilac, with crimson center, . . . . . . 25

## GAILLARDIA, page 31.
picta, or Painted, brownish-red, bordered with
yellow, . . . . . . . . . . . . . . . . . . . 5
Josephus, very brilliant; red and orange, . . . 5
albo-marginata, red, bordered with white, . . 5

## GILIA, page 31.
achillæfolia, mixed colors, . . . . . . . . . . 5
capitata, mixed colors, . . . . . . . . . . . 5
tricolor, mixed colors, . . . . . . . . . . . . 5
All varieties mixed, . . . . . . . . . . . . . 5

## HELIANTHUS, page 31.
Californicus grandiflorus, flowers large and
double; orange; 5 feet, . . . . . . . . . . . 5

Helianthus globosus fistulosus, the best of
the Sunflowers; very large; double; saffron-
yellow; globular form, . . . . . . . . . . . . 10
Double Green-centered, a large flower with
green center when young; when old, perfectly
double flower; 5 to 8 feet in height, . . . . . . 10
New Mammoth Russian, single; very large, 5
Common Single, usually grown for the seed;
per lb. 60 cents, . . . . . . . . . . . . . . . 5

## HUNNEMANNIA, page 32.
fumariæfolia, herbaceous; yellow, tulip-shaped
flowers, . . . . . . . . . . . . . . . . . . . 15

## KAULFUSSIA, page 32.
amelloides, light, bright blue, . . . . . . . . 5
amelloides rosea, rose, with red center, . . . 5
amelloides atroviolacea, intense violet; the
richest color imaginable; new, . . . . . . . . 5

## LEPTOSIPHON, page 32.
Mixed varieties, . . . . . . . . . . . . . . . 5

## LINUM, page 32.
grandiflorum rubrum, a beautiful half-hardy
annual, . . . . . . . . . . . . . . . . . . . 5

## LOBELIA, page 33.
cardinalis, our native Cardinal Flower; spikes
of brilliant scarlet flowers; blooms first year if
well started with heat, . . . . . . . . . . . . 10
Queen Victoria, splendid large scarlet flowers;
dark leaves, . . . . . . . . . . . . . . . . . 25
hybrida grandiflora, large, dark blue flower,
with white eye, . . . . . . . . . . . . . . . 10
gracilis rosea, rose-colored; new, . . . . . . . 10
gracilis erecta, of fine, compact growth, . . . . 10
ramosa, branching; large, dark blue flowers, . 10
Erinus marmorata, marbled, blue and white, 10
Erinus compacta, deep, rich blue, . . . . . . 10
Erinus compacta alba, new; white, . . . . . 10
pumila grandiflora, a compact, erect little plant,
for pots or edgings, . . . . . . . . . . . . . 10

## LUPINUS, page 33.
affinis, blue and white; 1 foot, . . . . . . . . 5
Cruikshankii, blue, white and yellow; 3 feet, . 5
Hartwegii, 2 feet; mixed colors, . . . . . . . 5
hirsutissimus, hairy; 2 feet . . . . . . . . . . 5
hybridus superbus, superb; purple, lilac and
yellow; 2 feet, . . . . . . . . . . . . . . . . 5
hybridus atrococcineus, bright crimson-scarlet, white tip; spikes large, . . . . . . . . . . 5
tricolor mutabilis, new; cream color, changing
to mottled purple, . . . . . . . . . . . . . . 5
Mixed varieties, . . . . . . . . . . . . . . . 5

## LYCHNIS, page 33.
Chalcedonica, bright scarlet; has a fine appearance when grown in masses; 2 feet, . . . . . 5
Chalcedonica carnea, flesh-colored; 2 feet, . 5
Chalcedonica flore-albo, white; 2 feet, . . . 5
Haageana, very beautiful vermillion-colored
flowers; plant dwarf; 1 foot, . . . . . . . . . 10
Haageana hybrida, large flowers, white, rose,
red, etc.; 1 foot, . . . . . . . . . . . . . . . 10
Sieboldii, new; large and superb; white; 1 foot, 15
fulgens, very brilliant; 18 inches, . . . . . . . 10
grandiflora gigantea, new; flowers very large,
of various colors, . . . . . . . . . . . . . . 10

## MALOPE, page 34.
grandiflora, large, purple flowers, . . . . . . 5
grandiflora alba, pure white, . . . . . . . . 5

**MARIGOLD**, page 34.
African Marigold, (Tagetes erecta,) Tall Orange, double, . . . . . . . . . . . . . 5
Tall Sulphur, light yellow; double, . . . . . 5
Tall Quilled Orange, double, . . . . . . . 5
Tall Quilled Sulphur, light yellow; double, . 5
All the above mixed, . . . . . . . . . . . 5
French Marigold, (Tagetes patula,) Tall Orange, double, . . . . . . . . . . . . . . 5
Tall Brown, double; branching; 18 inches, . 5
Tall Striped, yellow and brown striped; 18 inches, . . . . . . . . . . . . . . . . . 5
Dwarf Sulphur, double, . . . . . . . . . 5
Dwarf Brown, double, . . . . . . . . . . 5
Striped Dwarf, double; yellow and brown, . 5
Dunnett's New Orange, very superior; new, 5
Tall varieties mixed, . . . . . . . . . . . 5
Dwarf varieties mixed, . . . . . . . . . . 5
Tagetes pulchra punctata, spotted; double, 5
Tagetes signata pumila, a beautiful plant, forming a globular, dense mass, . . . . . . . 5

**MARTYNIA**, page 34.
formosa, (fragrans,) purple; sweet-scented, . 10
lutea, yellow, . . . . . . . . . . . . . . . 10
craniolaria, white, . . . . . . . . . . . . 10
proboscidea, bluish flowers; seed-vessels, when tender, used for pickles, . . . . . . . . 10
All the above mixed, . . . . . . . . . . . 10

**MEDICAGO**, page 34.
Snail, clover-like plant, with small, yellow flowers, 10
Hedge-hog, like above, except seed-pod, . . 10

**MESEMBRYANTHEMUM**, page 35.
crystallinum, (Ice Plant,) prized for its singular icy foliage, . . . . . . . . . . . . . 5
tricolor, (Dew Plant,) pink, with purple center, 5
tricolor album, white, . . . . . . . . . . 5
glabrum, light yellow, . . . . . . . . . . 5

**MIGNONETTE**, page 35.
Reseda odorata, (Sweet Mignonette,) a well-known, fragrant, little, hardy annual; per oz. 25 cents, . . . . . . . . . . . . . . . . . 5
grandiflora ameliorata, a large variety of Mignonette, reddish tinge to flowers, . . . . . 5
Parson's New White, a robust Mignonette; flowers larger and showing more white than the common sort, . . . . . . . . . . . . . . 10

**MIRABILIS**, page 35.
Marvel of Peru, (Mirabilis Jalapa,) chamois, crimson, lilac, lilac striped with white, tricolor, red striped with white, violet, white, yellow, yellow and red; each color, . . . . . . . . . 10
All the above mixed, . . . . . . . . . . . 10
foliis-variegatis, flowers of a variety of colors; leaves light green, faintly marbled, . . . . 10
longiflora, white, exceedingly sweet-scented; flower tube 3 or 4 inches long, . . . . . . 10
longiflora violacea, same as above, but violet, color, . . . . . . . . . . . . . . . . . 10

**MIMULUS**, page 36.
roseus pallidus, new and very fine, . . . . 10
cupreus, beautiful, orange and crimson, . . 10
hybridus tigrinus, as beautifully spotted as the finest Calceolarias, . . . . . . . . . . . 10
hybridus tigrinus bruneus, stems and leaves dark brown, with very large, deep yellow, dotted flowers, . . . . . . . . . . . . . . . 10
cardinalis, fine scarlet, . . . . . . . . . . 10

Mimulus hybridus tigrinus flore-pleno, a double Mimulus with flowers more durable than those of any other variety, . . . . . . . . 25
moschatus, (Musk Plant,) . . . . . . . . . 10
quinquevulnerus maximus, from best named varieties, . . . . . . . . . . . . . . . . 10

**MYOSOTIS**, page 36.
alpestris, blue; 6 inches, . . . . . . . . . 10
alpestris, white; 6 inches, . . . . . . . . . 10
alpestris rosea, a new rose-colored variety of the Alpine Forget-me-not, . . . . . . . . 10
palustris, (Forget-me-not,) white and blue, . 10
Azorica, dark blue; new; 1 foot, . . . . . . 15
Azorica var. cælestina, flowers sky-blue, and produced in great profusion, . . . . . . 15

**NEMOPHILA**, page 36.
insignis, beautiful light blue, . . . . . . . 5
insignis striata, white and blue striped, . . 5
insignis marmorata, blue, edged with white, 5
maculata, large, white, blotched with violet, 5
atomaria, white; spotted, . . . . . . . . 5
atomaria oculata, very pretty light blue, with large, dark eye, . . . . . . . . . . . . 5
discoidalis elegans, rich, velvety maroon, bordered with white, . . . . . . . . . . . . 5
The above mixed, . . . . . . . . . . . . 5

**NIEREMBERGIA**, page 37.
gracilis, plant slender, very branching, spreading; fine for baskets, pots, or the border, . 10
frutescens, taller, and of more erect habit than preceding, with flowers larger and more open, 10

**NIGELLA**, page 37.
Damascena, light blue; double; about 1 foot, 5
Damascena nana, dwarf; variety of colors; 6 inches, . . . . . . . . . . . . . . . . . 5
Hispanica, large-flowered; very fine; 6 inches, 5
Fontanesiana, much like N. atropurpurea, but blooms two weeks earlier, . . . . . . . 5

**NOLANA**, page 37.
atriplicifolia, blue, white and yellow, . . . 5
grandiflora, large; variety of colors, . . . . 5
grandiflora alba, . . . . . . . . . . . . . 5
paradoxa violacea, violet, with white center, 5

**ŒNOTHERA**, page 38.
Veitchii, a pretty, half-hardy annual; flowers yellow, with a red spot at the base of each petal; 1 foot, . . . . . . . . . . . . . . . . . 5
acaulis alba, a very dwarf or rather stemless plant, the leaves lying close to the ground; flowers snowy white, about four inches across. Grow plants in frame or seed-bed, and set about six inches apart, . . . . . . . . . . . . 10
Lamarckiana grandiflora, one of the most showy of the genus; flowers yellow, 4 inches in diameter; plant grows 4 feet in height, . 5

**OBELISCARIA**, page 38.
pulcherrima, ray flowers rich velvety crimson, edged with yellow, . . . . . . . . . . . 5

**OXYURA**, page 38.
chrysanthemoides, a hardy annual, about 18 inches in height, a beautiful flower, . . . 5

**PALAFOXIA**, page 38.
Hookeriana, a very fine new annual, of a dwarf, branching habit, . . . . . . . . . . . . 5

### PANSY, page 39.
King of the Blacks, almost coal black, coming true from seed, . . . . . . . . . . . . . . . 15
Sky Blue, with lovely new shades of light and nearly sky blue, . . . . . . . . . . . . . 15
Violet, with white border; somewhat resembling the fancy Geraniums, . . . . . . . . . . 20
Red, bright coppery colors, but not strictly red, 15
Pure Yellow, generally true to color, . . . . . 15
White, sometimes slightly marked with purple, 15
Striped and Mottled, extra, and very showy, . 20
Yellow Margined, beautiful color, with margin or belt of yellow, . . . . . . . . . . . . . . 20
Marbled Purple, new colors, . . . . . . . . . . 15
Mahogany-colored, a very fine variety, . . . 15
Cliveden Purple, very rich, deep purple, . . . 20
Emperor William, a new variety from Germany; fine, large flower, ultramarine-blue with purple-violet eye, . . . . . . . . . . . . . 25
Odier, or Large-Eyed, dark spots on each petal, and large eyes, . . . . . . . . . . . . . . . 25
Mixed seed of above sorts, . . . . . . . . . . 15

### PERILLA, page 39.
Nankinensis, an ornamental-leaved, half-hardy annual; leaves deep mulberry, . . . . . . . 5

### PETUNIA, page 40.
hybrida grandiflora Kermesina, . . . . . . . 25
grandiflora maculata, splendid spotted, . . . 25
grandiflora venosa, variety of colors, beautifully veined, . . . . . . . . . . . . . . . . 25
grandiflora rosea, splendid large flowers, bright rose, white throat, . . . . . . . . . . . . . 25
grandiflora marginata, large flowers, bordered and veined with green, . . . . . . . . . . . 25
grandiflora violacea, one of the noblest of the large-flowered Petunias, and of a rich violet, . 25
Choicest mixed, from show flowers, . . . . . 25
Vick's New Fringed, a new strain, with fringed and frilled edges, very distinct and beautiful, and coming unusually true to seed. Packet, 50 seeds 25
Double. The seed I offer is the best to be obtained, I think. The double Petunia bears no seed, and but little pollen. Packet of 50 seeds, 25
Countess of Ellesmere, dark rose, with fine white throat, . . . . . . . . . . . . . . . . 10
Blotched and Striped, . . . . . . . . . . . . 10
Fine mixed, . . . . . . . . . . . . . . . . . 10

### PHACELIA, page 40.
congesta, light blue, . . . . . . . . . . . . . 5
tanacetifolia alba, white, . . . . . . . . . . . 5

### PHLOX DRUMMONDII, page 41.
Deep Blood Purple, . . . . . . . . . . . . . . 10
Brilliant Scarlet, . . . . . . . . . . . . . . . 10
Large Blue, white eye, the nearest to blue of the Phloxes, but really a fine purple, . . . . . . 10
rosea, beautiful rose color, . . . . . . . . . . 10
rosea albo-oculata, beautiful rose, with distinct white eye, . . . . . . . . . . . . . . . . . 10
Leopoldii, splendid deep pink, with white eye, 10
Radowitzii, rose, striped with white, . . . . . 10
Radowitzii Kermesina striata, crimson, striped with white, . . . . . . . . . . . . . 10
Radowitzii violacea, violet, striped with white, 10
flore-albo, pure white, . . . . . . . . . . . . 10
flore-albo oculata, pure white with purple eye, 10
Chamois Rose, very delicate and fine; new, . 10
variabilis, violet and lilac, . . . . . . . . . . 10
Isabellina, new; light, dull yellow, . . . . . . 10

Phlox, Violet Queen, violet, with a large white eye, very large, . . . . . . . . . . . . . . . 10
Scarlet Fringed, . . . . . . . . . . . . . . . 10
All varieties mixed, . . . . . . . . . . . . . 10
grandiflora, an improved annual Phlox, with flowers unusually large, round, and of great substance. This we may call a perfect Phlox, . . 25

### POPPY, page 41.
Ranunculus-flowered, small, double, various colors, . . . . . . . . . . . . . . . . . . . 5
Murselli, mixed colors, very showy, double, . . 5
Carnation, double, mixed colors, . . . . . . . 5
Pæony-flowered, large flowers, very double, mixed colors, . . . . . . . . . . . . . . . . 5
somniferum, (Opium Poppy,) true, single, per lb. $2.00; per oz. 20 cents, . . . . . . . 5
somniferum fl. pl., (Double Opium Poppy,) splendid large flowers; mixed colors, . . . . 5

### PORTULACA, page 42.
alba striata, white, striped with rose and red, . 5
caryophylloides, rose, striped with deep carmine, . . . . . . . . . . . . . . . . . . . . 5
New Rose, fine rose color, . . . . . . . . . . 5
Thellussonii, fine crimson, . . . . . . . . . . 5
splendens, rosy purple, . . . . . . . . . . . . 5
aurea, straw-colored, . . . . . . . . . . . . . 5
aurea vera, deep, golden yellow, . . . . . . . 5
aurea striata, sulphur yellow, striped with gold, 5
Fine mixed, . . . . . . . . . . . . . . . . . . 5
Double Rose-flowered, a perfectly double variety, as much so as the most perfect Rose, and of many brilliant colors, as well as striped. First quality, mixed colors, . . . . . . . . . . . . 20
Double Rose-flowered, seven different colors—crimson, rosy purple, rose, white, rose striped with carmine, orange, yellow—each color, . . 25

### RICINUS, page 42.
macrocarpus, whitish foliage, beautiful; 6 feet . 10
purpureus, purple, magnificent; 6 feet, . . . 10
Borboniensis, beautiful, splendid large leaves; 10 feet, . . . . . . . . . . . . . . . . . . . 10
sanguineus, blood red stalks, scarlet fruit, one of the best; 5 feet, . . . . . . . . . . . . . 10
Africanus hybridus, new and fine, stalk and fruit rose; 6 feet, . . . . . . . . . . . . . . 10
giganteus, new, large, fine and showy; 6 feet, . 10
New species from the Phillippines, gigantic leaves; 6 to 10 feet, . . . . . . . . . . . . . . . . 15
nanus microcarpus, dwarf, only 2 to 3 feet in height; fine for outside groups, . . . . . . . 10
communis, (Palma Christi,) common Castor Oil Bean, . . . . . . . . . . . . . . . . . . 5

### SALPIGLOSSIS, page 43.
coccinea, splendid scarlet, . . . . . . . . . . 10
azurea grandiflora, large, blue, . . . . . . . 10
purpurea, purple, . . . . . . . . . . . . . . 10
sulphurea, yellow, . . . . . . . . . . . . . . 10
atrococcinea, deep scarlet, beautifully spotted, . 10
Mixed colors, extra, from selected seed, . . . 10
Dwarf, finest mixed colors, . . . . . . . . . . 10

### SALVIA, page 43.
Rœmeriana, scarlet, beautiful, . . . . . . . . 10
punicea nana, scarlet, dwarf, splendid, tender; 18 inches, . . . . . . . . . . . . . . . . . 10
coccinea, scarlet, small, but good, . . . . . . 10
coccinea splendens, scarlet, large and showy, 10
bicolor, blue and white, . . . . . . . . . . . 10
splendens, true; large, scarlet, . . . . . . . . 25

**SANVITALIA, page 43.**
procumbens flore-pleno, a beautiful, low plant, creeping, with bright, double, yellow flowers, fine for pots, baskets, etc., . . . . . . . . . 10

**SAPONARIA, page 43.**
calabrica, rich, deep pink, . . . . . . . . . 5
alba, white, . . . . . . . . . . . . . . . 5

**SCABIOSA, page 44.**
Dark purple, brick color, dark purple and white, lilac and purple, lilac, white, each color, . . . 5
All colors mixed, . . . . . . . . . . . . . 5
Dwarf, mixed colors, . . . . . . . . . . . 5
stellata, starry seed vessels; excellent for winter bouquets, . . . . . . . . . . . . . . 5
nana fl.-pl. var., double, dwarf Scabiosa. Variety of colors, and a free bloomer, . . . . . 5

**SCHIZANTHUS, page 44.**
grandiflorus oculatus, various shades, fine, blue center, new, . . . . . . . . . . . . 5
pinnatus, rose and purple, very pretty, . . . . 5
retusus, scarlet, rose and orange, . . . . . . 5
retusus albus, white and yellow, . . . . . . 5
Grahami, deep rose, . . . . . . . . . . . 5
papillionaceus, delicately spotted and laced with purple and yellow, shading to orange and crimson 5
Above varieties mixed, . . . . . . . . . . 5

**SENSITIVE PLANT, page 44.**
Mimosa pudica, a tender, sensitive annual, . . 5

**SPRAGUEA, page 45.**
umbellata, a pink flower, in umbels; will dry and keep like Everlastings, . . . . . . . . 25

**STOCK, TEN-WEEKS, page 45.**
New Largest-flowering Dwarf, a plant of dwarf habit, with magnificent large spikes of very large double flowers; all colors mixed, . 20
New Largest-flowering Dwarf, white, flesh-color, rose, rose-carmine, carmine, crimson, light blue, deep blue, lilac, violet, purple, light brown, dark brown, brick red, aurora color, chamois, canary yellow, ash color, etc., each color, 20
New Largest-flowering Dwarf, Blood Red, the richest, deepest colored Stock grown; new, and a great acquisition in color, . . . . . . 20
Newest Large-flowering Pyramidal Dwarf, a plant of pyramidal habit, with long spikes of large flowers, many choice colors mixed, . . . 25
New Large-flowering Pyramidal, Celestial Blue, new and excellent color, . . . . . . . 30
Dwarf German, a fine dwarf variety, very free bloomer, mixed colors, . . . . . . . . . . 20
Branching German, pretty large growth, habit of plant branching, spikes of flowers numerous, long and rather loose, mixed colors, . . . . 20

Stock, Wallflower-leaved, smooth, dark, shining leaves, like the Wallflower, dwarf habit. Set only six inches apart. Mixed colors, . . . . . 20
Early Autumn-flowering, commences flowering in the autumn, and if removed to the house will bloom during the winter; mixed colors, . 25
New Hybrid, the foliage between rough and Wallflower-leaved, flowers large and splendid, mixed colors, . . . . . . . . . . . . . . 20
semperflorens, or Perpetual-flowering, dwarf, free-bloomer, but late in the season, . . . . 20
Large-flowering Dark Blood Red, Wallflower-leaved, new, . . . . . . . . . . . 20

**TROPÆOLUM MINUS, page 46.**
Dark Crimson, . . . . . . . . . . . . . . 10
Crystal Palace Gem, sulphur, spotted with maroon, . . . . . . . . . . . . . . . . 10
Dwarf Spotted, yellow, spotted with crimson, . 10
Tom Thumb Beauty, orange and vermilion, . 10
Tom Thumb Yellow, . . . . . . . . . . . 10
Carter's Tom Thumb, scarlet, . . . . . . . 10
Tom Thumb Rose, a new color in Nasturtions; habit similar to *Scarlet Tom Thumb*, . . . . 10
King of Tom Thumbs, foliage dark bluish green; flowers brilliant scarlet, . . . . . . . 15
King Theodore, flowers very dark, . . . . . 15
Mixed varieties, . . . . . . . . . . . . . 10

**VERBENA, page 46.**
hybrida, choice seed, saved only from the most beautiful named flowers, . . . . . . . . . 20
Striped, excellent flowers, with broad Carnation like stripes. Inclined to sport, . . . . . . . 25
Scarlet, all the brightest scarlet sorts, generally coming quite true, . . . . . . . . . . . . 25
Montana, a hardy Verbena from the Rocky Mountains, that bears our winters well. Flowers bright rose, changing to lilac, . . . . . . 20

**VINCA, page 46.**
rosea, rose; 2 feet, . . . . . . . . . . . . 10
rosea alba, white, red eye, . . . . . . . . . 10
rosea nova spec. pure white, . . . . . . . . 10

**WHITLAVIA, page 47.**
grandiflora, hardy annual, 10 inches high, violet-blue, bell-shaped flowers, . . . . . . . . . 5
grandiflora alba, similar to above, but white, . 5
gloxinoides, an elegant variety of the same habit as *W. grandiflora*, but larger flowers; tube of the corolla pure white, limb delicate light blue, . . . . . . . . . . . . . . . . . . 5

**ZINNIA, page 47.**
Double, Choicest, all the best colors mixed, . 10
Eight separate colors — scarlet, yellow, orange, purple, salmon, etc.— each color, . . . . . 10
Pure white, . . . . . . . . . . . . . . . 10

# CLIMBERS

Nothing can excel the beautiful natural drapery of the Climbers. In the hands of the tasteful gardener they are almost invaluable, transforming an unsightly fence or out-house into an object of real beauty. For arbors, verandahs, etc., all know their value. As the annual Climbers come to perfection in a few weeks they are just the things to cover in a hurry any unsightly spot.

**CALAMPELIS**, page 48.
scabra, (*Eccremocarpus scaber*,) a very beautiful climber, foliage very pretty, flowers bright orange, and produced in racemes; blooms profusely the latter part of the season, . . . . . . 10

**CARDIOSPERMUM**, page 48.
Halicacabum, . . . . . . . . . . . . . . . . . . 10

**COBŒA**, page 49.
scandens, . . . . . . . . . . . . . . . . . . . . 10

**CONVOLVULUS MAJOR**, page 49.
White, . . . . . . . . . . . . . . . . . . . . . . . 5
White and violet striped, . . . . . . . . . . . . 5
White striped with blue, . . . . . . . . . . . . 5
Dark blue, . . . . . . . . . . . . . . . . . . . . . 5
Rose, . . . . . . . . . . . . . . . . . . . . . . . . 5
Lilac, . . . . . . . . . . . . . . . . . . . . . . . . 5
Violet striped, . . . . . . . . . . . . . . . . . . 5
Michauxii, fine striped, . . . . . . . . . . . . 5
incarnata, bright red, . . . . . . . . . . . . . 5
atrosanguinea, dark red, . . . . . . . . . . . 5
tricolor, new and fine, three-colored, . . . . 5
All the above mixed, . . . . . . . . . . . . . . 5

**DOLICHOS**, page 49.
Lablab, (Hyacinth Bean,) a fine climber, with purple and lilac flowers, . . . . . . . . . . 10
albus nanus, white, dwarf, . . . . . . . . . . 10
spec. giganteus, large, free grower, . . . . 10

**GOURDS AND CUCUMBERS**, page 50.
Bryonopsis laciniosa, foliage elegant; fruit scarlet, striped with white, . . . . . . . . 10
Hercules' Club, large, long, club-shaped, . . 10
Smallest Lemon, yellow. . . . . . . . . . . . 10
Pear-formed, yellow and green, striped with cream, . . . . . . . . . . . . . . . . . . . . . 10
Gooseberry, small, bright green, . . . . . . 10
Striped Apple, small, yellow, beautifully striped, 10
Egg-formed, like the fruit of White Egg Plant, 10
Orange, the well known Mock Orange, . . . 10
Calabash, the old-fashioned Dipper Gourd, . . 10
Momordica Balsamina, orange and red. . . . 10
Tricosanthes Colubrina, true Serpent Gourd, striped like a serpent, changing to carmine, . 10
Cucurbita leucantha longissima, . . . . . . . 10
Echinocistis lobata, very strong, free growing climber, with Ivy-like leaf, and small fruit, . . 20
Cucumis dipsaceus, Teasel-like, yellow, . . . 10

**IPOMŒA**, page 50.
limbata elegantissima, large, Convolvulus-like blossoms, of a rich, mazarine blue, with a conspicuous white margin or belt, . . . . . . . . 10
grandiflora superba, fine large flowers, sky-blue, with broad border of white, . . . . . . 10
Bona Nox, (Good Night, or Evening Glory,) flowers large, white, . . . . . . . . . . . . . 10
coccinea, sometimes called Star Ipomœa, with small, scarlet flowers, . . . . . . . . . . . . 10

Ipomœa, Quamoclit, (Cypress Vine,) tender climber; flowers small but elegant and striking; foliage beautiful; mixed colors, . . . . . . . 10
Scarlet, white, rose, each color, . . . . . . . . 10

**LOASA**, page 50.
nitida, yellowish, light green leaves, . . . . . 5
lateritia, large, dark red flowers in abundance, . 10
Herbertii, fine scarlet, . . . . . . . . . . . . . . 10

**MAURANDYA**, page 51.
Barclayana, blue and white, . . . . . . . . . . 10
Barclayana purpurea grandiflora, dark blue, 10
Barclayana Scarlet, mauve, . . . . . . . . . . 10
Finest mixed, . . . . . . . . . . . . . . . . . . . 10

**PEAS, FLOWERING**, page 51.
Scarlet Winged, beautiful, small flowers; low creeper, . . . . . . . . . . . . . . . . . . . . . 10
Yellow Winged, same habit as Scarlet Winged, 10
Sweet, Scarlet Invincible, a beautiful new deep scarlet variety; lb. $1.50; oz. 15 cents, . 10
Scarlet, per lb. $1.50; per oz. 15 cents, . . . . 10
Scarlet, striped with White, per lb. $1.50; per oz. 15 cents, . . . . . . . . . . . . . . . . 10
Painted Lady, rose and white; per lb. $1.50; per oz. 15 cents, . . . . . . . . . . . . . . . . 10
Blue Edged, white and pink, edged with blue; per lb. $2.50; per oz. 20 cents, . . . . . . . 10
White, per lb. $1.50; per oz. 15 cents, . . . . . 10
Black, very dark, brownish purple; per lb. $1.50; per oz. 15 cents, . . . . . . . . . . . . . . . . 10
Black, with light Blue, brownish purple and light blue; per lb. $1.50; per oz. 15 cents, . . 10
All colors mixed; per lb. $1.00; oz. 10 cents, . . 5

**THUNBERGIA**, page 51.
Bakeri, pure white, very fine, . . . . . . . . . 15
alata, yellow or buff, with dark eye. . . . . . . 15
alata unicolor, yellow, . . . . . . . . . . . . . 15
aurantiaca, bright orange, with dark eye, . . . 15
aurantiaca unicolor, bright orange. . . . . . . 15
Above mixed, . . . . . . . . . . . . . . . . . . 15

**TROPÆOLUM**, page 52.
majus, atropurpureum, dark crimson, . . . . . 10
coccineum, scarlet, . . . . . . . . . . . . . . . 10
Dunnett's Orange, dark orange, . . . . . . . . 10
Edward Otto, splendid bronze, silky and glittering, . . . . . . . . . . . . . . . . . . . . . 10
Scheuerianum, straw color, striped with brown, 10
Scheuerianum coccineum, scarlet, striped, . . 20
Schulzii, brilliant scarlet, . . . . . . . . . . . . 10
luteum, yellow, . . . . . . . . . . . . . . . . . 10
Common mixed; the green seed pods used for pickles; per oz. 15 cents, . . . . . . . . . . . 5
peregrinum, (Canary Flower,) . . . . . . . . . 15
Lobbianum, mixed varieties, . . . . . . . . . . 20
Caroline Smith, spotted, . . . . . . . . . . . . 25
Lilli Smith, orange scarlet, . . . . . . . . . . 25
Napoleon III, yellow, striped with vermilion, 25
Giant of Battles, brilliant carmine, . . . . . . 25
Queen Victoria, vermilion, scarlet striped, . . 25

# EVERLASTINGS

The Everlastings have no moisture in their petals, consequently never wilt or decay, but will keep their form as long as a piece of straw. Secured from dust, they retain both color and form for years, and are valuable for winter ornaments.

**ACROCLINIUM, page 53.**
roseum, bright rose color, . . . . . . . . . . . 5
roseum album, pure white, . . . . . . . . . 5
Both colors mixed, . . . . . . . . . . . . . 5

**AMMOBIUM, page 53.**
alatum, white; hardy; 2 feet, . . . . . . . . 5

**GOMPHRENA, page 54.**
globosa, (Globe Amaranth,) alba, pure white, 5
globosa carnea, flesh-colored, . . . . . . . . 5
globosa rubra, dark purplish crimson. . . . . 5
globosa striata, pink and white striped, . . . 5
aurea superba, orange; large and fine. Pick before the lower scales drop, . . . . . . . . . 10
Above mixed, . . . . . . . . . . . . . . . . 5

**HELICHRYSUM, page 54.**
monstrosum, large, showy flowers; variety of colors; double, . . . . . . . . . . . . . . . . 10
monstrosum, Double Rose, fine color, . . . 10
monstrosum, Double Red, very bright, . . . . 10
monstrosum, Double White, pure, . . . . . 10
monstrosum, Double Yellow, . . . . . . . 10
bracteatum, bright yellow; 18 inches, . . . . 10
minimum, dwarf; both flowers and buds excellent for wreaths, etc.; various colors, . . . . . 10
nanum atrosanguineum, brilliant crimson; new; 1 foot, . . . . . . . . . . . . . . . . . 10
brachyrrhinchum, dwarf; 6 inches, . . . . . 10

**HELIPTERUM, page 54.**
Sanfordi, one of the choicest Everlastings; a foot in height; flowers small, rich, yellow, . . . . 15
corymbiflorum, clusters of white, star-like flowers, . . . . . . . . . . . . . . . . . . . 15

**RHODANTHE, page 54.**
Manglesii, fine for house culture, but delicate for out-door; often, however, makes a most beautiful display in the garden, . . . . . . . 10
maculata, more hardy and robust than E. Manglesii; rosy purple, . . . . . . . . . . . . . 10
maculata alba, pure white, yellow disc, . . . 15
atrosanguinea, flowers dark purple and violet, 25

**WAITZIA, page 55.**
aurea, new; fine yellow, . . . . . . . . . . 30
grandiflora, new; flowers large, golden yellow, 25

**XERANTHEMUM, page 55.**
Large Purple-flowered, the largest-flowered, very double and fine, . . . . . . . . . . . . 10
cœruleum, double; light blue, . . . . . . . . 10
cœruleum compactum, very compact, round-headed plant; dwarf, . . . . . . . . . . . 10
Double White, very fine, . . . . . . . . . 10
Mixed colors, . . . . . . . . . . . . . . . . 10

**GYPSOPHILA, page 55.**
elegans, hardy annual; white; 6 inches, . . . . 10
muralis, hardy annual; rose colored flowers, dwarf, . . . . . . . . . . . . . . . . . . . 10
paniculata, perennial; white, . . . . . . . . 10

**STATICE, page 55.**
Bonducella, annual; golden yellow flowers; 1 foot, . . . . . . . . . . . . . . . . . . . 10
Besseriana rosea, perennial; small rose colored flowers; very pretty, . . . . . . . . . . 10
coccinea, perennial; fine, . . . . . . . . . . 10
incana hybrida nana, perennial; mixed colors, 10
latifolia, perennial; one of the best, . . . . . 10
sinuata, beautiful annual; blue flowers; 1 foot, 10
Thouinii, dwarf annual; free flowering, flowers in spikes, . . . . . . . . . . . . . . . . . 10

**ORNAMENTAL GRASSES, page 56.**
Agrostis nebulosa, the most elegant of Ornamental Grasses; fine and feathery; delicate, . . . 10
Steveni, beautiful light panicles, . . . . . . . 10
Andropogon bombycinus, small heads covered with silky hairs; hardy perennial, . . . . . . 25
Arundo Donax variegatis aureus, perennial; strong stem, with golden yellow striped leaves, 6 feet high, . . . . . . . . . . . . . . . . . 15
Avena sterilis, ('Animated Oat,' 30 inches high. 10
Briza maxima, an elegant Shaking Grass, one of the best of the Ornamental Grasses, perfectly hardy; sow in the open ground any time in the spring; 1 foot, . . . . . . . . . . . . . . . 5
geniculata, small, flowers freely, and is always desirable; 8 inches, . . . . . . . . . . . . 5
minor, small and pretty. sow early; 6 inches, 5
compacta, an erect, compact variety of Quaking Grass, . . . . . . . . . . . . . . . . 10
Brizopyrum siculum, dwarf, with shining green leaves, very pretty; 8 inches, . . . . . . . . 5
Bromus brizæformis, a very fine Grass with elegant hanging ears, well adapted for bouquets, either in summer or winter; flowers second summer, something like Briza maxima; 1 foot, . 5
Chloris radiata, small growth and tassel-like, hardy; may be sown in the garden; 1 foot, . 10
Chrysurus cynosuroides, (Lamarkia aurea,) dwarf; yellowish, feathery spikes, . . . . . 5
Erianthus Ravennæ, as fine as Pampas Grass, which it resembles, and very much superior for a Northern climate, being quite hardy. Plants 25 cents each; seeds, . . . . . . . . . . . 10
Coix Lachryma, 'Job's Tears,) grows about two feet, broad, corn-like leaves, . . . . . . . . 10
Gynerium argenteum, 'Pampas Grass, a noble grass, flowers second season, not hardy here, . 10
Hordeum jubatum, (Squirrel Tail Grass,) fine, 10
Isolepis gracilis, perennial; very graceful, fine for flower baskets, . . . . . . . . . . . . . 20
Lagurus ovatus, dwarf; showy heads; called Hare's Tail Grass; 1 foot, sow early, . . . . 5
Panicum sulcatum, perennial; very decorative, with palm shaped foliage, . . . . . . . . . 10
Pennisetum longistylum, a very graceful grass, growing 18 inches, . . . . . . . . . . . . 10
Stipa pennata, 'Feather Grass,) magnificent grass, flowering the second season, . . . . . 15
Trycholæna rosea, a very beautiful rose tinted grass; 2 feet, . . . . . . . . . . . . . . . 10

# PERENNIALS.

The PERENNIALS that are found in this Department do not flower until the second year. As will be seen by the names below, it contains some of our oldest and best flowers, like the Canterbury Bell, Hollyhock, &c. These Perennials, many of them, though wonders of beauty when in bloom, flower only for a limited period, and therefore should be planted a little in the background. They will not answer for a bed on the lawn, which should make a show of flowers all through the summer.

**ADLUMIA, page 57.**
cirrhosa, or Alleghany Vine, and sometimes called Wood Fringe, . . . . . . . . . . . . . 10

**ADONIS, page 58.**
vernalis, a handsome perennial border plant, . 5

**ALYSSUM, page 58.**
saxatile compactum, golden yellow flowers, compact, free growing; 18 inches high, . . . 10

**AQUILEGIA, page 58.**
Carnation, or Striped, white, with broad red stripes; double, . . . . . . . . . . . . . . . 10
Skinneri, very beautiful; colors scarlet and yellow, 10
lucida, light blue, large, strong grower, . . . 10
lucida fl. pl., very double and perfect, . . . . 10
cœrulea, flowers very large; sky blue and white, 25
Mixed varieties, . . . . . . . . . . . . . . . 10

**CAMPANULA, page 58.**
Carpatica, blue and white mixed, . . . . . . 10
Medium, (Canterbury Bell,) flowers large, blue; plant 2 feet in height, . . . . . . . 10
White, . . . . . . . . . . . . . . . . . . . . 10
Rose, . . . . . . . . . . . . . . . . . . . . . 10
Double Rose, . . . . . . . . . . . . . . . . . 10
Double Blue, . . . . . . . . . . . . . . . . . 10
Double White, . . . . . . . . . . . . . . . . 10
Double Lilac, . . . . . . . . . . . . . . . . . 10
calycanthema, a new and beautiful variety, . 50
Single varieties mixed, . . . . . . . . . . . . 10
Double varieties mixed, . . . . . . . . . . . 10
grandiflora, large, star-like, blue and white flowers, . . . . . . . . . . . . . . . . . . 10
Leutweinii, new; splendid light blue and white flowers, as large as Canterbury Bell; dwarf, 1 foot, . . . . . . . . . . . . . . . . . . . . 20

**DIANTHUS, page 59.**
Carnation, German seed from named flowers, . 25
Extra Italian seed, saved from prize flowers only, 50
Choicest, with white ground, . . . . . . . . 50
Choicest, with yellow ground, . . . . . . . . 50
Picotee, German seed, from named flowers only, 25
Italian seed, saved from prize flowers only, . 50
Pink, best double, mixed colors, . . . . . . . 25

**DELPHINIUM, page 60.**
formosum, brilliant blue, with white eye, . . . 10
formosum cœlestinum, new; celestial blue; flowers large, spikes long, . . . . . . . . . 10
nudicaule, a beautiful bright scarlet variety; native of Californian mountains; new, . . . . 25
Chinense, fine; blue, white and pink, mixed, . 5
New varieties mixed, . . . . . . . . . . . . . 5

**DIGITALIS, page 60.**
purpurea, purple flowers; 3 feet, . . . . . . . 5
purpurea alba, white; 3 feet, . . . . . . . . 5

Digitalis, lanata, white and brown; 2 feet, . . 5
gloxinæflora, new; beautifully spotted; 4 feet, 5
Nevadensis, red, purple spots; 3 feet, . . . . 5
ferruginea gigantea, tall and fine, . . . . . . 5
Mixed varieties, . . . . . . . . . . . . . . . 5

**HEDYSARUM, page 60.**
coronarium, fine scarlet, . . . . . . . . . . . 5
coronarium flore albo, white, . . . . . . . . 5

**HOLLYHOCK, page 61.**
Double, very double and fine, from the best named collection in Europe, . . . . . . . 10
Good plants sent out in the spring, of any color desired, each, . . . . . . . . . . . . . . . 50

**HONESTY, page 61.**
Purple, very hardy, free-flowering perennial, . 10

**IPOMOPSIS, page 61.**
aurantiaca, orange, . . . . . . . . . . . . . . 5
Beyrichii, scarlet, . . . . . . . . . . . . . . 5
elegans superba, orange scarlet, . . . . . . . 5
rosea, new; fine, . . . . . . . . . . . . . . . 5
cupreata, new, . . . . . . . . . . . . . . . . 5
Jaune Canarie, canary yellow, . . . . . . . . 5

**LINUM, page 62.**
perenne, blue, . . . . . . . . . . . . . . . . 10
perenne album, white, . . . . . . . . . . . . 10
perenne roseum, beautiful rose colored, . . . 10
luteum, yellow, . . . . . . . . . . . . . . . . 10
Narbonense, splendid, . . . . . . . . . . . . 10

**PAPAVER, page 62.**
bracteatum, scarlet; 3 feet, . . . . . . . . . 10
croceum, orange; 1 foot, . . . . . . . . . . . 10
orientale, very large, red; 3 feet, . . . . . . 10
involucratum maximum, fine large flowers, . 10

**PENTSTEMON, page 62.**
Wrightii, splendid scarlet, . . . . . . . . . . 15
Murrayanus, magnificent vermilion, . . . . . 25
cordifolius, scarlet; fine for conservatory, . . 25
gentianoides coccinea, splendid scarlet, . . . 25
grandiflorus, lilac-purple; 3 to 4 feet in height, 10
barbatus Torreyii, fine; crimson and yellow, . 10
Mixed varieties, . . . . . . . . . . . . . . . 15

**PEAS, PERENNIAL, page 63.**
Lathyrus latifolius, red, . . . . . . . . . . . 15
latifolius albus, white, . . . . . . . . . . . . 25
latifolius roseus, rose-colored, . . . . . . . . 15
grandiflorus splendens, large-flowered; showy 25
rotundifolius, round leaves; purple, . . . . . 25
Mixed varieties, . . . . . . . . . . . . . . . 15

**PRIMULA, page 63.**
auricula, fine mixed, . . . . . . . . . . . . . 25
auricula, from named flowers, . . . . . . . . 50
elatior, (Polyanthus,) . . . . . . . . . . . . . 10
vulgaris, common wild English Primrose, . . 10

## PYRETHRUM, page 63.
hybrida, double varieties mixed, . . . . . . . . 25
Parthenium flore-pleno, the double Feverfew, 10
parthenifolium aureum, Golden Feather, prized for its yellow foliage, . . . . . . . . 10

## ROCKET, page 64.
Sweet Purple, . . . . . . . . . . . . . . . 5
Sweet White, . . . . . . . . . . . . . . . 5

## STOCK, page 64.
Brompton, Violet, dwarf habit; new, beautiful, 25
White, . . . . . . . . . . . . . . . . . . . 25
Carmine, the largest-flowering and most beautiful of the winter Brompton Stocks, . . . . 35
Best mixed colors, . . . . . . . . . . . . 25
Emperor, hybrid between Brompton and Annual, 25
Tree Giant Cape Winter, . . . . . . . . . 25

## SWEET WILLIAM, page 64.
Perfection, . . . . . . . . . . . . . . . . 10
Common Double, . . . . . . . . . . . . . 10
Dunetti, blood red; velvety texture, . . . . . . 10

## VALERIANA, page 65.
coccinea, fine scarlet, . . . . . . . . . . . . 5
rubra, red, . . . . . . . . . . . . . . . . . 5
alba, white, . . . . . . . . . . . . . . . . 5

## WALLFLOWER, page 65.
Fine mixed colors; double, . . . . . . . . . 20

## DICTAMNUS, page 65.
Fraxinella, seedling plants, 30 cents; seeds, . . 15

## HARDY CLIMBERS.
The following are Perennial Climbers, and all useful for covering Arbors, Porches, etc. They are hardy and hard-wooded. Seeds, 10 cents; plants, 50 cents.
Ampelopsis quinquefolia, Virginia Creeper.
Bignonia radicans, Trumpet-Vine.
Celastrus scandens, climbing Bitter-Sweet.
Clematis flammula, European Sweet, white.
Clematis Vitalba, Virgin's Bower, white.

## GREENHOUSE.

For Suggestions on Greenhouse Culture, see page 66 of Flower and Vegetable Garden.

Abutilon, finest varieties mixed, . . . . . . . 50
Boston Smilax, (Myrsiphyllum asparagoides,) the most popular plant now known for decorative purposes; fine climber, furnishing yards of glossy green trimming, . . . . . . . . . . . 25
Calceolaria hybrida tigrina, spotted; seeds saved from the best collection in Europe, . . 50
hybrida tigrina nana, six or eight inches in height, and of very compact habit, . . . . . 50
hybrida grandiflora, very large, superb flowers, 50
James' International Prize, saved from the choicest varieties only, . . . . . . . . . . . 50
Campanula Vidalis, white; very showy, . . . 25
Carnation, Remontant, or Tree Carnation, choicest Italian seed, . . . . . . . . . . . . 50
Centaurea gymnocarpa, desirable for its delicately cut and graceful white foliage, . . . . 25
candidissima, an effective white-leaved bedding plant, . . . . . . . . . . . . . . . . 25
Chrysanthemum Indicum, finest double, . . . 25
Pompon, or Dwarf, splendid; seeds from choicest named flowers, . . . . . . . . . . 25
Cineraria hybrida, of first quality; most perfect, 25
hybrida, New Dwarf, of compact growth, . . 25
maritima, white foliaged plant, similar to the Centaureas, . . . . . . . . . . . . . . . . 10
Clianthus Dampieri, magnificent green-house shrubby climber, fine foliage and clusters of brilliant scarlet flowers. Finely adapted for outdoor culture in the Southern States, as it delights in great heat and a light, sandy soil. In California it grows most luxuriantly in the dry season. We keep it in the house in the winter, and put it out in the spring, . . . . . . . . . . 20
Dampieri, new varieties mixed, . . . . . . . 50
Convolvulus mauritanicus, desirable for hanging baskets, bearing many lavender blue flowers, 10

Cuphea platycentra, Cigar, or Fire Cracker plant, 25
Fuchsia, choice mixed, . . . . . . . . . . . 50
Geranium, common mixed, . . . . . . . . . 25
Choicest fancy varieties, mixed sorts, packet of 5 seeds, . . . . . . . . . . . . . . . . 50
Apple-scented, . . . . . . . . . . . . . . 25
Gloxinia hybrida, best quality, choice flowers, from Benary's choice collection, . . . . . . 50
hybrida erecta, fine variety; upright flowers, . 50
Heliotrope, best mixed, . . . . . . . . . . . 15
Hibiscus immutabilis, rosy flowers; 3 feet, . . 10
coccinea, scarlet; 3 feet, . . . . . . . . . . 15
Humea elegans, a beautiful ornamental biennial, 4 feet high, with graceful dark flowers, . . . 10
Lantana, finest mixed, . . . . . . . . . . . . 15
Mandevilla suaveolens, ornamental climber, . . 15
Nerium Oleander, common Oleander, . . . . 10
Passion Flower, several choice varieties, desirable for green-house culture, . . . . . . . . 25
Passiflora coerulea, the most hardy of the Passion Flowers, . . . . . . . . . . . . . . . . 15
Primula Sinensis (Chinese Primrose,) fimbriata rubra, red; extra, . . . . . . . . . 50
fimbriata alba, white; extra, . . . . . . . . 50
fimbriata striata, new; white, fringed, striped with red, . . . . . . . . . . . . . . . . . 50
fimbriata erecta superba, new; fine variety, 50
fimbriata erecta superba albo-violascens, pure white on opening, changing to lilac-violet with red border; habit very fine; free bloomer, 75
Above varieties mixed, . . . . . . . . . . . 50
Fern-leaved, very pretty fern-like foliage, . . . 50
flore-pleno, a large per centage of the flowers perfectly double, and good colors, . . . . . . 1.50
Solanum ciliatum, very fine; red-fruited, fruit hanging on the plant a long time, . . . . . . 10
Tropæolum pentaphyllum, . . . . . . . . . . 25

## TENDER BULBS AND TUBERS.

The Tender or Summer Bulbs, in all places subject to winter frosts, must be planted in the spring. In August or September they are in perfection. Before hard frost the Bulbs must be taken up and stored away in some place secure from frost until spring. We need say nothing more of the great beauty of this class of Bulbs than merely to mention the fact that the *Gladiolus*, the *Dahlia* and the *Tuberose* are its leading members. When Seeds and Bulbs are ordered together, the Seeds will be sent at once, and the Bulbs as soon as possible without danger of injury from frost. The figures show the price of each bulb.

### GLADIOLUS.

[See pages 67 and 68 Flower and Vegetable Garden.]

Addison, rose tinged, with lilac white ground, . $2.00
Adonis, large cherry, marbled with white, .... 15
Agatha, large flower; rose, orange-tinged, blazed with amaranth and yellow spotted, ...... 25
Amalthee, pure white, with red blotch, lower petals tinted with lilac, .............. 2.50
Ambroise Verschaffelt, carmine, garnet flamed, 2.50
Andromede, new; very tall spike, rose tinted with carmine, striped with white, ........ 4.00
Anna, cherry, orange tinged, cherry stripe on white ground, .................. 1.00
Aramis, long spike, large flowers, rose, tinged with orange, edged with carmine cherry ; lower division white, striped with bright carmine, ... 1.00
Arethuse, white, rose tinted, carmine striped, 3.00
Argus, fire-red center, lower petals white, .... 75
Ariane, white ground, tinged with rosy lilac, lower petals white, ................ 3.00
Armida, white slightly tinged with carmine, ... 3.00
Arsinoe, satin rose, flamed with carmine, .... 1.00
Asmodee, cherry purple, white stain and stripes, 3.00
Astree, new ; white with carmine blotch, beautifully striped ; extra, .............. 3.50
Athalia, long spike, large flowers, violet, slightly tinted with rose, blazed with purple, ..... 1.25
Beatrix, white ground, flushed with carmine lilac, 3.00
Belladonna, white, tinted with lilac, lower petals striped with carmine, ............ 3.00
Belle Gabrielle, lilac, rose and carmine, .... 50
Benvenuto, orange red, with white blotch, ... 2.50
Bernard de Jussieu, large, violet ground, shaded with cherry, stains purple on white ground, . . 45
Bertha Rabourdin, white, blotched with carmine, 30
Bijou, light cherry, flamed with scarlet, ..... 20
Bowiensis, vermilion scarlet ; very tall spike ; in flower a long time, ............. 15
Brenchleyensis, vermilion scarlet ; fine old variety 15
Calypso, flesh colored rose, blotched with carmine, 25
Canary, light yellow, rose striped, sometimes pink, 25
Cassini, rose, flamed with carmine, ....... 2.50
Celimene, light orange red, flamed with bright red, 1.50
Celine, rosy white, streaked with rose and purple, 15
Ceres, white, marbled and striped with rose and purple, .................. 35
Charles Dickens, light, tinted with chamois, and blazed and striped with carmine, ....... 35
Chateaubriand, cherry rose, carmine streaked, 25
Citrinus, a very fair yellow, ........... 45
Cleopatra, large flower ; soft lilac, violet tinged, . 75
Colbert, long spike, cherry red, tinted with orange divisions lined with white, ......... 25

Conde, long spike, large flowers, light orange red, white stain, striped with carmine, ...... $0 50
Coralie, white, tinted with rose and yellow, blazed with bright rose, stain yellow ; dwarf, .... 60
Cybelle, new ; white flamed with carmine, ... 3.00
De Candolle, cherry, suffused with red, ..... 60
De Humboldt, magenta, bright crimson border, . 2.00
Delicatissima, white, tinged with carmine lilac, . 1.50
De Mirbel, rose, tinted with lilac violet, striped with dark crimson, ............. 3.00
Didon, white and lilac ; large and fine, ..... 1.00
Don Juan, fiery orange red, whitish veins, .... 15
Dr. Lindley, large, ground delicate rose, edges of petals brighter rose, ............ 60
Edith Dombrain, long spike, large flowers, white ground, blazed with dark carmine, ...... 3.00
Eldorado, pure yellow, slightly striped with purple, 25
Elvire, white, flamed with carmine, ....... 3.00
Etendard, large flower, white. blazed with lilac, . 60
Eugene Scribe, flower large and wide, rose, blazed with carmine red ; very fine, ..... 35
Eurydice, white, shaded off to bright carmine, . . 75
Eva, spike long, flower large, white, violet-tinged, 2.50
Fanny Rouget, bright rose, striped with carmine, 15
Fenelon, rose, violet-tinged, flamed with carmine, 75
Flavia, very deep red, splendid white throat, . . 25
Ginevra, new ; cherry rose flushed with red, each center of petal veined with white, ...... 4.00
Giganteus, new ; large flower, rose shading to cherry, carmine blotch, whole flower stained with white, ................ 3.50
Gil Blas, cherry red, variegated with carmine, . . 25
Goliah, light rosy red, base striped with carmine, . 15
Grand Lilas, new ; delicate lilac, novel shade, . 4.00
Henrietta, large flower, white, tinted with lilac, . 50
Hercules, new ; very large flower ; scarlet, flamed with orange red, violet blotch, ........ 5.00
Homer, light amaranth, blazed with bright purple, 1.50
Horace Vernet, long spike of large flowers, bright purplish red, pure white stain, ........ 3.00
Ida, large flower, white, rose-tinted, blazed with carmine rose, ............... 20
Imperatrice, white, striped and dashed with carmine 15
Imperatrice Eugenie, (*Souchet*,) large flowers, white, blazed with violet rose inside, and violet lilac outside, ............... 60
James Carter, light orange red, very bright, with a large, pure white throat, .......... 25
James Watt, large flower, light vermilion, pure white throat, striped to tip of petals, ..... 60
John Bull, whitish, sometimes striped with lilac, . 20
Juno, white, lilac-striped, purple stains in throat, 75
Jupiter, large flower, light red, blazed with dark crimson, ................. 3.00

La Candeur, large flower, white, slightly striped
  with violet, . . . . . . . . . . . . . . . . . . 2.00
La Favorite, large flower, rose and dark carmine,
  lower divisions light yellow, . . . . . . . . . 60
La Fiancee, pure white, with bluish violet stains, 75
La Poussin, light red, white ground ; very pretty, 35
Leda, new ; bright flesh, striped with lilac carmine, 4.50
Le Phare, brilliant fiery red ; very showy, . . . . 3.00
Le Tintoret, cherry rose, carmine blotch on yellow
  ground, . . . . . . . . . . . . . . . . . . . . 3.00
Le Vesuve, intense fiery red ; very rich, . . . . 4.00
Lord Byron, brilliant scarlet, stained and rib-
  boned with pure white, . . . . . . . . . . . . 30
Lord Granville, light yellow, stained with deep
  yellow and striped with lilac, . . . . . . . . 30
Lord Raglan, salmon, spotted with scarlet, ver-
  milion throat, . . . . . . . . . . . . . . . . 30
L'Ornement des Parterres, white ground, blazed
  with lilac rose and carmine, . . . . . . . . . 30
Louis Van Houtte, velvety carmine, branches
  freely, and flowers a long time, . . . . . . . 15
Lulli, bright cherry, lower petals carmine-streaked, 2.50
L' Unique Violet, dark lilac, tinted with violet, . 4.00
Lydia, new ; white striped with carmine, yellow
  ground with carmine blotch, . . . . . . . . . . 4.00
Macauley, large, bright crimson, violet stained, . 3.00
Madame Binder, white, purple and lilac striped, . 40
Madame Desportes, large, white, inferior divi-
  sions striped with white, . . . . . . . . . . . 2.50
Madame Furtado, rose, with carmine rose, large, 75
Madame Leseble, white, purplish rose stains, . . 45
Madame Place, rosy pink, white base and stripes, 45
Madame Sosthene des Jardins, white, with car-
  mine stripe ; very late, . . . . . . . . . . . 20
Madame Vilmorin, rose, with white center, and
  edged with dark rose, fine, . . . . . . . . . . 60
Marechal Vaillant, deep pink, white throat and
  stripes, splendid, . . . . . . . . . . . . . . 1.25
Margarita, white, suffused with dark crimson, . . 1.50
Marie, white, stained with carmine, . . . . . . . 35
Mars, beautiful scarlet, . . . . . . . . . . . . . 25
Mary Stuart, white, rose tinged, carmine flamed, . 1.50
Mathilda de Landevoisin, very large, rosy white,
  shaded with carmine, . . . . . . . . . . . . . 30
Mazeppa, rosy orange, large yellow stains, striped
  with carmine, fine, . . . . . . . . . . . . . . 20
Merville, cherry rose, flamed with carmine, with
  lighter center, . . . . . . . . . . . . . . . . 4.00
Meteor, dark red, brilliant, pure white stain, . . 60
Meyerbeer, red, blazed with vermilion, . . . . . . 75
Michel Ange, dark crimson and purple, with white, 2.50
Minerve, crimson, carmine feathered, with white, 2.50
Mons. Legouve, fiery red with blotch, white line
  on each petal . . . . . . . . . . . . . . . . . 1.50
Murillo, rose, white blotch and line on each petal, 4.00
Nelly, white, carminate rose, dark stain, . . . . 25
Nestor, yellow, lower part darker, striped with red, 1.25
Newton, dark red, light ground, lined with white, 60
Octavia, light rose, blazed with red, white stain, . 3.00
Ondine, white, tinted with lilac, violet blotch, . . 2.50
Ophir, dark yellow, mottled with purple, . . . . 40
Osiris, purple, marked with white, dwarf, late, . . 20
Ossian, bright rose, violet and carmine tinted, light
  ground, . . . . . . . . . . . . . . . . . . . . 1.25
Pactole, new ; yellow tinged with rose at the edges,
  blotch of darker shade, . . . . . . . . . . . . 1.50
Phebus, fire red, with large showy white stain, . 3.00
Phedre, long spike, pure white, bordered and blazed
  with cherry rose, . . . . . . . . . . . . . . . 2.50
Phidias, fine spike, brilliant purple, violet-tinted,
  white stain, striped with cherry, . . . . . . . 2.50

Picciola, satin rose, carmine-flamed, white blotch, . 60
Picturata, carmine lilac, flamed with violet, dark
  carmine blotch, . . . . . . . . . . . . . . . . 50
Primatice, long spike, large flowers, fine rose, lilac-
  tinged, blazed with bright carmine, carmine stain
  on white ground ; showy, . . . . . . . . . . . 1.00
Prince Imperial, very large, white, slightly flesh-
  colored, stained with carmine and violet, . . . 15
Prince of Wales, bright fiery red, white-stained
  and violet-striped, . . . . . . . . . . . . . . 75
Princess Marie de Cambridge, large flower,
  white, with carmine stains, . . . . . . . . . . 2.00
Princess of Wales, white, blazed with carmine
  and rose, stained with deep carmine, . . . . . 25
Psyche, satin rose, bordered with dark crimson,
  with lighter center, . . . . . . . . . . . . . 5.00
Queen Victoria, very large flower, pure white,
  stained with carmine ; splendid, . . . . . . . 25
Racine, cherry, tinged with violet, white center, . 50
Rebecca, white, shaded with lilac, . . . . . . . . 20
Redoute, large flowers, fine rose, tinted with violet,
  blazed with bright carmine, white stain, . . . 75
Reine Blanche, pure white, dark crimson blotch, 1.50
Richard Cœur-de-Lion, new ; large flower ; crim-
  son red, flamed with garnet, . . . . . . . . . 3.50
Roi Leopold, rose, crimson-blazed, carnation stripe, 40
Rosa Bonheur, white and lilac, stain dark violet, 2.50
Rosea Perfecta, fine rose, tinged violet, center
  light, white veins, . . . . . . . . . . . . . . 1.00
Rossini, long spike, amaranth red, lined with
  white, . . . . . . . . . . . . . . . . . . . . 75
Rubis, carmine, cherry center, light carmine blotch
  on white, . . . . . . . . . . . . . . . . . . . 60
Sappho, long spike, large, fine cherry, orange-tinted,
  lower division white-stained, bright red-striped, 1.50
Shakspeare large and perfect shape, white, blazed
  and stained with carmine rose, . . . . . . . . 1.50
Sirene, delicate rose, flamed with red, red blotch on
  yellow ground, . . . . . . . . . . . . . . . . 2.50
Sir John Franklin, long spike, large flowers, fine
  satin-like rose, inferior divisions white, . . 2.50
Spectabilis, delicate rose, shaded to cherry, pur-
  ple blotch on white, . . . . . . . . . . . . . 75
Sulphureus, sulphur colored, . . . . . . . . . . . 25
Sultana, satin rose, flamed with carmine, purplish
  blotch on white, . . . . . . . . . . . . . . . 2.00
Surprise, rose amaranth ; dwarf ; very late ; this
  and Mad. Sosthene des Jardins do finely only
  with a long season, . . . . . . . . . . . . . . 10
Sylphide, white, flamed with carmine, large purple
  carmine blotch, . . . . . . . . . . . . . . . . 1.50
Sylvie, new ; white edged with cherry rose, throat
  clear, . . . . . . . . . . . . . . . . . . . . 3.00
Talisman, long spike, large flowers, violet, carmine
  cherry, ground white, divisions lined with white, 3.00
Themis, new ; satin rose flushed with carmine,
  cream blotch, . . . . . . . . . . . . . . . . . 4.00
Triumphans, cherry, shading off to currant red, . 2.50
Van Spandonk, long spike, fine flowers, fiery
  red, . . . . . . . . . . . . . . . . . . . . . 1.50
Velleda, delicate rose, lilac stains, large flower, . 45
Venus, long spike, ground pure white, blazed with
  light rose, . . . . . . . . . . . . . . . . . . 3.00
Virginalis, pure white, bordered and flamed with
  carmine, . . . . . . . . . . . . . . . . . . . 3.00
Variabilis, white, sometimes blotched and flamed
  with lilac, . . . . . . . . . . . . . . . . . . 3.00
Zelinda, long spike, rose, carmine-blazed, dwarf, 1.00
Zenobia, fine spike, rose, violet-tinted, blazed with
  dark carmine, center well lighted, white stain
  edged with carmine, fine, . . . . . . . . . . . 20

## MIXED GLADIOLUS.

**FULLY ONE-HALF AMERICAN SEEDLINGS.**

Very fine Mixed Varieties, of various shades of red, per doz., 75c.; half doz., . . . . . . . 40
Fine Mixed Varieties of light colors and white, per doz., $1.50; half doz., . . . . . . . . . . . 75
Fine Mixed Varieties, assorted colors, per doz., 75c.; half doz., . . . . . . . . . . . . . . . 40
Mixed Gladiolus, assorted colors, per 100, . . . 5.00
Mixed Gladiolus, light and white, per 100, . . . 8.00

Not less than 50 at 100 rates.

## DAHLIAS, pages 68 and 69.

Tubers can be sent as soon as danger from frost is passed—about first of April. Price, except in the select list of scarce sorts, 30 cents each, and $3.00 per dozen. To those who wish to make a large collection, or plant extensive beds, we will sell at $20.00 per hundred, our selection.

### GENERAL COLLECTION.

Acme of Perfection, yellow.
Ada Tiffin, light peach tinged with rose.
Adonis, French white, tipped with lilac.
Alexander Cramond, crimson and maroon.
Amy Creed, yellow and salmon.
Arthur, deep lilac, full size.
Autumn Glow, saffron red.
Bird of Passage, white, tipped with pink.
Bishop of Durham, deep buff.
Blushing Fifteen, rosy lilac, perfect form.
British Triumph, rich crimson.
Buck's Lass, buff yellow, tipped with white.
Butterfly, scarlet and brown stripes, light ground.
Carnation, clear white flaked with rosy purple.
Caroline Tetterell, white, slight lilac tip.
Celestial, bluish lilac.
Charles Turner, yellow, edged with crimson.
Chairman, buff.
Copperhead, copper color; large flower.
Constance, blush, fine form.
Cremorne, yellow, tipped with rose, fine; new.
Crown Prince, dark maroon.
Duchess of Cambridge, blush tipped with lake.
Earl of Radnor, plum, large and fine.
Ebor, chocolate, dark maroon stripes.
Emily, blush, suffused with rose.
Emily Williams, light ground, edged with vermillion.
Emperor, bright claret, tinted purple.
Fancy Boy, light scarlet.
Fancy Queen, dark cherry, white tip.
Fanny Purchase, bright yellow.
Firefly, deep scarlet.
Flamingo, vermilion scarlet.
Flora Wyatt, orange, flaked with red.
Flossie Williams, violet flaked, great depth and substance.
Flossy Gill, light, heavily edged with violet purple.
Formosa, pale pink.
Glory of Summer, rich, glowing salmon scarlet.
Golden Eagle, yellow, heavy red tip.
Grand Sultan, buff, striped with red.
Hero of York, crimson, striped with maroon.
High Sheriff, very dark
Incomparable, yellow, heavy claret tip, fine and large.
James Cocker, purple, fine color and form.
James Wilder, rich velvet maroon.
Jenny Deans, orange, striped with purple.
J. Neville Keynes, large, shaded yellow.
John Harrison, very dark maroon.
John Powell, buff, tinted rose.
John Standish, bright red.
King of Primroses, primrose yellow.
Lady Bird, rose ground, shaded.
Lady Derby, blush, purple tip.
Lady Dunmore, yellow, crimson and white.
Lady Jane Ellis, cream, tipped with purplish rose.
Lady Paxton, red, tipped with white.
Lady Popham, white, tipped with lavender.
Livonia, fine shaded lilac; free, and good flower.
Lord Napier, bright purple; a fine dark variety.
Lord Salisbury, lake.
Lothair, yellow, deeply edged with carmine.
Lottie Atkins, white and lilac; small.
Madame Zahler, yellow, tipped with rose.
Maid of Essex, pale, tipped purple rose.
Marchioness of Lorne, yellow, edged purple.
Marquis of Lorne, light, striped purple.
Mirefield Beauty, fine red.
Miss Bateman, yellow, delicately suffused with red
Monarch, large, dark, sometimes tipped.
Mr. Dix, crimson scarlet.
Mr. Sinclair, rose, tipped with purple.
Mrs. Bennett, fine shaded lilac.
Mrs. Brunton, white, laced deep purple.
Mrs. Bunn, creamy white, striped with purple.
Mrs. Dorling, light ground, purple tip; constant.
Mrs. Fordham, French white, tipped with purple.
Mrs. Waite, French white.
Nelly, white, tipped with purple; new and distinct.
Nemesis, white, shaded blush.
Nettie Buckell, light blush, tinted pink; fine.
One in the Ring, yellow, edged purple.
Othello, dark purple.
Paradise Williams, bright claret, always ready, good for cutting.
Pauline, buff, distinct white tip.
Poins de Belge, a standard white variety.
Prince Arthur, clear yellow.
Princess, white, large, free bloomer.
Princess of Wales, blush, slightly lilac edged.
Provost, salmon and buff, fine flower.
Purity, white, medium size; constant.
Queen of Beauties, straw, purple tip.
Queen of Sports, white and lilac, purple striped.
Queen of York, blush, edged violet purple.
Redan, deep buff, good form.
Rev. J. B. M. Camm, yellow, flaked with red.
Richard Dean, yellow, flaked crimson.
Rose Unique, soft rosy purple.
Rosy Queen, rosy purple.
Royalty, golden yellow, dark tips at center.
Sarah Read, straw, edged rosy purple.
Snowdrift, clear white, full flower.
Startler, dark with white tip.
Summertide, chocolate, white tipped and striped.
Thomas Goodwin, very dark, large.
Thomas White, fine dark crimson maroon.
Vice President, orange buff, free.
William Newman, pure purple.
Wm. Keynes, fine, orange.
Wm. Lucas, yellow, lightly edged with puce
Woman in White, large, white.
Wonderful, lilac, purple flakes.
Yellow Boy, deep yellow.

### POMPON OR BOUQUET.

Ardens, brilliant scarlet.
Bird of Roses, rose, tipped with carmine.
Burning Coal, yellow, with intense scarlet tip
Cochineal Rose, cochineal red.

Conflagration, orange, tinted scarlet.
Crusader, pale yellow, slightly tipped.
Dr. Schwebes, crimson scarlet.
Emotion, crimson, tipped with white.
Herman, pale yellow with white tips.
Infancy, pure white.
Little Bird of Kostriz, blush, tipped with carmine.
Little Bob, fine, deep scarlet.
Little Fireball, bright scarlet.
Little Goldlight, gold, tipped with scarlet.
Little Julius, carmine red.
Little Lina, blush, tipped with violet purple.
Little Madonna, crimson, tipped with white.
Little Minnie, red, tipped white.
Little Model, rosy crimson.
Little Philip, creamy buff, edged with lilac.
Little Virginie, bright rosy purple.
Lurline, primrose yellow.
Patti, rosy ground, tipped with carmine.
Sappho, rich shaded maroon crimson.
Seraph, buff, tipped with orange red.
White Aster, pure white.

#### DWARFS OR BEDDERS.

Alba Floribunda, white, free bloomer.
Dawn, creamy ground, tipped with rose.
Dwarf Queen, purple, tipped with white.
Gem of the Dwarfs, red, tipped with white.
Golden Bedder, fine yellow.
Goldfinder, golden yellow.
Leah, fine shade of orange, tinted with rose.
Mt. Blanc, clear white.
Orange Boven, orange.
Pearl, pearly white.
Puritanii, primrose yellow.
Queen Victoria, canary yellow.
Rising Sun, large, scarlet.
Royal Purple, fine purple.
Sambo, dark maroon.

#### NEW VARIETIES.

This section embraces new and scarce varieties.
Price, 60 cents each; $6.00 per dozen.

Duke of Cambridge, shaded orange.
Duke of Edinburg, deep yellow.
Florence Pontin, white ground, crimson tip.
Gil Blas, crimson and purple on buff.
Harlequin, white striped with purple.
Herbert Purchase, rosy ground, mottled crimson stripe.
Herbert Turner, French white, tinged with lilac.
Her Majesty, white, deeply edged purple.
James Service, dark crimson.
Jennie, white, delicately edged rose.
John Sealey, lilac, striped purple.
Julia Davis, clear yellow.
Letty Coles, rose, striped red.
Lord Hawke, yellowish buff, tinged with red.

Maggie Smith, fine blush, perfect form.
Miss Dennis, white, tipped with lilac.
Mrs. Lewington, rosy purple.
Mrs. Saunders, yellow, with white; extra fine.
Mrs. Stancomb, canary yellow, tipped fawn.
Negro Boy, dark shaded maroon.
Orient, light, distinctly striped and marked with purple.
Ovid, dark purple.
Parrot, yellow, striped with scarlet.
Queen's Messenger, fine purple.
Rival, most beautiful new purple.
Spot, light ground, spotted and striped.
The Pet, dark ground, tipped with white.
Willie Eckford, shaded crimson, [bedder.]

### CANNA, page 70.
Good roots, $2.50 per dozen, each, . . . . . . . 25

### CALADIUM ESCULENTUM, page 70.
One of the most showy foliage plants; roots, . . 50

### OXALIS, page 70.
lasiandra. Per 100, 2.50; per dozen, . . . . . 25

### TUBEROSE, page 71.
Large flowering tubers, $1.50 per dozen; each, . . 15
New Dwarf Tuberose, "Pearl," per dozen, $2.50; each, . . . . . . . . . . . . . . . 25

### MADEIRA VINE, page 71.
A beautiful climber for the house or garden; 75c. per dozen; each, . . . . . . . . . . . . . . . 10

### TIGRIDIA, page 72.
conchiflora, yellow and orange, with dark spots; $1.50 per dozen; each, . . . . . . . . . . . . 15
pavonia, red crimson spots; $1.50 per dozen; each, . . . . . . . . . . . . . . . . . . . . 15

### AMARYLLIS, page 72.
Valotta purpurea, Brilliant scarlet flowers; bulbs, each, . . . . . . . . . . . . . . . . 75

### ERYTHRINA, page 72.
Crista-galli, Dark carmine coral-like flowers; the roots can be kept like Dahlias; each, . . . 50

### TRITOMA, page 73.
uvaria, or Red-Hot Poker, fine roots, per dozen, $3.00; each, . . . . . . . . . . 30

### CALLA, page 73.
Calla, or Egyptian Lily. Our Calla roots are unusually large and fine, as we have them grown for us in California, where the Calla is perfectly at home and grows magnificently, . . . . . . 50

### BEGONIA.
Tuberous-rooted varieties, dry roots, . . . . . . 75
These bulbs produce fine plants either for pots in summer or for bedding out, flowering profusely till frost comes, and doing well either in the shade or sun.

# HARDY PLANTS, BULBS, &c.

**ANEMONE, page 74.**
Japonica alba, flowers white; blossoms in fall, . . 25
Coronaria, dry roots, double mixed, per dozen, . 25
Dry roots, single mixed, per dozen, . . . . . 25

**DAY LILY, page 74.**
White, . . . . . . . . . . . . . . . . . 30
Blue, . . . . . . . . . . . . . . . . . . 20

**LILIES.**
(See pages 75, 76, 77, 78 and 79.)
|  | each. | doz. |
|---|---|---|
| auratum, the magnificent Japan Lily, . . | $0.50 | $5.00 |
| atrosanguineum, red, orange-marbled, . | 25 | 2.50 |
| candidum, common white, . . . . . . . | 25 | 2.50 |
| excelsum, delicate, cream or buff, . . . | 1.00 | |
| speciosum album, (*Præcox*,) new, white, . | 2.00 | |
| Chalcedonicum, scarlet, . . . . . . . . | 1.00 | |
| Japonicum longiflorum, white, trumpet-shaped; 5 inches long, . . . . . . . | 25 | 2.50 |
| Takesima, large, trumpet-shaped, . . . | 75 | |
| Eximium, large, white, trumpet-shaped, . | 75 | |
| lancifolium rubrum, white and red, . . . | 25 | 2.50 |
| lancifolium roseum, white and rose, . . | 25 | 2.50 |
| lancifolium, extra large bulbs of the above, . | 50 | 5.00 |
| lancifolium album, white, . . . . . . | 50 | 5.00 |
| lancifolium punctatum, . . . . . . . . | 75 | |
| tigrinum, Tiger Lily, . . . . . . . . . | 20 | 2.00 |
| Thunbergianum citrinum, citron yellow, with dark spots; dwarf, . . . . | 35 | 3.50 |
| Thunbergianum grandiflorum, large cluster of dark red flowers; 2 feet, . . | 25 | 2.50 |
| Washingtonianum, white, changing to pink, . . . . . . . . . . . . . . | 1.00 | |
| Bloomerianum, or Humboldtii, yellow, spotted, . . . . . . . . . . . . . | 75 | |
| Pardalinum, yellow and red, spotted, . . | 75 | |
| Parvum, rich, dark yellow, red spots, . . | 1.00 | |
| croceum, orange, . . . . . . . . . . | 20 | 2.00 |
| Canadense, our native Lily, . . . . . . | 25 | 2.50 |

**PÆONIES.**
(See page 80.)
Fragrans, one of the best pink varieties, fragrant, . 25
Double White, . . . . . . . . . . . . . . 50
Active, rose, very large flower and very compact . 35
Alice, outside petals white, center yellow, . . . 35
Amabilis lilacina, outside petals blush, center cream and white, . . . . . . . . . . . . . 35
Amabilis lilaceus, outside petals blush, inner petals buff, center blush, . . . . . . . . . . . . 35
Anemoneflora alba, outside petals pale rose, center cream and rose, . . . . . . . . . . . 35
Anemoneflora striata, outer petals rosy violet, inside rose and salmon, . . . . . . . . : 35
Beauté Francaise, outside rose, center salmon, . 35
Buchanan, outside petals blush, center white with crimson markings, . . . . . . . . . . . 35
Buyckii, rose, shaded with salmon, . . . . . . 35
Centripetala, outside petals pink, second row fringed, center full, . . . . . . . . . . . 35
Comte de Paris, fine, bright rose, . . . . . . 35
Caroline Mather, purplish crimson, . . . . . 35
Congress, blush and white with purple markings in the center, . . . . . . . . . . . . . . . 35
Doyen d' Engheim, crimson, large and fine, . . 35
Duchesse d'Orleans, violet rose, salmon center, . 35
Dugnesline, rose, very fine, . . . . . . . . . 35
Elegantissima, outside petals blush, inside salmon . 35
Faust, blush center, tinged with salmon, . . . . 35
Festiva, white, a few carmine spots in the center, 35

Frances Ortegat, dark crimson; large and full, . 35
Fulgida, crimson; large flower, . . . . . . . . 35
General Bertrand, outside petals blush, center yellow, . . . . . . . . . . . . . . . . 35
Genesee, outside petals blush, center yellow, . . 35
Hericartiana, outside petals rose, inside salmon, . 35
Isabella, outside petals blush, center straw color, . 35
Lady Washington, outside petals blush, center yellow, . . . . . . . . . . . . . . . . 35
Lamartine, dark crimson, . . . . . . . . . . 35
Latipetala, outside petals flesh, center yellowish, . 35
Lilacina plena, pale rose, center salmon, . . . 35
Limbata, rose; large and fine, . . . . . . . . 35
Lutea plenissima, blush, . . . . . . . . . . 35
Lutesiana, outside petals blush, center white, . . 35
Mad. Morren, outside petals rosy pink, center salmon and rose, . . . . . . . . . . . . 35
Nivalet, rose, . . . . . . . . . . . . . . . 35
Perfection, outside petals rose, inside salmon, marked with purple, . . . . . . . . . . . 35
Pius the 9th, blush and white, purple markings in the center, . . . . . . . . . . . . . . 35
Pomponia, outside petals large, purplish pink, center salmon, . . . . . . . . . . . . . 35
Pottsii, dark purplish crimson, distinct and fine, . 35
Pulcherrima, rose and salmon, . . . . . . . 35
Purple Crown, very dark, velvety purple, . . . 35
Queen Isabella, blush, changing to white, inside petals striped with purple, . . . . . . . . 35
Reevesii, delicate rose, center petals fringed, . . 35
Rosea grandiflora, deep rose; early, . . . . . 35
Rosencrants, blush, changing to white, center fringed, . . . . . . . . . . . . . . . . 35
Striata speciosa, pale rose, center whitish, large and sweet, . . . . . . . . . . . . . . . 35
Unicolor grandiflora, outside petals rose, center salmon tinted with rose, . . . . . . . . . 35
Victoria tricolor, outer petals rose, center yellowish white, . . . . . . . . . . . . . . 35
Virance, purplish rose, . . . . . . . . . . . 35

**ASTILBE JAPONICA.**
Spirea Japonica, white feathery flowers; hardy, also very fine for forcing in the winter, . . . . 30

**CARNATIONS AND PICOTEES, p. 59.**
Strong plants, assorted colors; per dozen, $5.00; each, . . . . . . . . . . . . . . . . . 50

**DAISY, page 29.**
Double, Red and white; per dozen, $2.00; each, 20

**DICENTRA, page 81.**
spectabilis, (Bleeding Heart,) one of the most popular plants for the garden, and equally as desirable for the house in winter, . . . . . . . 25

**ENGLISH GARDEN PINKS, page 59.**
White, with colored margin and center; fragrant; quite hardy, and nothing better for a button-hole flower; per doz., $3.50; each, . . . . . 35

**ERIANTHUS RAVENNÆ, page 56.**
Ornamental Grass, resembling Pampas Grass; per dozen, $3.00; each, . . . . . . . . . . . 30

**GYPSOPHILA, page 55.**
paniculata, one of the very best of the Gypsophilas, desirable for bouquet making both in the summer and winter, as it dries elegantly, . . . 30

HOLLYHOCK, page 81.
  Double, per dozen, $5.00; each, . . . . . . . 50
IVY PLANTS, page 81.
  Not hardy far North; unsurpassed for in-door decorations, etc.; plants, according to size, each, 25 cents, 50 cents, and . . . . . . . . 1.00
LILY OF THE VALLEY, page 82.
  Very sweet and graceful; delicately hung; pips per dozen, . . . . . . . . . . . . . . . . 60
  Pips sent at any time for winter flowering.
PAMPAS GRASS.
  A beautiful, strong Grass, with large, elegant spikes, but not sufficiently hardy in the Northern States for out-door culture, . . . . . . . 50
PENTSTEMON, page 62.
  barbatus, scarlet, . . . . . . . . . . . . . 30
PERENNIAL PEA, page 63.
  Pink, strong roots, . . . . . . . . . . . . 30
PERENNIAL PHLOX, page 81.
  Flowers abundantly in the summer, and never suffers in the winter; strong roots, per dozen, $2.50; each, . . . . . . . . . . . . . . . 25
VIOLETS, page 80.
  Neapolitan, light blue, fragrant; fine clump, . . 30
  Maria Louise, light blue, new, clumps, . . . . 40
YUCCA.
  filamentosa, very fine hardy plant, with striking foliage and elegant trusses of flowers; described in No. 1 Floral Guide for 1876. Strong 1 year old roots, 50 cents; strong 2 year old roots, . . 75

## HARDY CLIMBERS.

AMPELOPSIS quinquefolia, or Virginia Creeper, sometimes called American Ivy and Woodbine; a native plant, very rapid grower, leaves turning to a beautiful crimson in autumn; the best Climber for verandas, porches, or for walls, . . . . . . . . . . . . . . . . . . 50
  Veitchii, from Japan; foliage smaller than the first named. This is considered by all who have seen it in perfection the finest hardy wall plant known, clinging to the smoothest surfaces perfectly, . . . . . . . . . . . . . . . . 50

AKEBIA quinata, a singular Japanese Climber, with small, pretty foliage, and small chocolate brown flowers, ; a rapid grower, very desirable; 20 feet, . . . . . . . . . . . . . . . . . 50
BIGNONIA radicans, or Trumpet Creeper, a rapid, strong grower, with clean, glossy foliage, bright, scarlet, trumpet-shaped flowers, three inches long; blooms in August, . . . . . . . 50
CELASTRUS scandens, or Climbing Bittersweet, another of our beautiful native plants, well worthy of cultivation; leaves pea green; flowers small, followed by clusters of orange capsuled berries, . . . . . . . . . . . . . . . . . 50
CLEMATIS flammula, European Sweet, flowers white, small and very sweet scented, . . . 50
  Virginiana, common Virgin Bower, another native plant, with clusters of small, white flowers, succeeded in autumn by fruit with conspicuous feathery tails, . . . . . . . . . . . . . . 50
  Jackmanii, an English hybrid; flowers large, intense violet purple, and from 4 to 6 inches in diameter, . . . . . . . . . . . . . . . 1 00
  Lanuginosa candida, flowers larger than the above; white, tinted with lavender. The two grown together form a pleasing contrast, . . . 1 00
LONICERA, (Honeysuckles,) Halleana, an evergreen variety from Japan; flowers pure white, changing to yellow; very fragrant, and covered with flowers from June to November; a strong grower, . . . . . . . . . . . . . . . . . 50
  Japan Golden-veined, foliage small, beautifully netted with yellow, flowers pure white, sweet, 25 feet, . . . . . . . . . . . . . . . . . 50
  Monthly Fragrant, or Dutch, flowers red and pale yellow, blooming through the whole summer; very desirable, . . . . . . . . . . . . 50
  Scarlet Trumpet, monthly, evergreen, or nearly so, flowers 2 inches long; scarlet outside and yellow inside, . . . . . . . . . . . . . . 50
WISTARIA Sinensis, Chinese Wistaria, a rapid, strong grower, when well established grows 20 feet in a season, with long racemes of light purple flowers; a large plant in bloom is a most gorgeous sight, . . . . . . . . . . . . . . 50

# HOLLAND BULBS for Autumn planting

A class of Hardy Bulbs, the leading members being the Hyacinth, Tulip, and Crocus, are known as *Holland Bulbs*, because for a great number of years they have been grown almost exclusively in that country, from whence the flowering bulbs have been exported to nearly every quarter of the world. For winter flowering in the house few things are more beautiful, and nothing easier of culture, while for early spring flowers, in cold climates, we are almost dependent upon this elegant and popular class of Bulbs.

## NAMED HYACINTHS.

[See pages 85, 86 and 87.]

### DOUBLE BLUE.

#### DARK BLUE.
| | |
|---|---|
| Albion, late, low, | $0 35 |
| Grand Alfred, low, | 30 |
| King of Wurtemburg, tall, | 30 |
| Kroon van Indien, low, | 40 |
| La Renommee, low, | 35 |
| Laurens Coster, tall, new, | 70 |
| Othello, low, new, | 35 |
| Prince Albert, low, | 40 |
| Prince of Saxe-Weimar, tall, | 35 |

#### DEEP BLUE.
| | |
|---|---|
| Carl, Crown Prince of Sweden, tall, | 40 |
| Duc de Normandie, tall, | 45 |
| Frederic Soulie, late, low, | 30 |
| King of the Netherlands, low, | 30 |
| Lord Wellington, low, | 30 |
| Lord Raglan, low, | 55 |
| Mignon de Drijfhout, low, | 35 |
| Morillo, late, low, | 45 |
| Prince Frederick, tall, | 35 |

#### LIGHT BLUE.
| | |
|---|---|
| A la Mode, low, | 35 |
| Bloksberg, late, low, | 30 |
| Comte de St. Priest, tall, | 50 |
| Envoye, late, low, | 35 |
| General Antink, low, | 30 |
| Grande Vedette, low, | 40 |
| Habit Brilliant, late, tall, | 40 |
| Koning Ascingaris, tall, | 35 |
| La Fontaine, tall, | 35 |
| Pasqulu, tall, | 35 |
| Richard Steele, low, | 30 |
| Rudolphus, low, | 35 |

### DOUBLE WHITE.

#### PURE WHITE.
| | |
|---|---|
| Bucenthaurus, tall, | 35 |
| Duc de Berry, late, tall, | 70 |
| Gloria Florum, low, | 35 |
| La Deesse, late, low, | 30 |
| La Tour d' Auvergne, tall, | 35 |
| La Virginite, low, | 30 |
| Non Plus Ultra, late, tall, | 35 |
| Prince of Waterloo, late, tall, | 50 |
| Pyrene, low, | 30 |
| Sceptre d'Or, late, low, | 30 |
| Sphæra Mundi, late, low, | 40 |
| Sultan Achmet, late, low, | 35 |

#### BLUSH-WHITE.
| | |
|---|---|
| A la Mode, low, | 35 |
| Anna Maria, low, | 30 |
| Herman Lange, low, | 30 |
| Lord Anson, low, | 45 |
| Mathilda, tall, | 30 |
| Miss Kitty, low, | 40 |
| Triumph Blandina, tall, | 40 |
| Virgo, tall, | 35 |

### DOUBLE RED AND ROSE.

#### RED.
| | |
|---|---|
| Acteur, tall, | 25 |
| Alida Catharina, low, | 25 |
| Bouquet Constant, low, new, | 50 |
| Bouquet Tendre, low, | 30 |
| Cochinelle, (Eclipse,) low, | $0 35 |
| General von Ziethen, late, low, | 30 |
| La Gaiete, low, | 35 |
| Maria Louise, low, | 35 |
| Noble par Merite, low, | 35 |
| Panorama, low, | 25 |
| Princess Royal, late, low, | 25 |
| Queen Victoria, tall, | 25 |
| Sans Souci, low, | 50 |
| Sir Thomas Grey, late, low, fine, | 35 |

#### ROSE.
| | |
|---|---|
| Bouquet Royal, late, tall, | 35 |
| Cœur Fidele, late, low, | 25 |
| Comtesse de la Coste, tall, | 30 |
| Czar Nicholas, low, | 25 |
| Gœthe, tall, | 45 |
| Grootvorst, late, tall, | 30 |
| Honneur d'Amsterdam, tall, | 40 |
| L' Esperance, low, | 25 |
| Lord Wellington, low, very fine, | 40 |
| Medea, late, low, | 35 |
| Perruque Royale, late, tall, | 45 |

### DOUBLE YELLOW.
| | |
|---|---|
| Bouquet d'Orange, low, | 40 |
| Crœsus, late, low, | 50 |
| Gœthe, tall, | 35 |
| Jaune Supreme, tall, new, | 60 |
| La Grandeur, late, low, new, | 60 |
| Louis d'Or, late, tall, | 35 |
| Ophir, late, tall, | 35 |
| Piet Hein, low, | 35 |

### SINGLE BLUE.

#### VERY DARK.
| | |
|---|---|
| Ami du Cœur, tall, | 25 |
| Belle Africaine, tall, | 45 |
| La Nuit, low, | 35 |
| Mimosa, tall, | 30 |
| O'Connell, low, | 25 |
| Prince Albert, low, | 45 |
| Siam, low, | 35 |
| Uncle Tom, low, | 35 |
| William I, low, | 40 |

#### DEEP BLUE.
| | |
|---|---|
| Ami du Cœur, purple, low, | 25 |
| Baron van Tuijll, tall, | 30 |
| Bleu Mourant, late, low, | 25 |
| Charles Dickens, tall, | 25 |
| Emicus, low, | 25 |
| Emilius, low, | 30 |
| Graaf van Nassau, low, | 35 |
| Keizer Ferdinand, low, | 30 |
| L'Unique, purple, tall, | 25 |
| Nimrod, low, | 40 |
| Thunberg, tall, | 25 |

#### LIGHT BLUE.
| | |
|---|---|
| Bishop Royal, low, | 25 |
| Camper, tall, | 25 |
| Couronne de Celle, tall, | 35 |
| Grand Lilac, tall, | 25 |
| Grande Vedette, tall, | 40 |
| Iris, low, | 30 |
| La Peyrouse, low, | 25 |
| Orondates, tall, | 35 |
| Porcelaine Sceptre, low, | 35 |
| Regulus, low, | 25 |

## SINGLE WHITE.
### PURE WHITE.
| | |
|---|---|
| Alba Maxima, low, | 50 |
| Alba Superbissima, (Theba,) low, | 35 |
| Bella Donna, late, low, | 25 |
| Belle Blanchisseuse, tall, | 40 |
| Belle Esther, low, | 35 |
| Belle Galathe, low, | 40 |
| Blanchard, tall, | 40 |
| Emicus, low, | 30 |
| Grand Vainqueur, tall, | 35 |
| Grande Vedette, low, | 30 |
| Hannah Moore, low, | 25 |
| Kroonprincess, low, | 35 |
| La Candeur, low, | 30 |
| La Pucelle d'Orleans, low, | 30 |
| Madame Talleyrand, tall, | 35 |
| Queen Victoria, low, | 30 |

### PURE WHITE.
| | |
|---|---|
| Queen of the Netherlands, tall, | 40 |
| Themistocles, late, low, | 30 |

### ROSY WHITE.
| | |
|---|---|
| Anna Paulowna, late, tall, | 30 |
| Cleopatra, low, | 25 |
| Elfride, tall, | 30 |
| Grande Blanche Imperiale, tall, | 30 |
| Grandeur a Merveille, low, | 30 |
| Hercules, low, | 35 |
| Lord Grey, tall, | 35 |
| Mammoth, low, | 35 |
| Rousseau, low, | 25 |
| Vesta, tall, | 25 |
| Voltaire, low, | 25 |

## SINGLE RED AND ROSE.
### DEEP AND DARK RED.
| | |
|---|---|
| Agnes, low, | 35 |
| Amphion, low, | 40 |
| Amy, tall, | 25 |
| Appeltus, low, | 30 |
| Belle Quirine, low, | 25 |
| Charilaus, low, | 25 |
| Deliah, low, | 25 |
| Dibbitz Sabalkanski, low, | 25 |
| Dunois, low, | 35 |
| Eldorado, low, | 30 |
| Herstelde Vrede, tall, | 30 |
| L'Adorable, low, | 40 |
| Madame Hodson, tall, | 30 |
| Mdlle Rachel, low, | 30 |
| Mars, low, | 25 |
| Monsieur de Faesch, low, | 25 |
| Prosper Alpini, late, low, | 50 |
| Queen Victoria Alexandrina, low, | 35 |
| Robert Steiger, tall, | 25 |
| Satella, low, | 35 |
| Veronica, low, | 30 |

### ROSE AND PINK.
| | |
|---|---|
| Ami du Cœur, low, | 25 |
| Duchess of Richmond, tall, | 35 |
| Emmeline, low, | 25 |
| Hermina, low, | 25 |
| Homerus, low, | 45 |
| Jenny Lind, low, | 30 |
| Johanna Christina, low, | 25 |
| La Dame du Lac, low, | 45 |
| Lord Wellington, low, | 35 |
| Maria Theresa, tall, | 25 |
| Neerlands Glorie, low, | 25 |
| Norma, tall, | 25 |
| Princess Victoria, late, low, | 30 |
| Prof. von Zwinden, tall, | 40 |
| Sultan's Favorite, tall, | 30 |
| Temple of Apollo, tall, | 30 |
| Tuba Flora, late, tall, | 35 |

## SINGLE YELLOW.
| | |
|---|---|
| Adonia, tall, | 25 |
| Alida Jacoba, low, | 25 |
| Anna Carolina, late, low, | 30 |
| Conqueror, low, | 25 |
| Fleur d'Or, low, | 25 |
| Heroine, tall, | 30 |
| Koning van Holland, low, | 25 |
| La Pluie d'Or, tall, | 25 |
| Piet Hein, low, | 35 |
| Rhinosceros, tall, | 35 |

To those who prefer to *leave the selection to me*, I will furnish Hyacinths from the above list at $3.00 per DOZEN, each dozen to contain a good selection of the different and most desirable colors, single and double, and all first class Bulbs. Those who desire them for particular purposes, as for pots and glasses for winter flowering, will please state the fact, and I will select the kinds best adapted for the purpose. Those who have a particular choice of one or more varieties that they wish sent in the dozen, shall be accommodated as far as possible.

## UNNAMED HYACINTHS.

The mixed or unnamed Hyacinths will do well for out-door culture, and they can be obtained at comparatively little cost; but the flowers will not usually be as fine as those from named Bulbs, every one of which is selected particularly with reference to flowering in the house. These unnamed Hyacinths, however, are all large, excellent Bulbs, imported directly from Holland, and will give good satisfaction. Indeed, they often flower admirably in the house, though we do not recommend them for this purpose. I have placed them at the lowest possible price — only a trifle over cost — so as to bring them within the reach of all.

**MIXED HYACINTHS,** 15 cents each; or $1.50 per dozen.

| | | |
|---|---|---|
| Double Blue. | Double White. | Double Red. |
| Single Blue. | Single White. | Single Red. |

## ROMAN HYACINTHS.
Early Roman White Hyacinths; desirable for early flowering, each, 20 cts.; doz. $2 25; 100 $17 00

## NAMED TULIPS.
[See pages 88 and 89.]

### DUC VAN THOL
| | each | per doz |
|---|---|---|
| Single Red, | $0 10 | $0 95 |
| Rose, | 15 | 1 45 |
| Scarlet, | 10 | 1 00 |
| Yellow, | 15 | 1 70 |
| Crimson, | 10 | 1 00 |
| White, true, | 25 | 2 80 |
| Gold Striped, | 15 | 1 50 |
| Double Red, | 5 | 50 |

### TOURNESOL.
| | | |
|---|---|---|
| Orange and Red, | 10 | 1 00 |
| Yellow, true, fine, | 15 | 1 50 |

### SINGLE EARLY.
| | each |
|---|---|
| Abbesse de St. Denis, cherry striped, | $0 15 |
| Admiral Florida, purple striped, | 25 |
| Alida Maria, white striped, | 30 |
| Alpherus, violet, tipped with white, | 25 |
| Arthus, beautiful deep red, | 15 |
| Bacchus, deep crimson, | 15 |
| Bakhuizen, violet, | 35 |
| Bizard Pronkert, red and yellow, | 10 |
| Breughel, purple, | 15 |
| Bride of Haarlem, red and white, | 20 |
| Brutus, gold striped, | 15 |
| Caiman, white, striped with purple, | 10 |
| Canary Bird, yellow, | 25 |
| Cerise de France, white and red striped, | 25 |
| Chrysolora, yellow and red, striped, | 15 |
| Claremont Striped, red, white flaked, | 10 |
| Commandant, flame, yellow margin, | 10 |
| Compte de Vergennes, white and red, | 25 |
| Couleur Cardinal, brilliant red, | 15 |
| Couleur Ponceau, crimson border, whitish ground, | 10 |
| Cour de France, yellow and red, | 10 |
| Cramoisi Royal, splendid crimson, | 15 |

Donna Maria, red and white, . . . . . . . . . $0 20
Dorothea Blanche, white ground, marbled with pink; new, . . . . . . . . . . . . . . . 25
Duc de Claremont, carmine and white, . . . . 15
Duc Major, fine, brownish red, edged with yellow, 5
Duc d' Orange, brownish red, marbled with orange, . . . . . . . . . . . . . . . . . 10
Duchesse de Parma, red, edged with yellow; splendid, . . . . . . . . . . . . . . . . 5
Eleonore, purple edged with white, . . . . . . 10
Feu de Muscovie, yellow, striped with red; new, 25
Feu Superbe, flame-colored, . . . . . . . . . 10
Franciscus I, splendid red and yellow, . . . . . 15
Globe de Rigaud, purple striped, . . . . . . . 20
Graaf Floris, white and rose, . . . . . . . . . 15
Grand Duke of Russia, red, deeply edged with yellow, . . . . . . . . . . . . . . . . . 15
Grootmeester, white and crimson, striped; large, 15
Hebee, deep red and yellow, fine, . . . . . . . 15
Hecuba, white, striped with red, . . . . . . . 15
Hobbema Feuillemont, violet, bordered with white, . . . . . . . . . . . . . . . . . . 15
Lac Bontlof, purple and white, variegated leaves, 10
Lac Dore, purple, . . . . . . . . . . . . . . 5
Lac van Rijn, purple and white, . . . . . . . . 5
La Precieuse, rose and white, . . . . . . . . . 15
La Reine, beautiful rosy white, . . . . . . . . 5
Ma Plus Aimable, red, striped with orange, . . 10
Marmont, red and white striped, . . . . . . . 20
Paragon Guldebloem, violet and yellow, . . . 10
Pax Aba, very fine white, . . . . . . . . . . 10
Pigeon, white, . . . . . . . . . . . . . . . . 7
Pottebakker, white, . . . . . . . . . . . . . 10
Prince of Austria, red and yellow, . . . . . . . 15
Proserpine, crimson; large and splendid; new, . 25
Pure d'Or, golden yellow, red striped, . . . . . 15
Purpurmantel, purple striped, . . . . . . . . 15
Purple Crown, purplish crimson, . . . . . . . 10
Reine des Cerises, cherry and white, . . . . . 10
Red and Yellow of Leiden, fine red, striped with yellow, . . . . . . . . . . . . . . . 15
Rose Brilliant, white, edged with red, . . . . . 25
Rose Gris de Lin, very fine rose, . . . . . . . 10
Samson, red, . . . . . . . . . . . . . . . . 10
Souvenir, red, yellow striped, dwarf, . . . . . 5
Standard Royal, white and red striped, . . . . 8
Thomas Moore, orange, . . . . . . . . . . . 7
Van Goijen, rose, . . . . . . . . . . . . . . 10
Vermillion Brilliant, glittering red, . . . . . . 20
Violet Blanche, white, tipped with red, . . . . 15
Wapan van Leiden, white and rose, . . . . . . 10
White and Red Bordered, white, delicately mottled with red, . . . . . . . . . . . . . 7
Yellow Prince, fine yellow, . . . . . . . . . . 5

### DOUBLE TULIPS.

Admiral Kingsbergen, golden yellow, striped with bronze, large; late, . . . . . . . . . 10
Aimable, coppery yellow, shaded with violet; early, . . . . . . . . . . . . . . . . . . 15
Alexander, red, yellow striped; late, . . . . . 10
Atrium, yellow striped, fine; late, . . . . . . . 10
Blue Flag, fine blue; late, . . . . . . . . . . 10
Bouquet d'Orange, salmon red, with tinge of orange; late, . . . . . . . . . . . . . . . 10
Brunello, brownish red, edged with yellow; late, 10
Buonaparte, orange red; late, . . . . . . . . 5
Comte de Pompadour, purplish red, large; early, . . . . . . . . . . . . . . . . . . . 15
Conqueror, white and violet striped, large; late, 10
Cafe Noir, rich, velvety, deep crimson, . . . . 10
Courronne d'Or, red, edged white; late, . . . 15
Crown Imperial, red striped, large; early, . . . 20
Crown of Roses, splendid double rose, large; early, . . . . . . . . . . . . . . . . . . . 15
Duke of York, puce and white; fine, large; early, . . . . . . . . . . . . . . . . . . . 20
Extremite d' Or, yellow and red; early, . . . . 5
Gloria Solis, bronze, orange and crimson; early, 5
Grand Alexandre, yellow, beautifully striped with red; early, . . . . . . . . . . . . . 10
Imperator Rubrorum, fine red; early, . . . . . 10
Incarnat Gris de Lin, copper color, striped with violet; late, . . . . . . . . . . . . . . . 10
Incomparable, deep rose, edged with white; early, 15

La Candeur, white; fine, large, early, . . . . $0 10
La Fidele, yellow and red; large, late, . . . . . 10
Le Blason, fine rosy; large, early, . . . . . . . 15
Madame Catalani, purplish rose, edged and mottled with white; late, . . . . . . . . . 15
Mariage de ma Fille, pure white, striped with rose, large; late, . . . . . . . . . . . . . . 15
Milton, reddish purple, large; late, . . . . . . 5
Mina, white, striped with rose; late, . . . . . . 15
Nosor, rich purplish; early, . . . . . . . . . . 10
Orange Boom, rose, carmine striped; late, . . . 15
Orange Troon, deep rose, edged with white; late, 10
Pæony Gold, yellow and red; early, . . . . . . 10
Pæony Rose, scarlet; early, . . . . . . . . . . 5
Phoedor, splendid purple, fine; late, . . . . . . 15
Purple Crown, splendid dark velvety crimson; early, . . . . . . . . . . . . . . . . . . . 10
Purple, White Bordered, early, . . . . . . . . 5
Regina Rubrorum, red, striped with creamy yellow; early, . . . . . . . . . . . . . . . 25
Rex Rubrorum, fine scarlet; early, . . . . . . 5
Rhinosceros, purple, large; early, . . . . . . . 10
Rose Eclatante, rich crimson; late, . . . . . . 5
Rose Hortense, white and purplish crimson, large and fine; early, . . . . . . . . . . . . . . 15
Violet de Paris, violet striped, . . . . . . . . 20
William Rex, purple and yellow; late, . . . . . 20
Xenophon, crimson and yellow; late, . . . . . 15
Yellow Rose, variegated foliage; late, . . . . . 10
Yellow Rose, beautiful golden yellow, large; late, 5
Zebra, dark, velvety red, lightly striped with yellow; late, . . . . . . . . . . . . . . . . 10
Zwinglius, deep rose; early, . . . . . . . . . 25

### PARROT TULIPS.

Belle Jaune, beautiful yellow, . . . . . . . . . 10
Cafe Brun, rich brown, . . . . . . . . . . . . 5
Large Scarlet, large and bright, . . . . . . . . 10
Perfecta, red striped . . . . . . . . . . . . . 10

Those who wish to leave the selection to me, I will supply *Duc Van Thol* and *Single Early* Tulips at $1.25 per dozen; *Double* at $1.00 a dozen, and *Parrots* at 90 cents a dozen.

### LATE FLOWERING SHOW TULIPS.

Of this splendid class I have OVER TWO HUNDRED of the finest named prize varieties.

|  | each | per doz |
|---|---|---|
| Bizarres, named varieties, | $0 10 | $1 00 |
| Byblooms, " | 18 | 1 75 |
| Roses, " | 25 | 2 50 |
| Bizarres, mixed varieties, |  | 65 |
| Byblooms, " |  | 70 |
| Roses, " |  | 75 |

### BEDDING TULIPS.

We know of no flower that will make such a perfect and showy ribbon bed as the Tulip, properly selected for the purpose. It should be formed of three distinct colors, at least, as yellow, white and red, and not less than three rows of each color. For the purpose of encouraging this kind of planting, I have selected and imported in large quantities several varieties best adapted for the purpose, which I sell so low as to bring them within the reach of all.

|  | per doz | per 100 |
|---|---|---|
| Duchesse de Parma, red, bordered with yellow, splendid, tall, | $0 50 | $3 50 |
| Feu Superbe, bright red, | 1 00 | 7 00 |
| Samson, beautiful red, | 1 00 | 7 50 |
| Duc Major, red, edged with yellow, | 50 | 3 50 |
| La Reine, white, fine, | 50 | 3 00 |
| Yellow Prince, pure yellow, | 55 | 3 80 |
| Thomas Moore, orange, | 60 | 4 20 |
| Pigeon, pure white, | 65 | 4 60 |

### TULIPS FOR BORDERS.

Some of the low growing early Tulips are unsurpassed for bordering beds. They grow from four to eight inches in height, and when planted close together so as to make an unbroken row, the effect is delightful. The effect is destroyed if a variety of improper height is

planted. For this reason we give a list of varieties suitable for borders. The following are the most desirable varieties for this purpose:

|  | per doz | per 100 |
|---|---|---|
| Standard Royal, red and white striped, beautiful, | $0 75 | $5 50 |
| White and Red Bordered, fine, | 60 | 4 20 |
| Souvenir, red and yellow striped, | 50 | 3 00 |
| Lac van Rijn, violet, white bordered, very fine, | 55 | 3 80 |
| Duc Van Thol, Double Red, | 50 | 3 40 |
| Duc Van Thol, Single Red, | 95 | 7 00 |

### UNNAMED TULIPS.

The Mixed Tulips I offer are not small or inferior bulbs, but are large, and of fine varieties, and will make a showy, splendid bed, at little cost. Where it is not considered important to have the colors separate, they will give the best of satisfaction, especially to that highly respectable class whom Providence has blessed with fine taste and little money. To accommodate such I have reduced the price to about cost.

|  | per doz | per 100 |
|---|---|---|
| Mixed Single early, splendid flowers, | $0 50 | $3 00 |
| Mixed Double, splendid flowers, | 50 | 3 00 |
| Mixed Parrot Tulips, fine flowers, | 55 | 3 80 |
| Bizarres, Byblooms and Roses, Mixed, | 60 | 4 20 |

### CROCUSES, page 90.

UNNAMED, 20 cents per dozen; $1.50 per 100.

Large Blue,     Large Striped,
Large White,     Large Yellow.

Those ordering the above by the dozen or hundred can select of one or all the varieties.

NAMED CROCUSES, 40 cents per dozen; $3.00 per 100. Of the FINE NAMED CROCUSES, mostly new varieties, I have about thirty sorts, white, blue and striped. They are unusually large and fine.

### COLCHICUM, page 90.

|  | each |
|---|---|
| Autumnalis, | $0 10 |
| Agrippina, new and fine, | 40 |

### SNOW-DROP, page 90.

|  | per doz | per 100 |
|---|---|---|
| Single Snow-Drop, | $0 25 | $1 75 |
| Double Snow-Drop, | 70 | 6 00 |
| Leucojum æstivum, Large Snow-Flake, | each, | 15 |

### NARCISSUS, page 91.

#### POLYANTHUS NARCISSUS.

|  | each |
|---|---|
| Bazelman Major, fine white, | $0 60 |
| Double Roman, white and yellow, fragrant, | 10 |
| Gloriosum superbum, white, with deep orange cup, fine, | 15 |
| Grand Monarque, white, yellow cup, | 20 |
| Grand Primo White, | 20 |
| Grand Primo Yellow, very fine, | 30 |
| Grand Soliel d'Or, bright yellow, deep orange cup, splendid, | 15 |
| Grootvorst, white, | 15 |
| Luna, white, | 15 |
| Newton, yellow and orange, extra, | 30 |
| Staten General, fine lemon, | 15 |

#### DOUBLE NARCISSUS.

|  | each |
|---|---|
| Albo pleno odorato, white, fragrant, | 10 |
| Incomparable, fine light yellow, | 10 |
| Noblissimus, fine, new, | 25 |
| Orange Phœnix, orange and lemon, | 10 |
| Tratus Cantus, new, fine, | 10 |
| Sulphur Crown, light yellow, | 10 |
| Van Sion, (Yellow Daffodil,) | 7 |

### SINGLE NARCISSUS.

|  | each |
|---|---|
| Bulbocodium, or Hoop Petticoat, fine, | $0 25 |
| Campernel, (Great Jonquil,) yellow, fragrant; per dozen, 50 cents, | 5 |
| Etoile d'Or, | 10 |
| Muschatos, fine, new, | 20 |
| Poeticus, per dozen, 50 cents, | 5 |
| Trumpet, Gold, | 15 |
| Trumpet, Silver, | 15 |

### JONQUILS.

|  | each | per doz |
|---|---|---|
| Largest Double, sweet-scented, | $0 30 | $3 00 |
| Single, sweet-scented, | 5 | 50 |

### SCILLAS, page 91.

|  | each |
|---|---|
| Siberica, bright intense blue, | $0 10 |
| Campanulata, | 10 |
| Hyacinthoides alba, | 10 |
| Hyacinthoides cœrulea and rosea, | 10 |

### CROWN IMPERIAL, page 92.

|  | each |
|---|---|
| Crown upon Crown, | $0 50 |
| Maximum Red, | 55 |
| Maximum Yellow, | 1 25 |
| Red, gold striped foliage, | 70 |
| Double Red, | 1 50 |
| Double Yellow, | 2 00 |
| Red, | 30 |

### SMILAX, page 92.

Boston Smilax, fine bulbs, . . . . . . each, 30

### ANEMONE, page 93.

|  | per doz |
|---|---|
| Anemone, single, brightest colors, | $0 25 |
| double, best mixed colors, | 25 |
| single scarlet, | 30 |

|  | each | per doz |
|---|---|---|
| Anemone, double scarlet, | $0 06 | $0 60 |
| best double named sorts, (100 varieties,) | 10 | 75 |

The Anemone can be kept until spring or longer without injury. It is well to save some for spring planting. The Ranunculus can also be kept for spring planting.

### RANUNCULUS, page 93.

|  | each | per doz |
|---|---|---|
| Ranunculus, 100 best named varieties, | $0 10 | $0 75 |
| Ranunculus, best mixed varieties, | | 25 |

### IRIS, page 93.

|  |  |  |
|---|---|---|
| Anglica, mixed sorts, . . . . each, | $0 07 | doz., $0 70 |
| Hispanica, mixed varieties, | " | 25 |
| Pavonia, (Peacock,) beautiful, | " 10 | " 1 00 |
| Persica, dwarf fragrant, fine, | " 30 | doz., 3 00 |
| Susiana major, rose, tinted with brown, | each, | 80 |
| Tuberosa, rich velvet, marked with black, | | 25 |

### OXALIS, page 94.

|  | each |
|---|---|
| Bowii, bright rose, | $0 10 |
| Lutea, yellow; one of the best for winter blooming, | 10 |
| multiflora, white, | 10 |
| Versicolor, a beautiful variety; white, yellow eye, crimson outside, | 10 |
| About twenty-five of the finest named varieties, | 10 |

### CYCLAMEN, page 94.

Cyclamen Persicum, . . . . . . . . each, 50

### IXIAS, page 95.

Ixias, Twenty best named varieties, . . . . each, 10

[HOLLAND BULBS are received about the middle of September, and are for sale until the last of November.]

# VEGETABLES.

THE VEGETABLE DEPARTMENT embraces almost every article of value known. We have excluded everything our experience has proved unworthy of culture, as also some untried and not very promising kinds. As fast as new Vegetables establish their good character we shall add them to our list, but we do not propose to admit any bad or untried characters into our goodly company.

**ASPARAGUS, pages 96 and 97.**
Conover's Colossal, large, and of rapid growth; per lb. $1.00; per oz. 10 cents, . . . . . . . . . 5
Giant Ulm, a popular German variety, large and superior; per lb. $1.00; per oz. 10 cents, . . . 5
Roots—1 year, by mail, per 100, prepaid, . . . $1.50
    2 years, by mail, per 100, prepaid, . . . 3.50
    2 years, by express, per 100, not paid, . 1.50

**BEANS, pages 97 and 98.**
DWARF OR SNAP BEANS.
Early Rachel, the earliest, and very hardy; desirable as a String Bean; per pint 25 cents, . . 10
Long Yellow Six-Weeks, one of the earliest; an excellent and productive String Bean; per pint 25 cents, . . . . . . . . . . . . . . . . 10
Early Mohawk, a hardy, productive and excellent String Bean; per pint, 25 cents, . . . . . 10
Wax or Butter, a popular variety wherever known; the pods a waxy yellow, solid, very tender and almost transparent, stringless, seeds black when ripe; per pint 35 cents, . . . . . . 15
Early Valentine, early and tender for String Beans; per pint 25 cents, . . . . . . . . . . 10
Early China, early, tender for String Beans, good for shelling; per pint 25 cents, . . . . . 10
Refugee, hardy, abundant bearer, flesh thick and tender, one of the very best for pickling, on account of its thick flesh; not very early, will produce pods fit for eating in about eight weeks from planting; per pint 25 cents, . . . . . . . 10
White Kidney or Royal Dwarf, one of the very best for shelling, either green or dry; per pint 25 cents, . . . . . . . . . . . . . . . 10
White Marrowfat, clear white, almost round, fair as a String Bean, and first class for use shelled, either green or dry; per pint 25 cents, 10
Broad Windsor, the celebrated *Broad Bean* of England, growing on a strong, erect stalk, about two feet in height. Beans eaten shelled. About twice as large as the Lima and not half as good. Not very well adapted to our climate; pint 25 cts. 10

RUNNING BEANS.
Large Lima, the most buttery and delicious Bean grown. Plant in a warm, sandy soil, if possible, not too early; per pint 40 cents, . . 15
London Horticultural, or Speckled Cranberry, a round, speckled Bean, tender for Snap Beans, and excellent for shelling; pint 35 cents, 15
Giant Wax, thick, fleshy, creamy yellow, waxy looking pods, very tender and excellent as a Snap Bean; productive, keeping in bearing a very long time; seeds red, rather tender; per pint 50 cents, . . . . . . . . . . . . . . 20
Scarlet Runner. This is the favorite Snap Bean of Europe, and nothing else will sell as soon as this appears in market. It is planted in rows and allowed to run on the ground; per pint 35 cents, . . . . . . . . . . . . . . 15

**BORECOLE, or KALE, page 98.**
Dwarf German Greens, or Sprouts, bluish green, resembling Ruta Baga tops, and of fine flavor. The plan is to sow in rows, about a foot apart, in September, and gather in early spring, like Spinach; per lb. $1.50; per oz. 15 cents, . 5
Green Curled, or Scotch Kale, dwarf in habit, very spreading, nicely curled, and bright green. Very hardy, and may be cut from the open ground all the early part of winter. Frost improves it; per lb. $1.50; per oz. 15 cents, . . 5
Purple Kale, like the Scotch Kale, except in color, and will endure more frost; oz. 25 cents, 5
Cottagers' Kale, the favorite English variety, dwarf in habit, and most beautifully curled. Hardy. Treatment as for Cabbage, except that it should remain in the ground until needed for use; per oz. 25 cents, . . . . . . . . . . . 5

**BRUSSELS SPROUTS, page 98.**
Per lb. $2.25; per ounce 20 cents, . . . . . 5

**BEETS, page 99.**
Egyptian Blood Turnip, the earliest variety grown, and valuable on this account; not very productive; per lb. $2.50; per oz. 25 cts., . . 15
Extra Early Bassano, an early, good Beet, tender and juicy; flesh white and rose; grows to a good size; when sown late, it keeps well in the winter, and by some is preferred over all others for a winter Beet; per lb. $1.00; oz. 15 cents, 10
Early Blood Turnip, turnip-shaped, smooth, tender and good; about ten days after Bassano; per lb. $1.00; per oz. 15 cents, . . . . . . . 10
Dewing's Turnip, a good red, but not dark, Turnip Beet, about a week earlier than Blood Turnip; smooth skin and small top, and growing much above ground; flesh tender and delicate, but not very solid · good for summer use; per lb. $1.00; per oz. 15 cents, . . . . . . . 10
Early Yellow Turnip, a variety of the Blood Turnip Beet, differing mainly in color; the roots are bright yellow, as are also the leaf-stems and nerves; a good early Beet; per lb. $1.00; per oz. 15 cents, . . . . . . . . . . . . . . . 10
Henderson's Pine Apple, compact, short-top variety; roots medium sized and of a deep crimson; much liked here by gardeners and amateurs; per lb. $2.50; per oz. 25 cents, . . 15
Long Blood Red, a popular winter sort; long, smooth, blood red; sweet and tender; per lb. $1.00; per oz. 15 cents, . . . . . . . . . . 10
Imperial Sugar, the sweetest and best Sugar Beet; per lb. 75 cents; per oz. 10 cents, . . . 5
Carter's St. Osyth, new and excellent; per lb. $2.50; per oz. 25 cents, . . . . . . . . . . 15
Beck's Improved Sea Kale, a variety of Beet with beautiful and tender leaves, becoming very popular in Europe for cooking as "greens"; per oz. 15 cents, . . . . . . . . . . . . . . 10

Beets, Swiss Chard, Large Ribbed Scarlet Brazilian, per lb. $1.00; per oz. 15 cents, . . 10
Large Ribbed Yellow Brazilian, per lb. $1.00; per oz. 15 cents, . . . . . . . . . . . 10
Large Ribbed Silver, per lb. $1.00; oz. 15 cts., 10
Mangel Wurtzel, Long Red, for cattle; per lb. 75 cents; per oz. . . . . . . . . . . . . 10
Carter's Mammoth Long Red, of very large size and good quality; per lb. 85 cents; per oz. 10
Long Yellow, for cattle; per lb. 75 cents; oz. . 10
Olive-Shaped Red, large, for cattle; per lb. 75 cents; per oz. . . . . . . . . . . . . . . . 10
Carter's Improved Orange Globe, the very best round Mangel; per lb. 85 cents; per oz. . 10

## BROCOLI, page 102.

Purple Cape, one of the hardiest and most popular varieties, and the most certain to form a good head; the earliest of the purple varieties; per oz. 70 cents, . . . . . . . . . . . . . . 10
Southampton, fine, hardy, large, yellow variety — one of the old popular sorts, like Portsmouth, Sulphur, etc.; per oz. 30 cents, . . . . 5

## CABBAGES, pages 100 and 101.

Early Dwarf York, small, very early; per lb. $2.00; per oz. 20 cents, . . . . . . . . . . . 5
Large York, larger than above, round head; good summer and fall sort; lb. $2.00; oz. 20 cts. 5
Wheeler's Imperial. This is one of the best early varieties we have ever tried. Every plant heads if it has but half a chance; per lb. $2.50; per oz. 25 cents, . . . . . . . . . . . . . . 10
Little Pixie, very early, small, and of delicate flavor; per lb. $2.50; per oz. 25 cents, . . . . 10
Early Wakefield, (American seed,) the great favorite with market gardeners for the New York Market; the earliest and sure to head. The seed is true and the best; per lb. $7.00; per oz. 60 cents; per half oz. 40 cents, . . . . 15
Early Wyman, a comparatively new variety, almost as early as Wakefield, larger, but not as solid; very popular around Boston, for market; but with us it has seemed very variable in character; per oz. $1.00; per half oz. 60 cents, . . 25
Fearnaught, a new, early, English Cabbage, claimed to be the earliest known; per lb. $3.00; per oz. 30 cents, . . . . . . . . . . . . . . 10
Large French Oxheart, a fine, heart-shaped Cabbage, coming in use after Early York and other earlier sorts; very tender and fine flavored, and heads freely; lb. $3.00; oz. 30 cents, . 10
Enfield Market, large, compact head, early and superior; per lb. $2.50; per oz. 25 cents, . . . 10
Sugar-loaf, a very good early variety, with a conical or sugar-loaf shaped head, a great favorite with many; per lb. $2.00; per oz. 20 cents, 5
Winningstadt, a fine tender variety, sugar-loaf in form; one of the best summer sorts; if sown late, good for fall or even winter; per lb. $3.00; per oz. 30 cents, . . . . . . . . . . . . . . . 10
Early Schweinfurth, an early Cabbage, for summer and autumn use, and of large size, but not solid; per oz. $1.20; per half oz. 75 cents, 30
Filderkraut. This is comparatively new, but has become the general favorite in Germany, and is excellent in America. I import the seed directly from Stuttgart; lb. $4.00; oz. 40 cents, . 10
Stone Mason Marblehead, a large, solid, tender and excellent free heading winter Cabbage; per lb. $5.00; per oz. 40 cents, . . . . . . . 10

Cabbages, Marblehead Mammoth, very large winter Cabbage; heads freely, and with good soil will grow to an enormous size; per lb. $6.00; per oz. 50 cents; per half oz. 30 cents, 15
Robinson's Champion. This is one of the largest Cabbages grown, very much resembling Marblehead Mammoth, and of good quality for so large a growth. It sometimes weighs 60 lbs.; per lb. $2.00; per oz. 20 cents, . . . . . . . 5
Large Late Drumhead, a very superior drumhead variety, grown from choice heads; per lb. $5.00; per oz. 40 cents, . . . . . . . . . . . 10
Premium Flat Dutch, heads well and keeps over finely; per lb. $5.00; per oz. 40 cents, . . 10
Large Flat Dutch, good for fall or winter crop, resembling the Drumhead; lb. $2.00; oz. 20 cts. 5
Flat Brunswick Drumhead, fine, late; per lb. $4.00; per oz. 40 cents, . . . . . . . . . . . 10
Fottler's Improved Brunswick, per lb. $5.00; per oz. 40 cents, . . . . . . . . . . . . . . 10
Drumhead Savoy, one of the very best winter Cabbages; per lb. $2.00; per oz. 20 cents, . . 5
Dwarf Green Curled Savoy, heads small and rather loose, very hardy and excellent; per lb. $2.00; per oz. 20 cents, . . . . . . . . . . . 5
Early Dwarf Ulm Savoy, heads round and very solid and of fine quality; forms its head very early; per lb. $2.00; per oz. 20 cents, . . 5
Chappell's Red Pickling, of brighter color and more true to the kind than any other variety of red or pickling Cabbage; lb. $3.75; oz. 35 cts., 10
Large Late Blood Red, pure; for pickling; per lb. $4.00; per oz. 40 cents, . . . . . . . 20
Early Blood Red, early variety; will make fine winter Cabbage if sown quite late in the open ground; per lb. $4.00; per oz. 40 cents, . . . . 10

## COLLARDS, page 101.

Creole, the popular Creole Collard, so well known and prized at the South, and so nicely adapted to the Southern climate. We have taken pains to secure this at the special request of our customers in the Southern States; per lb. $3.00; per oz. 30 cents, . . . . . . . . 10

## CAULIFLOWER, pages 101 and 102.

Early Paris, early and fine; short stalk, white; per oz. $1.50; half oz. 90 cents, . . . . . . . 20
Erfurt Large Early White, a large and excellent early Cauliflower; oz. $2.50; half oz. $1.50, 30
Erfurt Earliest Dwarf, the earliest variety grown; low, with pure white curd; the best and surest to head; per oz. $2.00; per half oz. $1.20, 25
New Imperial, a new French variety, represented as large and very early, and in every way superior; per oz. $2.00; per half oz. $1.20, . . 25
Lenormand's, one of the largest and hardiest of the Cauliflowers; very fine; per oz. $2.50; per half oz. $1.50, . . . . . . . . . . . . . . . 30
Lenormand's Short-Stemmed, new; extra fine; per oz. $2.00; per half oz. $1.20, . . . . 25
Veitch's Autumn Giant, a new, large and very superior variety; per oz. $2.50; half oz. $1.50, . 30
Large Asiatic, a fine, large, late variety, one of the best large sorts; per oz. $1.00; per half oz. 60 cents, . . . . . . . . . . . . . . . . . 15
Stadtholder, a large German variety; very large head and fine flavor; oz. $1.00; half oz. 60 cts., 15
Walcheren, a very hardy variety, and by many considered the best; per oz. $1.00; per half oz. 60 cents, . . . . . . . . . . . . . . . . 15

Cauliflower, Carter's Dwarf Mammoth, early, dwarf, compact and hardy; per oz. $1.75; half oz. $1.00, .......... 25

### CRESS, page 102.
Fine Curled, superior; will bear cutting several times; per oz. 10 cents, .......... 5
Plain-Leaved, tender and delicate, fine for salad; per oz. 10 cents, .......... 5
Broad-Leaved Garden, sometimes used for soups; per oz. 10 cents, .......... 5
Australian, leaves delicate green, flavor mild and fine; per oz. 10 cents, .......... 5
Perennial American, resembles the Water Cress; may be cut through the season; oz. 20 cts. 10
Water, does pretty well in moist situations, but better on the edges of streams in shallow water; per oz. 60 cents; per half oz. 40 cents, .... 15

### CORN SALAD, page 102.
Per lb. $1.50; per oz. 15 cents, .......... 5

### CARROTS, page 103.
Early Very Short Scarlet, the most desirable for forcing, and much prized in Europe for soups; per lb. $1.50; per oz. 15 cents, .......... 5
Early French Short Horn, small; best for table; preferred by some for all purposes, even for stock; per lb. $1.25; per oz. 15 cents, ... 5
Half Long Scarlet Stump Rooted, larger than Short Horn, and a desirable table variety; per lb. $1.50; per oz. 15 cents, .......... 5
Half Long Scarlet Pointed Rooted, a very desirable Carrot either for table or feeding, sweet and productive; lb. $1.25; oz. 15 cents, 5
Long Orange, per lb. $1.25; per oz. 15 cents, . 5
Altringham, selected, red; lb. $1.25; oz. 15 cts., 5
Large Orange Belgian Green-Top, rich, fine for feeding; per lb. $1.25; per oz. 15 cents, .. 5
Long White Belgian Green-Top, fine for cattle; per lb. 75 cents; per oz. 10 cents, .... 5

### CHICORY, page 103.
Large-Rooted Long Magdeburg, per lb. $1.25; per oz. .......... 10

### CELERY, page 104.
Turner's Incomparable Dwarf White, one of the very best varieties, growing stout, crisp and of exceedingly fine nutty flavor; per oz. 25 cts., 5
Lion's Paw, fine, large, white; per oz. 25 cents, 5
Goodwin's White, fine, solid; per oz. 25 cents, 5
Sandringham Dwarf White, a new variety, gaining much popularity in Europe; produced by the gardener to the Prince of Wales; solid, crisp, and of fine flavor; per oz. 30 cents, .. 10
Boston Market, of low growth, somewhat branching, white, crisp, and a favorite of the market gardeners in the vicinity of Boston; per oz. 35 cents, .......... 10
Sealey's Leviathan, white, very large and solid, unsurpassed in flavor; per oz. 25 cents, . 5
Laing's Mammoth Red, fine flavor, large; excellent keeper; per oz. 25 cents, ...... 5
Carter's Incomparable Dwarf Dark Crimson, like Turner's Incomparable Dwarf in everything but color, being crimson; oz. 30 cts., 10
Turnip-Rooted, (Celeriac,) forming Turnip-shaped bulbs, of Celery flavor; per oz. 25 cts., 5
Seeds for Flavoring. This is seed too old for vegetation, but excellent for flavoring pickles, etc.; per lb. $1.00; per oz. .......... 10

### CORN, page 105.
Early Minnesota, by far the best *very early* Sweet Corn we have ever tried. Plant rather dwarf, ears fine for so early a variety, and of good quality; per pint 25 cents, ...... 10
Campbell's Extra Early Sixty Days, an early, good Corn, sweet, with very small cob, nearly as early as the Minnesota; per pint 25 cents, . 10
Russell's Prolific, a very superior early variety. It is the earliest first-class Sweet Corn. Ears eight to ten inches in length; per pint 25 cents, 10
Moore's Early Concord, a very good Corn, very much prized in the neighborhood of Boston; ears large; ripens after Russell's, and in earliness about with Early Eight Rowed, or Crosby's; per pint 25 cents, .......... 10
Crosby's Early, nearly as early as Russell's Prolific, ears about as long, or a little longer, very thick, having from twelve to sixteen rows. A very desirable Corn for the private garden and for market, like the old Asylum, but earlier; per pint 25 cents, .......... 10
Early Eight-Rowed Sugar, following the preceding in time of maturity; excellent; ears about nine inches long and very fine; per pint 25 cents, .......... 10
Stowell's Evergreen, late; very select and pure; per pint 25 cents, .......... 10
Parching, best white; per pint 25 cents, ... 10

### CUCUMBERS, pages 105 and 106.
#### AMERICAN VARIETIES.
Early Russian, very early, hardy and productive; small, growing in pairs; per lb. $2.00; per oz. 20 cents, .......... 10
Early Netted Russian, new, and very promising 25
Early Green Cluster, next in earliness to the Russian; small, prickly, in clusters, productive; per lb. $1.25; per oz. 15 cents, ..... 5
Early Frame, a good variety for pickling and table, of medium size; per lb. $1.25; per oz. 15 cents, .......... 5
Early White Spine, an excellent variety for table; very pretty and a great bearer; a favorite with market growers, and called "New York Market;" per lb. $1.25; per oz. 15 cents, .. 5
Improved Long Green, a very fine long fruit of excellent quality; per lb. $1.50; per oz. 15 cents, .......... 5

#### FOREIGN VARIETIES.
Long Green Southgate, one of the finest old English varieties, pretty hardy, ....... 15
Chinese Long Green, long, productive and hardy, .......... 15
Stockwood, fine, hardy, standard sort; every way superior, .......... 15
Wood's Long Ridge, a fine, hardy variety, . 15
Bedfordshire Surprise, hardy and excellent, . 15
Giant of Arnstadt, one of the finest, good bearer, 25
Rollisson's Telegraph, one of the best, ... 25
General Grant, new and excellent, ..... 25
Carter's Champion, a fine winter variety, .. 25
Lord Kenyon's Favorite, a very fine, large, black-spined English variety, ....... 25
Cuthill's Highland Mary, very superior and productive; hardy; fine for forcing, ..... 25
Sion House Improved, fine; constant; good bearer; one of the best English sorts, .... 25
Mills' Jewess, .......... 25
Sir Colin Campbell, fine, large, black-spined, . 25
Swan Neck, a new variety; very promising, . 25

**EGG PLANT**, page 106.
　Early Long Purple, eight or nine inches long, productive; per oz. 45 cents, . . . . . . . . . 5
　Round Purple, medium size; per oz. 40 cents, 5
　Improved New York Purple, very large and fine, the best; per oz. 60 cents; half oz. 40 cts., 10
　Striped, fine fruit and beautiful, . . . . . . . . 10
　Black Pekin, per oz. 75 cents; half oz. 45 cents, 10

**ENDIVE**, page 118.
　Green Curled, per lb. $2.50; per oz. 25 cents, . 5
　White Curled, per lb. $2.50; per oz. 25 cents, . 5
　Batavian, per lb. $2.25; per oz. 25 cents, . . . 5

**KOHL RABI**, page 107.
　Large Early Purple, beautiful purple, tender, and excellent for the table; lb. $2.00; oz. 20cts., 5
　Large Early White, fine and tender for table; per lb. $2.00; per oz. 20 cents, . . . . . . . . 5
　Large Late Green, large and excellent for stock; per lb. $2.00; per oz. 20, . . . . . . . . . . . 5
　Large Late Purple, large and fine for stock; per lb. $2.00; per oz. 20 cents,'. . . . . . . . . 5
　Early White Vienna, delicate, much prized for forcing; per lb. $5.00; per oz. 40 cents, . . . 10
　Early Purple Vienna, another forcing variety, similar to above except in color; per lb. $5.00; per oz. 40 cents, . . . . . . . . . . . . . . . . 10

**LEEK**, page 118.
　Broad Flag, per lb. $3.00; per oz. 30 cents, . . 10
　Musselburg, per lb. $6.00; per oz. 50 cents, . 20

**LETTUCE**, page 107.
　Malta Drumhead, or Ice Cabbage, very large and superb; per oz. 25 cents, . . . . . . . . . 5
　Large Pale Green Asiatic, a large and good Cabbage variety; per oz. 25 cents, . . . . . . 5
　Victoria Cabbage, hardy and fine for early sowing; per oz. 25 cts., . . . . . . . . . . . . 5
　Neapolitan Cabbage, very large; best variety for summer; per oz.; 30c., . . . . . . . . . . 5
　Imperial White, large Cabbage; hardy, desirable for winter sowing; oz., 25 cts., . . . . . . 5
　All the Year Round, a very hardy, compact growing Cabbage Lettuce, with small, close heads; in perfection a long time; oz., 40c., . . 10
　Satisfaction, a new English variety, large, unusually tender; remaining in head a long time, . . . . . . . . . . . . . . . . . . . . . . . . 20
　New Premium Cabbage, good solid head, keeping in good condition without going to seed longer than any other variety; excellent for all uses and seasons; per oz., 50c., . . . . . . . . 10
　Wheeler's Tom Thumb, a new dwarf variety, of excellent quality, with fine, white, solid heart; per oz. 50 cents, . . . . . . . . . . . . 10
　Early Tennis Ball, one of the earliest and best heading varieties; per oz., 25c., . . . . . . . . 5
　Early Egg, very early; the best for forcing; small, beautiful yellow head; per oz.,30c., . . 5
　Hardy Green Winter, the old Hammersmith; considered the best Winter Lettuce; oz., 25c., . 5
　Green Curled, a very beautiful sort for garnishing, fair quality, early; per oz., 25c., . . . . 5
　White Silesian, early; rather loose head; tender; per oz., 25c., . . . . . . . . . . . . . . . . 5
　Carter's Giant White Cos, new; superb, large and exceedingly tender; per oz., 25c., . . . . 10
　Paris White Cos, one of the best of the Cos varieties; per oz., 25c., . . . . . . . . . . . . 5
　Cut Leaved, a new, handsome, hardy sort. See FLORAL GUIDE for 1876, No. 1, page 45, for description, . . . . . . . . . . . . . . . . . . . 20

**MARTYNIA**, page 92.
　proboscidea, per oz. 75 cents, . . . . . . . . . 10

**MELONS**, page 93.
　MUSK MELONS.
　Early Christina, early, yellow fleshed; per lb. $2.00; per oz. 20 cents, . . . . . . . . . . . . 10
　Jenny Lind, small fruit, but very fine quality, moderately early; per lb. $2.00; oz. 20 cents, . 10
　Prolific Nutmeg, a very good, hardy and prolific variety, fruit medium size, sometimes pretty large, roundish, netted, flesh thick, green and of very excellent flavor; per lb. $2.50; oz. 25 cts. 10
　Nutmeg, medium size, round, flesh green, of good quality; per lb. $1.50; per oz. 15 cents, . . . 5
　White Japanese, deliciously and delicately sweet, flesh thick, very pale green, skin creamy white and very thin; per lb. $2.50; oz. 25 cents, 10
　Fine Netted, an early, delicious melon; per lb. $2.00; per oz. 20 cents, . . . . . . . . . . . . 10
　Green Citron, large, with thick, green flesh, good flavor; per lb. $2.00; oz. 20 cents, . . . . 10
　Pineapple, dark green, oval, netted, flesh thick, sweet and juicy; per lb. $2.00; oz. 20 cents, . . 10
　Persian, very large, rather late, green fleshed; per lb. $2.00; per oz. 20 cents, . . . . . . . . 10
　Casaba, a new variety, oblong, and very large. fine flavor, yellowish green flesh and netted skin; per lb. $2.50; per oz. 25 cents, . . . . . . . . 10
　WATER MELONS.
　Mountain Sweet, dark green, flesh red, sweet and rich, early and hardy; lb. $1.00; oz. 10 cts. 5
　Mountain Sprout, long, striped; scarlet flesh, one of the best, but not quite as early as *Mountain Sweet*; per lb. $1.25; per oz. 15 cents, . . 10
　Black Spanish, an old variety and one of the richest; round, rather small, dark green; red flesh, sweet and rich; per lb. 1.25; oz., 15c., 10
　Goodwin's Imperial, a good melon for amateurs, of fine quality; per oz. 30 cents, . . . . 10
　Vick's Early. Long, smooth, rather small, flesh bright pink, solid, sweet, and the earliest Melon we are acquainted with, . . . . . . . . 25
　Orange. The flesh separates easily from the rind, fair quality; per oz. 25 cents, . . . . . . 10
　Citron, for preserves; per lb. $1.25; oz. 15 cents, 10

**MUSTARD**, page 93.
　White, best for salad or culinary purposes; per lb. 50 cents, per oz. 10 cents, . . . . . . . . 5
　Chinese, a variety with larger leaves and more succulent stems than the other sorts, and prized for salad; per lb. 50 cents, per oz. 10 cents, . . 5
　Black, this is the kind usually used for commercial Mustard, being stronger than the White; per lb. 50 cents; per oz., 10 cents, . . . . . . 5

**ONIONS**, pages 94 and 95.
　AMERICAN VARIETIES.
　*A good deal of cheap Western and California Onion Seed will be offered this season. Ours is all of home growth, from pure selected Onions.*
　Wethersfield Red, one of the best varieties for a general crop; of good size; red, roundish, productive; heads and keeps well; per lb. $2.50; per oz., 25c., . . . . . . . . . . . . . . 10
　Early Red, early; good; per lb., $3.00; oz., 30c., 10
　Danvers Yellow, a fine, large, round Onion; very choice; per lb., $3.00; per oz., 30c., . . . 10
　Large Yellow, a fine, large, flat Onion; forms bulbs readily; per lb., $2.50; per oz., 25c., . . 10
　White Globe, a large, white Onion, as large as Danvers Yellow; per lb. $4.00; per oz. 40 cents, 10

#### FOREIGN VARIETIES.

**Onions, Large Strasburg**, flesh-colored; large; good keeper and productive; lb., $2.00; oz., 20c., 10
**Large Oval Madeira, or New Giant**, flat; very large and good; per lb., $2.00; oz., 20c., . 10
**Large Round Madeira, or New Giant**, per lb., $2.00; per oz., 20c., . . . . . . . . . . . . 10
**White Lisbon**, a very pretty, round, white Onion, almost 4 inches in diameter, a fair keeper, and a splendid variety for warm climates, like the South or South-west; per lb., $2.00; per oz., 20c., . . . . . . . . . . . . 10
**Silver-Skinned**, true, white; delicate; early; not a good keeper; per lb., $2.00; per oz., 20c., 10

#### NEW ITALIAN ONIONS.

**New Giant Rocca**, of Naples, a splendid large Onion, of globular shape, and light brown skin; weight as exhibited at the Royal Horticultural Society, of London, 3 pounds, 9 ounces; per lb., $5.00; per oz., 40c., . . . . . . . . . . . . . 15
**Large Blood Red Italian Tripoli**, more flat than the preceding, quite as large, and blood red; per lb., $6.00; per oz., 50c., . . . . . . 15
**Large Flat White Italian Tripoli**, very pure white skin, flat, very mild flavor; and as large as either of the above; per lb., $6.00; oz., 50c., 15
**Early Flat White Italian Tripoli**, beautiful white skin, very mild, of rapid growth, early; per lb. $6.00; per oz. 50 cents, . . . . . . . . 15
**Marzajola**, new, and represented as the earliest Onion grown. In warm climates seed sown in autumn produces large bulbs in March; per lb $6.00; oz., 50c., . . . . . . . . . . . . . . 15
**New Queen**, white skin, fine flavor, and the best keeper of the new foreign Onions; rather small; per lb., $8.00; per oz., 65c., . . . . . . . . . 25

### OKRA, page 111.

**Long Green**, long, pale green, and ribbed; per lb. $1.00; per oz 10 cents, . . . . . . . . . 5
**Dwarf White**, earliest and best for the North; per lb. $1.00; per oz. 10 cents, . . . . . . . . 5

### PARSLEY, page 111.

**Enfield Matchless**, one of the most delicate of the curled sorts; per lb. $1.00; oz. 10 cents, . 5
**Myatt's Garnishing**, large, finely curled, bright green; per lb. $1.00; oz. 10 cents, . . . . . . 5
**Carter's Champion Moss Curled**, somewhat similar to Myatt's Garnishing, but very much superior, especially for garnishing purposes; per lb. $1.00; per oz. 10 cents, . . . . . . . . . 5
**Giant Curled**, very large growth, finely curled; per lb. 75 cents / per oz. 10 cents, . . . . . . 5
**Covent Garden**, the most elegant curled Parsley grown for garnishing purposes; per lb. $1.00; per oz. 10 cents, . . . . . . . . . . . . . . . 5

### PUMPKINS, page 111.

**Large Cheese**, large, skin reddish orange; flesh thick, fine and sweet; lb. $1.00; oz. 10 cents, . 5
**Cushaw**, solid flesh, fine and sweet; keeps well; per lb. $1.00; per oz. 10 cents, . . . . . . . 5
**Connecticut Field**, lb. 50 cents; oz. 10 cents, . 5

### PARSNIPS, page 112.

**Long Hollow Crown**, one of the very best Parsnips grown, either for stock or the table; per lb. $1.00; per oz. 10 cents, . . . . . . . . . 5
**Carter's New Maltese**, claiming to be a marked improvement over all old sorts; per lb. $2.50; per oz., 25 cents, . . . . . . . . . . . . 10

### PEPPERS, page 112.

**Tomato-formed Red**, large—3 inches in diameter and 2 inches in length—ribbed; flesh thick, mild and pleasant; per oz. 30 cents, . . . . 5
**Large Bell** very large—nearly 4 inches long and 3 in diameter; glossy red, early, flesh thick and very mild; per oz. 30 cents, . . . . . . . . 5
**Sweet Mountain, or Mammoth**, much like Bell, perhaps a little larger; per oz. 50 cents, . 10
**Monstrous, or Grossum**, a French variety, the largest we have ever grown; per oz. 50 cents, . 10
**Long Red**, beautiful and productive, 4 inches in length and an inch or more in diameter; flesh thick and pungent; a good substitute for Cayenne; per oz. 30 cents, . . . . . . . . . . 5
**Long Yellow**, similar to the above except in color; both are late, and the plants should be started in a hot-bed; per oz. 30 cents, . . . . 5
**Cayenne**, small, pungent; the Cayenne Pepper of commerce; per oz. 35 cents, . . . . . . . 5
**Cherry-formed** small, round, very productive, makes a pretty plant; very hot; per oz. 35 cts., 5

### PEAS, page 113.

#### EARLIEST.

**Carter's First Crop**, earliest and most productive; height, 30 inches, and giving a large crop for so early a Pea; per quart, 60c., . . . . . . 10
**Kentish Invicta**, round, blue Pea, and the earliest blue variety grown, and only a day or so after First Crop, excellent; 2 feet in height; per quart, 80c., . . . . . . . . . . . . . . . . 20
**McLean's Little Gem**, a green, wrinkled, marrow Pea, as dwarf as Tom Thumb, of a delicious, rich, sugary flavor; very early; per quart, 80c., . . . . . . . . . . . . . . . . . 20
**McLean's Advancer**, a dwarf, green, wrinkled marrow, of fine flavor and very prolific; per quart, 70c., . . . . . . . . . . . . . . . . 15
**Laxton's Alpha**, an excellent wrinkled Pea, about as early as Little Gem, growing about 30 inches; per quart, 80c., . . . . . . . . . . 20
**Nutting's No. 1**, a very excellent Pea; dwarf, about 15 inches in height, very early, productive, and of fine quality; per quart, 80c., . . . 20
**Tom Thumb**, very dwarf, 8 or 10 inches; per quart, 70c., . . . . . . . . . . . . . . . . 15
**Blue Peter**, habit like Tom Thumb, but more robust, almost as dwarf, and immensely productive. We saw it in England, and it seemed to us the most promising of the new Peas for the American grower; per quart, 90c., . . . . 20
**Waite's Caractacus**, one of the best and most productive early Peas, strong grower and next in earliness to Carter's First Crop; per quart, 50 cents, . . . . . . . . . . . . . . . . . 10
**Early Kent**, 3 feet; the common early market Pea here; per quart, 50c., . . . . . . . . . 10

#### SECOND EARLY.

**Laxton's Prolific Early Long Pod**, a very productive, long-podded variety, having from 11 to 12 Peas in each pod; it is very hardy, and may be put in the ground as soon as the frost is out; per quart, 60c., . . . . . . . . . . . 10
**McLean's Premier**, a large, wrinkled Pea, in fact, the largest and finest looking Pea we have ever seen. It is claimed, in Europe, to be one of the best Peas in cultivation, both for productiveness and flavor; per quart, 70c., . . . . . 15
**Napoleon**, 30 inches; wrinkled; light green; rich, sweet; per quart, 70c., . . . . . . . . 15

Peas, **Eugenie**, 30 inches; wrinkled; white; sweet and rich; per quart, 70c., . . . . . . . . . . 15
**McLean's Princess Royal**, 1 foot; very productive, long podded, sweet; per quart, 60 cents, 10
LATE CROP.
**Carter's Surprise**, an improved large blue Pea, excellent in quality, and very productive; per quart, 60 cents, . . . . . . . . . . . . . 10
**Blue Imperial**, 3 to 4 feet; very hardy and productive; fair quality; per quart, 50 cents, . . 10
**Dwarf Waterloo Marrow**, a splendid Pea, of very dwarf Tom Thumb habit; per quart, 80 cents, . . . . . . . . . . . . . . . . . . 20
**Yorkshire Hero**, a very fine, large, dwarf, wrinkled variety, of good quality and productive; per quart, 60 cents, . . . . . . . . . . 10
**Champion of England**, 5 feet; rich; sweet; popular everywhere; per quart, 50 cents, . . 10
**Dwarf Sugar**, 3 feet; pods skinless and edible; good quality shelled; per quart, 80 cents, . . 20
**Tall Sugar**, 5 feet; edible pods, very large and long; per quart, 80 cents, . . . . . . . . . 20

## RHUBARB, page 113.
**Myatt's Victoria**, per oz., 25 cents, . . . . . 5
**Linnæus**, per oz., 25 cents, . . . . . . . . . 5

## RADISHES, page 114.
**Rose Olive-Shaped**, oval; very tender and excellent; an inch and a half long; flesh rose color; per ℔., $1.00; per oz., 10 cents, . . 5
**Scarlet Olive-Shaped**, like the above except in color; per ℔., $1.00; per oz., 10 cents, . . 5
**Scarlet Olive-Shaped, White Tip**, called New French Breakfast; very tender and beautiful; per ℔., $1.00; per oz., 10 cents, . . . . . 5
**White Olive-Shaped**, like the other olive-shaped varieties in everything except color; per ℔., $1.00; per oz., 10 cents, . . . . . . 5
**Long Scarlet Short-Top**, the favorite long market Radish everywhere; 6 or 7 inches long; per ℔., $1.00; per oz., 10 cents, . . . . . 5
**Salmon Color**, like Scarlet Short-Top, but lighter in color; per ℔., $1.00; per oz., 10 cents, 5
**Long White Naples**, a beautiful long, clear white Radish, tinged with green at the top; excellent for a late Radish; per ℔., $1.00 per oz., 10 cents, . . . . . . . . . . . . . 5
**Red Turnip**, round; about an inch in diameter; skin scarlet; flesh white; good; per ℔., $1.00; per oz., 10 cents, . . . . . . . . . . . . 5
**White Turnip**, similar to above except in color, and being less pungent and a few days later; per ℔., $1.00 per oz., 10 cents, . . . . . . 5
**Yellow Turnip**, similar to the above except in color; per ℔., $1.00; per oz., 10 cents, . . . 5
**Chinese Rose Winter**, sow in summer, same as Turnips; per ℔., $1.25; per oz., 15 cents, . 10
**Chinese White Winter**, an excellent white winter Radish, like Chinese Rose, except in color; per ℔., $1.25; per oz., 15 cents, . . . 10
**Black Spanish Winter, Round**, per ℔., $1.00; per oz., 10 cents, . . . . . . . . . . . . . 5
**Black Spanish Winter, Long**, per ℔., $1.00; per oz., 10 cents, . . . . . . . . . . . . . 5
**Large White Spanish Winter**, per ℔., $1.50; per oz., 15 cents, . . . . . . . . . . . . . 10
**California Mammoth White Winter**, is really a Chinese Radish, grown by the Chinese in California; 8 to 12 inches long, and from 2 to 3 inches in diameter; white, solid and good flavor; per ℔., $3.50; per oz., 30 cents, . . . 15

## SALSIFY, page 114.
**Salsify**, per ℔., $1.50; per oz., 15 cents, . . . 5
**Black**, or **Scorzonera**, a black variety, with a somewhat bitter root, not much used at present; per oz., 25 cents, . . . . . . . . . . . . . 10

## SEA KALE.
Per oz. 35 cents, . . . . . . . . . . . . . . . 10

## SQUASHES, page 115.
**Early Bush Scollop**, a good, early, Summer Squash, taking but little room, and bearing abundantly; plant in hills three feet apart; per ℔., 1.25; per oz., 15 cents, . . . . . . . . 10
**Early Bush Crook-Necked**, the richest summer Squash; very early and productive; plant in hills three feet apart; per ℔., $1.25; per oz., 15 cents, . . . . . . . . . . . . . . . . 10
**Hubbard**, an excellent Squash, almost as good as the Sweet Potato; per ℔., $1.50; per oz., 15 cents, . . . . . . . . . . . . . . . . 10
**Marblehead**, a very good winter Squash, resembling the Hubbard, sometimes quite as good, though more variable; per ℔., $1.50; per oz., 15 cents, . . . . . . . . . . . . . . . . 10
**Butman**. This is a new variety, evidently from the Hubbard, and in appearance almost like the light colored variety of the Hubbard, when first introduced. We have had some specimens for trial, and it is the driest Squash we have ever eaten, and on this account, if this good quality is constant, will be prized. The flavor does not suit our taste as well as the Hubbard, . . . . 25
**Turban**, or **Turk's Cap**, a good fall and early winter Squash, greenish in color, striped with white; in form it somewhat resembles a turban; flesh orange; almost as good as Hubbard, and weighing about six pounds; per ℔., $2.25; per oz., 25 cents, . . . . . . . . . . . . . . 10
**Boston Marrow**, a good, tender, rich variety, for fall and winter; per ℔., $1.50; per oz., 15 cents, 10
**Winter Crook-Neck**, of fair quality, very hardy and a good keeper; per ℔., $1.50; per oz., 15 cents, . . . . . . . . . . . . . . . . 10

## SPINACH, page 115.
**Prickly**, or **Fall**, hardiest and best for fall or very early spring sowing; per ℔., 75 cents; per oz., 10 cents, . . . . . . . . . . . . 5
**Round**, or **Summer**, for spring sowing; per ℔., 75 cents; per oz., 10 cents, . . . . . 5
**New Zealand**, very large and luxuriant; endures drouth well, and produces a large quantity of leaves; plants should stand at least two feet apart; per ℔., $2.00; per oz., 20 cents, . . . 10

## TOMATOES, page 116.
**Hubbard's Curled Leaf**, the earliest of all the Tomatoes; small to medium in size, some specimens irregular; plant dwarf in habit; set half the usual distance apart; the leaves curl as though the plants were drying up; oz., 25 cts., 5
**Early Smooth Red**, early, smooth, round, medium size, of fair quality, and productive; per oz., 30 cents, . . . . . . . . . . . . . . 5
**Gen. Grant**, a very superior, good sized Tomato, smooth, rather flat in form; of good quality, and ripens rapidly and thoroughly; oz., 30 cts., 5
**Hathaway's Excelsior**, early, medium to large, smooth as an apple; very solid, and of excellent quality every way; the best Tomato I have ever grown; per oz., 40 cents; per half oz., 25 cents, . . . . . . . . . . . . . . . . 5

Tomato, Trophy, very large, pretty smooth, very solid, and of fair quality; too late or it would be popular; per oz., 50 cents; half oz., 30 cents, . . 10
Green Gage, a new, smooth, orange-colored Tomato; less than medium size; of very good flavor, . . . . . . . . . . . . . . . . . . 10
Persian, a very large, solid variety, of delicate flavor, and beautiful creamy yellow in color; per oz., 25 cents, . . . . . . . . . . . . . 5
Large Yellow, bright yellow, large, smooth; per oz., 30 cents, . . . . . . . . . . . . . . 5
Pear-Shaped, fine for preserving and pickling, . 5
Plum-Shaped, Yellow, for preserving and pickling, . . . . . . . . . . . . . . . . 5
Cherry, Yellow and Red, for preserving or pickling, each, . . . . . . . . . . . . . . . 5
Strawberry, or Winter Cherry, a distinct species; prized for preserving, . . . . . . . . 10

## TURNIPS, page 117.

### ENGLISH TURNIPS.

Early White Flat Dutch, size medium; grows quick; per ℔. $1.00; per oz., 10 cents, . . . . 5
Early Yellow Dutch, one of the best for the garden; per ℔., $1.00; per oz., 10 cents, . . . 5
White Norfolk, a popular variety for feeding; per ℔., $1.00; per oz., 10 cents. . . . . . . 5
Strap-Leaved White-Top, roundish, of medium size; one of the best, either for market or family use; per ℔., $1.00; per oz., 10 cents, . . 5
Strap-Leaved Red-Top, similar to above, purple above ground; per ℔., $1.00; per oz., 10c, . 5
Early White Stone, a good, globe-shaped Turnip; per ℔., $1.00; per oz., 10 cents, . . . . 5
Early Yellow Stone, similar to above, except in color; per ℔., $1.00; per oz., 10 cents, . . . 5
Early White Six Weeks, or Snow Ball, very early and fine; per ℔., $1.00; per oz., 10 cents, 5
White Globe, large, white; fine for field culture; per ℔., $1.00; per oz., 10 cents, . . . . 5
Orange Jelly, a very beautiful yellow Turnip, one of the very best yellows for the table; per ℔., $1.00; per oz., 10 cents, . . . . . . . . 5
Long Red Tankard, good and productive sort for field crop. per ℔., $1.00; per oz., 10 cents, 5
Green-Top Yellow Aberdeen, excellent, per ℔., $1.00; per oz., 10 cents, . . . . . . . . 5
Yellow Malta, fine, rather small, very smooth; per ℔., $1.00; per oz., 10 cents, . . . . . . 5
Jersey Navet, a new, delicate, white Turnip, long, somewhat like the Parsnip in form; one of the best for the table, very sweet; per ℔., $1.50; per oz., 15 cents, . . . . . . . . . . 10
Teltow, a well-known German variety; flesh white, firm, sweet and of excellent flavor; per lb., $1.00; oz., 10c., . . . . . . . . . . . 5

### RUTA-BAGA, OR SWEDE TURNIPS.

White Sweet, a large, white, solid Swede, sometimes called White Russian; lb., $1.00; oz., 10c., 5
White Red-Top, a French Swede, with reddish purple top, sweet and solid; per lb., $1.00; per oz., 10 cents, . . . . . . . . . . . . . 5
Green-Top, a round, solid, sweet variety, very productive; per lb., $1.00; per oz., 10 cents, . 5
Laing's Purple-Top, an old and favorite variety, good keeper, solid and productive; per lb., $1.00; per oz., 10 cents, . . . . . . . . . 5
Carter's Imperial Purple-Top, claimed to be the best Purple-top grown; very hardy; per lb., $1.00; per oz., 10 cents, . . . . . . . . . 5

Turnips, Marshall's Extra Purple-Top, a celebrated English variety, and one of the very best; per lb., $1.00; per oz., 10 cents, . . . . . . 5
Skirving's Liverpool, very smooth, good quality, and of medium size, very solid and sweet; supposed to be the best for a shallow soil; per lb., $1.00; per oz. 10 cents, . . . . 5
Sutton's Champion, a good English variety, very much resembling Marshall's Extra Purple-top; per lb., $1.00; per oz., 10 cents, . . . . 5
Large London, a good and very reliable long keeping variety; per lb., $1.00; oz., 10 cents, . 5

## HERBS, page 119.

Anise; Arnica; Balm; Basil, Sweet; Bene; Borage; Caraway; Catnep; Coriander; Cumin; Dill; Fennel, Large Sweet; Horehound; Hyssop; Lavender; Marjoram, Sweet; Rosemary; Rue; Saffron; Sage; Savory, Summer; Savory, Winter; Tansy; Thyme, Broad-Leaved English; Thyme, Summer; Thyme, Winter; Wormwood; each, . . . . . . . . . . . . 5

## GRASSES AND CLOVER.

At the price per bushel we deliver to Express Company here or on board cars. No charge for bags or packing. By the quart we prepay postage.

Crested Dog's Tail, (Cynosurus cristatus,) quart, 75
Kentucky Blue Grass, (Poa pratensis,) clean seed; per bushel, $2.50; peck, 85 cents; quart, 25
Orchard Grass, (Dactylis glomerata,) per bushel, $4.00; peck, 1.25; quart, . . . . . . . . 30
Pacey's Perennial Rye Grass, (Lolium perenne,) per bushel, $4.00; peck, $1.35; quart, . . . 30
Red Top, (Agrostis vulgaris,) per bushel, $2.50; peck, 85 cents; quart, . . . . . . . . . . 25
Sheep's Fescue, (Festuca ovina,) per quart, . . 35
Slender-Leaved Fescue, (Festuca tenuifolia,) per quart, . . . . . . . . . . . . . . . 35
Sweet Vernal Grass, (Anthoxanthum odoratum,) per ℔., $2.00; per oz., . . . . . . . . . 10
Lawn Grass, fine mixed; per bushel, $4.00; per peck, $1.25; per quart, . . . . . . . . . 30
Clover, White, per ℔. by mail, 75 cents; per 100 lbs., delivered to railroad here, . . . . . . $50.00
Alsike, per lb., by mail, 75 cents; per 100 lbs., delivered to railroad here, . . . . . . . . 50.00
Scarlet, (Trifolium incarnatum), per lb., by mail, 50 cents; per 100 lbs., delivered here, . 25.00
Lucerne, (Alfalfa,) per lb., by mail, 75 cents; 100 lbs., delivered here, . . . . . . . . . . 50.00
Lucerne, (California Alfalfa,) per lb., by mail, 75 cents; per 100 lbs., delivered here, . 50.00
Spring Vetches, per lb., by mail, 35 cents; per 100 lbs., delivered here, . . . . . . . . . 10.00
Sainfoin, per lb., by mail, 60 cents; per bushel, delivered here, . . . . . . . . . . . . . 6.00

GRASS SEED IN BULK, BY MAIL.

|  | peck. | bush. |
|---|---|---|
| Blue Grass, post-paid, . . . . . . . | $1.25 | 5.00 |
| Orchard Grass, " . . . . . . . | 1.65 | 6.50 |
| Red Top, " . . . . . . . | 1.25 | 5.00 |
| Lawn Grass, " . . . . . . . | 1.75 | 7.00 |

## ONION SETS.

We keep on hand usually a good stock of Onion Sets of the best quality. As the prices by the bushel vary so much each season, we can give only approximate quotations, subject to market changes:

English Multipliers, or Potato Onions, per bushel $6.00; peck, $1.75; quart, . . . . . . 50

Top, or Button Onions, per bush., $8.00; peck,
$2.25; quart, . . . . . . . . . . . . . . . . . 50
Yellow Bottom Sets, per bush., $7.50; peck,
$2.00; quart, . . . . . . . . . . . . . . . 50
White Bottom Sets, per bushel, $8.00; peck,
$2.25; quart, . . . . . . . . . . . . . . . . 50
At bushel and peck rates, purchasers pay their own charges.
Although Onion Sets vary in price, as before noted, customers can depend upon being supplied at the very lowest market price, and of the best quality.
Garlic Sets, per lb., . . . . . . . . . . . . . . . 40
Horse Radish Sets, per 100, $1.25; dozen, . . . 30

### ASPARAGUS ROOTS.
Conover's Colossal, 1 year, by mail, prepaid, per
dozen, 30 cents; per 100, . . . . . . . . . . $1.50
2 years, by mail, prepaid, per dozen, 50 cents;
per 100, . . . . . . . . . . . . . . . . . . . 3.50
2 years, by express, not paid; per 100, . . . . 1.50
Not less than 50 roots at 100 rates.

### MUSHROOM SPAWN.
Per lb., . . . . . . . . . . . . . . . . . . . . 30
For culture, etc., see GUIDE No. 1, for 1875.

### HEDGE SEEDS.
Osage Orange, per lb., . . . . . . . . . . . . $0.75
Honey Locust, per lb., . . . . . . . . . . . . . 75

## EVERLASTING FLOWERS AND GRASSES.

I offer a choice assortment of Everlasting Flowers, Grasses and Immortelles, of natural colors or dyed, loose, as they are grown here or imported, so that persons ordering may arrange them as their taste suggests; also made up in Bouquets, Baskets, Wreaths, &c., as shown in the list below. All articles sent by mail or Express, free. A liberal discount allowed when ordered in large quantities for Churches, Fairs, &c. Prices to dealers on application.

**LOOSE FLOWERS TO BE MADE UP AT HOME.**
French Immortelles in white, red, blue, yellow, orange, green, purple, rose and lilac, separate or mixed, original bunch, . . . . . . . $1 00
Everlasting Flowers in variety, . . . . . . . . . 50
Immortelles, per bunch, mixed or separate, . . . 50
Ornamental Grasses, natural or dyed, per bunch, 50
" " natural colors, in great variety, per lb., . . . . . . . 3 25
" " other colors, as green, blue, rose, etc., per lb., . . . . 4 50
" " mixed—colored and natural, 4 00
Feather Grass, (*Stipa pennata*,) 15 inches high, in white, per lb., . . . . . . . . . . . . . . . 3 50
Feather Grass, 15 inches high, in 5 colors, per lb. 5 00
Mixed bunches of Feather Grass and Ornamental Grasses, . . . . . . . . . . . . . . . . . . . 50
Half a pound will be sufficient to fill two large Vases.
Statice *inc. hyb.*, resembling the white Erica, bunch 35
Moss, light and dark green, per bunch, 25 cts.; lb. 1 25

**COLLECTIONS.**
On account of the weak stems it will be necessary to put all the flowers and the Moss on fine wire; without doing this the bouquet never will look fine. If the flowers are for baskets, a little wooden stick can be tied on the flower stem, dipped in paste or gum, and then inserted in the moss, which will keep the flowers in just the position desired. (See little engraving.)
No. 1, Collection of Immortelles, Everlastings, Ornamental Grasses, Green Moss, sufficient to make up a good sized bouquet, . $1.00 to 3 00
The same on wire, . . . . . . . . . . . $1.25 to 4 00

No. 2, Collection of Immortelles, Everlastings, Grasses, Moss, sufficient for a good sized basket, basket included, any shape, $1.25 to 3 00
No. 3, Collection of Green Moss, White Immortelles, or White Everlastings, White Statice, and green leaves for a wreath or cross, $1.00 to 3 00
Bouquet Wire, fine, 200 stems, 8 inches long, . . 25
Wooden Spikes, per 500, 25 cents; per 2,500, . . 75
Round Hand Bouquets with Ornamental Papers, of all sizes, from 60 cents to $4.00 each.
Pyramidal Bouquets with Ornamental Papers, from 75 cents to $5.00 each.
Flat Bouquets, from 60 cents to $5.00 each.
Round Baskets without Handles, from 50 cents to $1.75.
Round Baskets with Handles, from 50 cts. to $1.50 each.
Oval Baskets with Handles, from 40 cents to $5.00 each.
The Baskets are fine White Willow, and imported.
Wreaths in White and Green, from $1.00 to $6.00 each.
Crosses, from $1.00 to $5.00.
Standard Crosses for Churches, &c., . . . 3.50 to 10 00
Anchors, Stars, in white or colors, from . . 1.50 to 5 00

**CROWNS IN WHITE AND GREEN.**
9 inch frame, . . . . . . . . . . . . . $4.50 to 6 00
12 inch frame, . . . . . . . . . . . . . . 5.00 to 10 00
If protected from dust these articles will last for years.

**FLOWERS FOR CEMETERIES.**
Made of Sheet Iron, endure the weather for years with a fresh coating of varnish each season.
Crosses, green Ivy leaves and white Lilies, 10 by 15 inches, $3 50; 12 by 20 inches, . . . . . . . $5 00
Of green leaves, . . . . . . . . . . . . . . . . . 3 00
Wreaths of green leaves, or green leaves and white or colored flowers, . . . . . . . $3.00 to 6 00

---

**VICK'S FLORAL GUIDE**, is published Quarterly at 25 cents a year. It is beautifully illustrated, and elegantly printed on the best tinted paper. To those who are getting up clubs among their neighbors, we desire to say that One Dollar will do for a Club of Five—that will give a free copy to every one who gets up a small Club. A German Edition published at the same price.

**THE FLORAL GUIDE** is published for the benefit of my customers, and the price charged is hardly enough to pay for the paper before it is printed, to say nothing of the postage, which we have to prepay. Still, anyone paying for the GUIDE, and afterwards ordering Seeds to the amount of One Dollar or more, may deduct the money paid for the GUIDE from the amount forwarded for Seeds.

**A CATALOGUE OF RUSTIC WORK**, Garden Tools, Vases, Ornamental Flower Pots, Ferneries and other Ornamental Goods and Garden Requisites, sent free to all who apply.

**PRICED CATALOGUE OF SEEDS.**—Those who possess the FLOWER AND VEGETABLE GARDEN can obtain a new copy of Vick's Priced Catalogue free, on the first of December each year, giving the prices of Seeds, Bulbs, &c., at date, by merely making the application.

## SUGGESTIONS TO EVERY ONE ORDERING SEEDS, &c.

### WHAT WE PROPOSE TO DO.

**All Seeds and Bulbs Free of Postage.**—I will send Seeds and Bulbs, by mail, to any part of the United States, AT THE PRICES NAMED IN THE CATALOGUE, POSTAGE PAID. This arrangement enables those who live at the most distant parts of the country to obtain good Seeds as cheap as those who reside in our large cities. Such persons will be no longer compelled to buy poor Seeds or none, but can send their orders with the money, and in a few days the articles will arrive in good order at their post office, where they can be obtained without further cost, as every package will be *paid through to its destination.* The only exceptions to this rule are when Grass Seed, and other heavy and bulky articles are ordered by the peck or bushel, or in cases especially noted. All Seeds will also be sent to other countries FREE OF UNITED STATES POSTAGE in all cases where payment is possible here.

**Free by Express.**—All orders over two pounds weight will be forwarded by Express, if possible. Our customers will oblige us very much by giving their nearest office and the Name of the Company delivering goods. Heavy orders can be forwarded by stage from the Express office. So please be particular and send special directions when on a Stage route. We ask this on account of the present postal law compelling us to pay 16 cents per pound. All Stage charges will be prepaid when it is possible for us to do so. This applies to Seeds and Bulbs at Catalogue rates, and not when special prices are made for large quantities, or on such by the peck or bushel, nor on miscellaneous articles, such as Brackets, Rustic Work, Pots, Implements, &c. *Goods C. O. D.*—Persons often order small packages sent in this way, and the Express charges sometimes amount to more than the order. We can send goods and collect the money on delivery, free of Express charges, only when orders amount to $10.00 and upward, and then not on long and expensive routes.

**Correction of Errors.**—I take the utmost care in filling orders, always striving to do a *little more* for my friends and patrons than justice and fair dealing require. Every order, after being filled, is carefully examined by an experienced person, to be certain that everything ordered is sent, and no error made in filling; yet it should be remembered that the seed trade of a year has to be done in a few months, and, in the rush of business, errors may occasionally occur. In such cases, I always desire to be informed of the fact, and promise to make such corrections as will be perfectly satisfactory. Customers will please keep a copy of all orders sent, so that they can see that they receive just what was ordered. Persons often forget the nature of their order, and complain without cause.

**Orders Lost or Stolen.**—Sometimes it happens that orders never reach us. When customers fail to receive their Seeds or Bulbs in a reasonable time, they should inform us of the fact, and at the same time send a duplicate of their order, which duplicate can be filled at once, and save much delay, if our conditions for remitting money have been complied with.

**The Safe Arrival of Packages Guaranteed.**—I guarantee the safe arrival of packages of Seeds and Bulbs in good condition in every case. If a package fails to reach a customer, I will send again as soon as informed of the fact; or if any part is injured or lost, I will replace it. My object is to supply all my customers with Seeds and Bulbs, &c., without any more expense or risk to them than if I had a *store in their own town*.

**Everything Supplied.**—We advertise nothing in the FLORAL GUIDE which we cannot supply—at least, we do not design to do so, but we have to print our GUIDE very early, having several hundreds of thousands to print and mail, which takes a long time. Occasionally a few things ordered from abroad fail to reach us, on account of bad crops or something of the kind. These are the only cases in which we fail to supply everything advertised.

**Our Customers in Canada.**—There is a duty on seeds sent from the United States to Canada. The expense is not great, but the trouble and delay is annoying. We have, therefore, made arrangements to pay all duties and postage on Seeds at a Canadian port, so that our customers will have no further trouble or expense. Bulbs are free of duty.

### WHAT WE ASK OF OUR CUSTOMERS.

**How to Send Money.**—ALL MONEY MAY BE SENT AT MY RISK AND EXPENSE, if forwarded according to directions, in either manner here stated.

1st. *Post Office Money Orders*, to be obtained at many Post Offices, but not at all, are perfectly safe, and will cost from 10 to 25 cents. This is the best way where practical.

2d. A *Draft on New York* can be obtained at any Bank for about 25 cents, and this is sure to come correctly.

3d. *Greenbacks*, in amounts not less than Five Dollars ($5.00), can be sent *by Express*, and these we are sure to get, and the cost is very little.

4th. REGISTERED LETTERS.—When money *cannot be sent by either of the first three methods*, it may be enclosed in a Registered Letter. The cost of registering is 10 cents.

☞ The expense of forwarding money in either of the above ways I will pay, and the cost may be deducted from the amount forwarded.

5th. SUMS LESS THAN ONE DOLLAR may be forwarded by mail at my risk without registering.

When remittances are not made according to these directions, we disclaim all responsibility.

**Forward Money with the Order.**—In the busy season we have to fill more than two thousand orders each day. To make out bills for customers, and mail, charge on our books, then, in a few days, receive the money, make the proper credit and send receipt, requires more work than we can possibly perform. Please, therefore, send money with the order, and it will so facilitate our business that your order will be promptly executed.

**Don't Forget your Name, Post Office or State.**—Those who order, will please remember to give their *Names, Post Office, County* and *State*, as plain as possible. Neglect of this causes us sometimes a great deal of trouble and our friends unnecessary uneasiness. Often we have a hundred letters without names on hand at one time. Please be sure the name you give is the name of your *Post Office*, and not of your town, or residence, or village.

## COLLECTIONS.

I have put up separate collections of the choicest seeds in neat envelopes, and these are very desirable to those who may wish a complete assortment of any particular class of flowers.

A FINE COLLECTION OF ASTERS, embracing most of the best sorts, . . . . . . . . . . . . . . . . $1 00
" " BALSAMS, " " " . . . . . . . . . . . . . . 50
" " DIANTHUS, " " " . . . . . . . . . . . . . . 1 00
" " COCKSCOMB, embracing six best varieties, . . . . . . . . . . . . . . 50
" " PANSIES, choice fancy colors, . . . . . . . . . . . . . $1 00 and 2 00
" " PHLOX DRUMMONDII, most brilliant sorts, . . . . . . . . . . . . . . 1 00
" " TEN-WEEKS STOCK, most superb lot, best sorts, . . . . . . . . . . . . . . 1 00
" " EVERLASTING FLOWERS, most desirable sorts, . . . . . . . 50 cents and 1 00
" " ORNAMENTAL GRASSES, the best and most beautiful, packages at 50 cents or 1 00

**Selection of Varieties.**—Some prefer to leave the selection of varieties to me; and in cases where purchasers are entirely unacquainted with the different varieties of flowers, this may be the better plan. Those who do so, should state what they have already, if any; for, unless informed of this fact, in some cases articles may be forwarded that are not needed. Those who are commencing the cultivation of flowers will find the collections named below suited to their wants.

No. 1. COLLECTION OF FINE ANNUALS, . . . . . . . . . . . . . . . . . $1 00
No. 2. " " " . . . . . . . . . . . . . . . . . 2 00
No. 3. " " BIENNIALS AND PERENNIALS, . . . . . . . . . . . 3 00
No. 4. " " " " . . . . . . . . . . . 5 00

No. 1 consists of about thirteen of the most hardy and popular Annuals; No. 2 about twenty varieties of hardy popular Annuals, and a few varieties that require a little more care in their culture; No. 3 is composed of about twenty varieties of Annuals, and twelve of the best Biennials and Perennials; No. 4 contains about twenty-five varieties of Annuals, and about the same number of Perennials.

**Collections of Vegetables.**—Hundreds of my customers prefer leaving the selection of Vegetables to me, and at a time when, in consequence of the press of business, I cannot give the time needed for a judicious choice. I have, therefore, taken a leisure time to make careful selections, and will have them put up in readiness for those who may desire.

No. 1. COMPLETE COLLECTION OF VEGETABLES for small family garden, . . . . . . . . . . . . $3 00
No. 2. " " " . . . . . . . . . . . . 5 00
No. 3. " " " for large family garden, . . . . . . . . . . . . 10 00

The very liberal premiums offered to Clubs are included in the above Collections.

## FORMATION OF CLUBS.

The lovers of flowers in any neighborhood may easily club together and send their orders in one letter, and thus avail themselves of the deductions I make on large orders. Those who desire Catalogues to aid them in the formation of Clubs will be furnished free. For the purpose of encouraging the formation of such Clubs, and as a slight compensation for the effort, I make the following liberal offer:

Persons sending $1 may select seeds at Catalogue prices amounting to . . . . . . . . . . . . . $1 10
" " 2 " " " " " . . . . . . . . . . . 2 25
" " 3 " " " " " . . . . . . . . . . . 3 45
" " 4 " " " " " . . . . . . . . . . . 4 70
" " 5 " " " " " . . . . . . . . . . . 6 00
" " 10 " " " " " . . . . . . . . . . . 12 50
" " 20 " " " " " . . . . . . . . . . . 26 00

These will be put up together and sent to *one* address, or in *separate packages*, and mailed to the address of each individual forming the club, as may be desired. In all cases the postage will be *prepaid*. The same deduction will, of course, be made to any one person ordering for himself alone. It must always be understood, however, that this discount is allowed only on **Flower and Vegetable Seeds by the packet**, and not on seeds by the **ounce** or **pound**, nor on **Bulbs**; nor can we pay this discount on **Bulbs**, or seeds by the **pound**. Otherwise, in many cases it would bring the price far below cost. Every person who sends us One Dollar or more for either Seeds or Bulbs is entitled to the FLORAL GUIDE for one year. Persons ordering Seeds for Clubs will please furnish Names and Post Office address of those who wish the GUIDE.

## OUR FLORAL CHROMOS.

For the purpose of increasing the love of Flowers, we have, for several years, published at least one Chromo each year. They are not cheap things, but beautiful pictures, true to nature, and superior to any Floral Chromos in Europe or America; every Flower is of natural size and color. We sell them at *the actual cost*, without profit. Each Chromo is accompanied by a Key, giving the names of all the Flowers. The little sketches will show their character.

CHROMO A is 16 by 20 inches, and contains portraits of 31 varieties of our most popular flowers, and has always been the favorite.

CHROMO C is an elegant piece, the flowers finely painted and exceedingly truthful. It contains 41 varieties, and all of natural size.

CHROMO D is composed of flowers of the spring-flowering bulbs, such as Tulips, Hyacinths, Crocuses, Narcissus, etc., 36 varieties.

CHROMO E represents Flora supporting a vase containing 36 varieties of our most elegant summer flowers.

PRICE OF CHROMOS.—On paper, sized and varnished, postage paid, 75 cents each. The whole collection of Eight for $5.00.

On Cloth and Stretchers, just like an oil painting, ready for the frame, $1.50 each, postage or Express charges paid by us. The collection of Eight, on Stretchers, $10.

**CHROMO F** is a beautiful Floral Cross, made for us in Germany. It was designed to be 19 by 24 inches, like the others, but by mistake it is only 18 by 23. It is an elegant ornament, either for the church or school or parlor.

**CHROMO G** is a basket of flowers, 26 varieties, and a very beautiful and artistic work. It is 12 by 16 inches, being made small at the request of some of my customers who desired at least one small one for convenience of arranging.

**CHROMO H** is called *Winter In-doors and Out*, and represents a stand covered with winter flowers, house plants, etc., while from the window is seen the leafless trees, the snow-covered hillside, and other evidences of winter.

**CHROMO I** is our new LILY CHROMO, including all the California varieties, and, we think, is the most complete and perfect group of Lilies in the world. It takes the place of our old Chromo B, which lacked some new sorts.

**PRICE OF CHROMOS.** — Framed in Black Walnut and Gilt, and very neat, $2.75. No charge for boxing or shipping, but those ordering must pay the freight. The whole Eight, framed, $20.00.

Our Chromos are about 19 by 24 inches, except otherwise noted. Our G Chromo, which is only 12 by 16 inches, we sell at 50 cents each, on paper, and $1.00 on stretchers, pre-paid. Framed in Black Walnut and Gilt, $2.00.

www.ingramcontent.com/pod-product-compliance
Lightning Source LLC
Chambersburg PA
CBHW031456160426
43195CB00010BB/995